Yale Historical Publications

YALE UNIVERSITY PRESS · NEW HAVEN & LONDON

Playing

Indian

Philip J. Deloria

Published under the direction of the Department of History of
Yale University with assistance from the income of the
Frederick John Kingsbury Memorial Fund.

Copyright © 1998 by Yale University. All rights reserved. This book
may not be reproduced, in whole or in part, including illustrations, in any
form (beyond that copying permitted by Sections 107 and 108 of the U.S.
Copyright Law and except by reviewers for the public press), without
written permission from the publishers.

Set in Monotype Joanna type by Keystone Typesetting. Printed in the United
States of America by BookCrafters, Inc., Chelsea, Michigan.

Library of Congress Cataloging-in-Publication Data
Deloria, Philip Joseph.
Playing Indian / Philip J. Deloria.
p.   cm. — (Yale historical publications)
Originally presented as the author's thesis (Ph. D.)—Yale University, 1994).
Includes bibliographical references and index.
ISBN 0-300-07111-6 (cloth : alk. paper)
ISBN 0-300-08067-0 (pbk. : alk. paper)
1. Indians of North America—Public opinion.   2. Indians in popular
culture—United States.   3. Indians of North America—Ethnic identity.
4. Indians of North America in literature.   5. Public opinion—United
States.   6. United States—Civilization—Indian influences.   I. Title.
II. Series: Yale historical publications (Unnumbered)
E98.P99D45   1998
973'.0497—dc21   97-30936

A catalogue record for this book is available from the British Library.

The paper in this book meets the guidelines for permanence and durability
of the Committee on Production Guidelines for Book Longevity of the
Council on Library Resources.

10   9   8   7   6   5   4   3   2

For Peg

Contents

Illustrations

Playing Indian

Introduction

American Indians

and American Identities

Benjamin [Franklin] knew that the breaking of the old
world was a long process. In the depths of his own under-
consciousness he hated England, he hated Europe, he hated the
whole corpus of the European being. He wanted to be
American. But you can't change your nature and mode of
consciousness like changing your shoes. It is a gradual
shedding. Years must go by and centuries must elapse before
you have finished. It is a long and half-secret process.

D. H. LAWRENCE,

Studies in Classic American Literature (1924)

In the fading evening light of December 16, 1773, Francis Rotch, the son
of a Boston shipowner, trudged away from the home of provincial governor
Thomas Hutchinson, his petition having been denied. Rotch's ship, the *Dartmouth*, had been anchored in Boston harbor for almost three weeks, the object of
a struggle between Hutchinson, who insisted that its cargo—East India Company tea—be landed, and the Sons of Liberty, who refused to allow dockworkers

to unload the tea, which had come packaged with an unpalatable import tax. Customs rules prevented the *Dartmouth* from leaving the harbor, and the governor had ordered the Royal Navy to fire on any vessels attempting to do so. Even if the ship had escaped Boston unscathed and returned to London, Rotch and the other owners would have borne the ruinous costs of two profitless voyages. And so, on the nineteenth day of the twenty-day customs period, a crowd of Bostonians gathered at Old South Church to discuss the dilemma yet again and to send Rotch to make one final petition. The next morning, customs authorities would be legally empowered to seize the *Dartmouth*'s cargo.

Hutchinson, we know, refused to make any concessions, and when Rotch relayed the news, the crowd inaugurated the night of purposeful craziness Americans have come to call the Boston Tea Party. A chorus of Indian war whoops sounded outside the hall, and a party of what looked like Indian men sprinted down the street to the wharves. Boarding the *Dartmouth* and two other tea ships, the *Eleanor* and the *Beaver*, the Indians "overpowered" the sympathetic guards and dumped tea into Boston harbor for the next three hours. No one tried to stop the tea party, least of all the crowd of spectators gathered on the well-lit wharf. When they had finished, the raiders cleaned up the ships, apologized to the guards for a broken lock, and went home to wash off their war paint. The tea party had been street theater and civil disobedience of the most organized kind. In full costume, the actors had waited patiently in the wings for Francis Rotch to deliver his lines. And the appointed guardians of social order at the harbor had willingly turned a blind eye and deaf ear in order to facilitate the citizens' effort to resolve an apparently unresolvable standoff.[1]

It has never failed to make a compelling story, retold by everyone from grade-schoolers to politicians. The tale has dramatic appeal of its own, but it also offers a defining story of something larger—American character. In the national iconography, the Tea Party is a catalytic moment, the first drumbeat in the long cadence of rebellion through which Americans redefined themselves as something other than British colonists.[2] For the next two hundred years, white Americans molded similar narratives of national identity around the rejection of an older European consciousness and an almost mystical imperative to become new. Although other Americans would appropriate and alter those stories, they often chose to leave the basic narratives in place. And so, in the "long and half-secret" struggle to define and claim American identity, the Boston Tea Party became thoroughly entrenched as a key origin story, one that resonates for a diverse range of people. And yet, one has to wonder. Why, of all the possible

stories of rebellion and re-creation, has the notion of disguised Indians dumping tea in Boston harbor had such a powerful hold on Americans' imaginations?

One hundred and fifty years, a continent, and a nationality removed, the British
writer D. H. Lawrence occupied himself with similar questions. In his most
significant work of literary criticism, *Studies in Classic American Literature*, Lawrence
focused on the issue of American identity, suggesting that American consciousness was essentially "unfinished" and incomplete. An unparalleled national
identity crisis swirled around two related dilemmas: First, Americans had an
awkward tendency to define themselves by what they were not. They had failed
to produce a positive identity that stood on its own. Americans were, as he put
it, "not so much bound to any haven ahead, as rushing from all havens astern."[3]
Second, Americans (and he did not hesitate to generalize) had been continually
haunted by the fatal dilemma of "wanting to have their cake and eat it too," of
wanting to savor both civilized order and savage freedom at the same time.[4]

Offering readings of classic nineteenth-century authors, Lawrence revealed a
string of contradictions at the heart of familiar American self-images. James
Fenimore Cooper, he claimed, was continually trying to work out the tension
between a society that promoted democratic equality and the undeniable fact
that some people are born more able than others. Nathaniel Hawthorne's *Scarlet
Letter* illustrated the indecisive battle between the equilibratory urges of in-
stinctual "blood consciousness" and self-aware "mind consciousness," the latter defining the former as sin yet never being able to eradicate it and, indeed,
often finding its animal wildness desirable. A range of American writers—
Hector St. John de Crèvecoeur, Henry David Thoreau, Herman Melville, Walt
Whitman, and others—had, even as they explored American contradiction,
found themselves captured and humbled by its incessant ambiguities.

Throughout the essays, Lawrence frequently turned to "the Indian," intuitively locating native people at the very heart of American ambivalence. Whereas
Euro-Americans had imprisoned themselves in the logical mind and the social
order, Indians represented instinct and freedom. They spoke for the "spirit
of the continent." Whites desperately desired that spirit, yet they invariably
failed to become aboriginal and thus "finished." Savage Indians served Americans as oppositional figures against whom one might imagine a civilized national Self. Coded as freedom, however, wild Indianness proved equally attractive, setting up a "have-the-cake-and-eat-it-too" dialectic of simultaneous desire
and repulsion.[5]

Lawrence's intuitive insight was hardly exclusive. Most of the writers he dissected in *Studies* had sensed the ambiguous but important place of Indians in the national psyches they sought to bring to life. Self-exiled to New Mexico, Lawrence himself would be quite literally surrounded by a circle of modernist writers, poets, and painters exploring the same theme.[6] "There has been all the time, in the white American soul, a dual feeling about the Indian," Lawrence claimed, unable, finally, to say much beyond the obvious. "The desire to extirpate [him]. And the contradictory desire to glorify him."[7]

This is, of course, the familiar contradiction we have come to label noble savagery, a term that both juxtaposes and conflates an urge to idealize and desire Indians and a need to despise and dispossess them. A flexible ideology, noble savagery has a long history, one going back to Michel de Montaigne, Jean-Jacques Rousseau, and other Enlightenment philosophers. If one emphasizes the noble aspect, as Rousseau did, pure and natural Indians serve to critique Western society. Putting more weight on savagery justifies (and perhaps requires) a campaign to eliminate barbarism. Two interlocked traditions: one of self-criticism, the other of conquest. They balance perfectly, forming one of the foundations underpinning the equally intertwined history of European colonialism and the European Enlightenment.[8]

Yet Lawrence, with his reckless prose and layering of unresolvable dualisms, seems (like his literary subjects) to be struggling to articulate something more. Indians, it is clear, are not simply useful symbols of the love-hate ambivalence of civilization and savagery. Rather, the contradictions embedded in noble savagery have themselves been the precondition for the formation of American identities. To understand the various ways Americans have contested and constructed national identities, we must constantly return to the original mysteries of Indianness.

Lawrence linked American incompleteness to an aboriginal "spirit of place" with which Americans had failed to come to terms. "No place," Lawrence observed, "exerts its full influence upon a newcomer until the old inhabitant is dead or absorbed."[9] Lawrence argued that in order to meet "the demon of the continent" head on and thus finalize the "unexpressed spirit of America," white Americans needed either to destroy Indians or to assimilate them into a white American world. These have, in fact, been two familiar options in the history of Indian-American relations, both aimed at making Indians vanish from the landscape. But loosing this unexpressed "spirit" required a difficult, collective, and absolute decision: extermination or inclusion. It is a decision that the American polity has been unable to make or, on the few occasions w

been relatively clear, to implement.

The indeterminacy of American identities stems, in p

inability to deal with Indian people. Americans wanted t

with the continent, and it was Indians who could teach

closeness. Yet, in order to control the landscape they had

inhabitants. Lawrence saw the problem demonstrated most clearly in the writ-

ings of Crèvecoeur: "[Crèvecoeur] wanted his ideal state. At the same time, he

wanted to know the other state, the dark, savage mind. He wanted both. Can't

be done Hector. The one is the death of the other!"[10] The nineteenth-century

quest for a self-identifying national literature that Lawrence took as his subject

continually replicated Crèvecoeur's dilemma, speaking the simultaneous lan-

guages of cultural fusion and of violent appropriation. Likewise, American

social and political policy toward Indians has been a two-hundred-year back-

and-forth between assimilation and destruction.

Recent scholarship has pointed to similar cultural ambiguities arising from

equally conflicted racial imaginings and relations with African Americans.

Blackness, in a range of cultural guises, has been an essential precondition for

American whiteness, and it has taken material shape in literature, minstrel

shows, class and gender relations, political struggles, and spatial geographies.[11]

This book will suggest that the figure of "the Indian" holds an equally critical

position in American culture. Race has, of course, been a characteristic Ameri-

can obsession—and the racial imagination has been at work on many different

groups of people, Indians included. But Americans—particularly white Ameri-

cans—have been similarly fixated on defining themselves as a nation. As we shall

see, those national definitions have engaged racialized and gendered Indians in

curious and contradictory ways. At the Boston Tea Party and elsewhere, Indian-

ness provided impetus and precondition for the creative assembling of an ul-

timately unassemblable American identity. From the colonial period to the

present, the Indian has skulked in and out of the most important stories various

Americans have told about themselves.

"The waves that wrought a country's wreck," observed Oliver Wendell

Holmes in 1874,

> have rolled o'er Whig and Tory;
> The Mohawks on the Dartmouth's deck
> Shall live in song and story.[12]

this and a thousand other songs and stories one can find Lawrence's half-secret, half-articulated Indianness, continually lurking behind various efforts at American self-imagination.

It is with this insight, however, that we part company with D. H. Lawrence, for, as suggestively quirky as it is, *Studies in Classic American Literature* deals almost exclusively in the world of texts and images. More interesting are the faux Mohawks slinking home down Boston alleyways on a chill December night. Their feathers, blankets, headdresses, and war paint point to the fact that images of Indianness have often been translated into material forms. Mohawk disguises allowed Bostonians not only to articulate ideologically useful Indian identities but also to perform and experience them. If Indianness is a key theme in this book, so too is the notion of disguise.

The Mohawk Indian disguise adopted by Tea Party participants has usually been explained as either an attempt to maintain secrecy and anonymity or as an effort—almost laughably transparent—to cast blame on a third party.[13] Neither explanation will suffice. As an attempt to deflect blame, dressing like an Indian had, at best, a limited rhetorical use. Few took the mammoth leap of imagination necessary to believe that a band of Mohawk raiders had traveled hundreds of miles through now-foreign territory solely to deprive Boston of its tea. The claim of anonymity is equally dubious. Although some participants donned feathers, for most a smear of soot and a blanket proved an easier choice. Others eschewed disguise altogether, making no effort to hide their identities. Having a recent history of political riot, Boston knew its popular street-gang leaders, and guessing the identities of many of even the disguised offenders was not an impossible task for informed observers. It was not the disguises that kept the participants' identities secret but the support of Boston residents and the social sanctions imposed by the enforcer wing of the Sons of Liberty.[14]

Even so, the participants took pains to offer up Indian identities, grunting and speaking stage Indian words that had to be "translated" into English.[15] If they did not care much about actual disguise, they cared immensely about the *idea* of disguise and its powerful imputation of Indian identity. Dressing as an Indian allowed these pretend Mohawks to translate texts, images, and ideologies into physical reality. In doing so, they lived out the cultural ideas that surrounded Noble Savagery as concrete gestures that possessed physical and emotional meaning.[16]

Costume and disguise—especially when associated with holidays, rituals, or the concealing dark—can have extraordinary transformative qualities. Almost everyone has experienced the sense of personal liberation that attends the wearing of disguise, be it Halloween masks, cross-gender clothing, or garments signifying a racial, ethnic, or class category different from one's own. Disguise readily calls the notion of fixed identity into question. At the same time, however, wearing a mask also makes one self-conscious of a real "me" underneath. This simultaneous experience is both precarious and creative, and it can play a critical role in the way people construct new identities. As they first imagined and then performed Indianness together on the docks of Boston, the Tea Party Indians gave material form to identities that were witnessed and made real. The performance of Indian Americanness afforded a powerful foundation for subsequent pursuits of national identity.[17]

Although these performances have changed over time, the practice of playing Indian has clustered around two paradigmatic moments—the Revolution, which rested on the creation of a national identity, and modernity, which has used Indian play to encounter the authentic amidst the anxiety of urban industrial and postindustrial life. In the beginning, British colonists who contemplated revolution dressed as Indians and threw tea in Boston Harbor. When they consolidated power and established the government of the early republic, former revolutionaries displayed their ideological proclivities in Indian clothing. In the antebellum United States, would-be national poets donned Indian garb and read their lyrics to each other around midnight backwoods campfires.

At the turn of the twentieth century, the thoroughly modern children of angst-ridden upper- and middle-class parents wore feathers and slept in tipis and wigwams at camps with multisyllabic Indian names. Their equally nervous post–World War II descendants made Indian dress and powwow-going into a hobby, with formal newsletters and regular monthly meetings. Over the past thirty years, the counterculture, the New Age, the men's movement, and a host of other Indian performance options have given meaning to Americans lost in a (post)modern freefall. In each of these historical moments, Americans have returned to the Indian, reinterpreting the intuitive dilemmas surrounding Indianness to meet the circumstances of their times.

Playing Indian is a persistent tradition in American culture, stretching from the very instant of the national big bang into an ever-expanding present and future. It is, however, a tradition with limitations. Not surprisingly, these cling tightly to the contours of power. The creation of what Carroll Smith-Rosenberg has called a "national subjectivity" has, from the constitutional convention forward, been largely the domain of white males. They have built that subjectivity on contrasts between their own citizenship and that denied to women, African Americans, Indians, and others.[18] Not until the early twentieth century, when national identity twined so intimately with questions surrounding modernist authenticity, did women don Indian costume on a regular basis. African-American Indian play—especially the carnivalesque revels of Mardi Gras—follows white practices to a degree, but it also stems from a different history of Afro-Caribbean cultural hybridity.[19] Europeans, too, have embraced Indianness, with summertime reenactment camps stretching from Great Britain to Germany to the former Soviet Union. Obviously linked to the United States, these practices are part of traditions that, in this book, must remain tangential. The groups I have chosen to pursue are by and large white American men. Although riven along class lines and differentiated by historical crises, they have been the primary claimants of an American cultural logic that has demanded the formulation and performance of national identities.

What is the connection between "the Indian" and American identity? What has been the role of disguise and costume in this identity play? How does this particular form of identity formation change over time and why? These questions define the primary themes explored in this book. One additional question, however, is essential to this inquiry: How have Indian people reacted to Europeans doing bad imitations of native dress, language, and custom?

It would be folly to imagine that white Americans blissfully used Indianness to tangle with their ideological dilemmas while native people stood idly by, exerting no influence over the resulting Indian images. Throughout a long history of Indian play, native people have been present at the margins, insinuating their way into Euro-American discourse, often attempting to nudge notions of Indianness in directions they found useful. As the nineteenth and twentieth centuries unfolded, increasing numbers of Indians participated in white people's Indian play, assisting, confirming, co-opting, challenging, and legitimating the performative tradition of aboriginal American identity. When, for example, the Seneca intermediary Ely S. Parker assisted Lewis Henry Morgan in establishing an Indian literary fraternity, he helped create a specific Indian image—one that proved useful in motivating Morgan's companions to help the Iroquois in their battles with a greedy land company and an unreliable federal government. Tracing the different manifestations of American Indian play invariably requires following the interlocked historical trajectory of native people as well.

The Boston Tea Party, as a generative moment of American political and cultural identity, serves as a likely beginning for the story D. H. Lawrence was trying to read out of the works of classic American authors. But just as America itself did not spring forth fully formed from the continent, neither was the Tea Party the manifestation of a purely American way of performing an identity. In fact, the Tea Party represents the collision of variant traditions in the colonies, themselves transformed from older European antecedents.

The American Revolution was both the beginning of the nation's struggle to assume an essential identity and the culmination of century-old traditions of popular rebellion. "You can't change your nature and mode of consciousness like changing your shoes," said Lawrence. "Years must go by and centuries must elapse before you have finished. . . . It is a long and half-secret process."[20] At the Tea Party one can witness both the beginning and the end of such half-secret processes. One process—centered in Europe—came to fruition in the new consciousness that was America. With the other, white Americans began a still-unfinished, always-contested effort to find an ideal sense of national Self and to figure out what its new mode of consciousness might be all about.

one

Patriotic Indians and Identities of Revolution

What, then, is the American, this new man?
HECTOR ST. JOHN DE CRÈVECOEUR
Letters from an American Farmer (1782)

"What is an American?" asked St. John de Crèvecoeur before
the Revolution, and the question has been repeated by every
generation from his time to ours.
HENRY NASH SMITH
Virgin Land: The American West as Symbol and Myth (1950)

When he was appointed the king's surveyor-general and assistant governor of New Hampshire in 1730, David Dunbar promised zealous enforcement of the Mast Tree law, an ordinance requiring him to claim trees suitable for ships' masts for the Royal Navy. During the forty-odd years preceding Dunbar's appointment, lax enforcement of the Mast Tree law and similar regulations had become status quo in New Hampshire. Local residents developed a system— juries that refused to indict or convict, paper townships created to evade private

property restrictions, political manipulation, and threats of violence—that en-
sured their control over the lucrative lumber and shipbuilding trades. Dunbar's
concern for renewed enforcement stemmed not from any deep devotion to the
lapsed laws, but from his desire to embarrass a political rival, Governor Jona-
than Belcher. Not coincidentally, his most serious enforcement efforts took
place in Exeter, a town controlled politically and economically by the Gilman
family, long-standing Belcher supporters.[1]

In 1734, Dunbar sent a party of men to enforce the Mast Tree law on the
residents of Exeter. Midway through their meal at the town inn one evening, the
party heard whoops and screams. The inn's door slammed open and a file of
men entered and headed directly for Dunbar's table. The intruders wore blankets wrapped Indian-style and sported caps and feathers on their heads. They
had blackened and painted faces, and they grimaced and brandished clubs at the
frightened group. When one of the stunned victims tried to speak, an Indian
clubbed him across the shoulders. As the king's men mounted a feeble resistance, war clubs rained down upon their heads. Bruised and bleeding, the
men lay dazed as the war party, whooping and howling, made for the door.

If Dunbar's men thought that the Indians' exit marked the end of the evening's excitement, they were gravely mistaken. Their assailants remained outside the public house, screaming curses, epithets, and threats. Concluding that
they were still in danger, the men fled out the back door and down to their boat,
only to find that the sails and rigging had been slashed. They pushed off into the
harbor anyway, hoping to find refuge offshore. Perhaps they breathed a collective sigh of relief as they floated away from the howling throng gathered on the
shore. Soon, however, the party realized that their vessel was taking on water,
the Indians having punched a hole in its bottom. They drifted ashore down-
stream and spent the rest of the night in hiding. Doubtless, during their hike
back to Portsmouth the next day each was reevaluating the relation between
zealous backwoods law enforcement and personal safety.

The Dunbar encounter may be the first recorded meeting with New England's
white Indians. It was certainly not the last. In 1768, for example, the *Boston
Evening Post* carried a similar story:

> We hear from the eastern parts of this province, that there have lately been
> disputes relating to the right of lands between some Claimers and the
> Possessors, which are very common in those parts: That a month ago
> at Woolwich a person there having built a house, about 20 or 30 men

disguised in an Indian dress, came upon him, and drove the people out, and they pull'd the house down; and afterwards threatened to serve some others in the same manner.[2]

In the years before the American Revolution, colonial crowds often acted out their political and economic discontent in Indian disguise.[3] The Boston Tea Party has given the practice its greatest notoriety, but white Indians attacked other tea ships as well, and they kept a tight watch on activities involving tea. When a tea vessel did manage to land south of Boston the following spring, Samuel Adams wrote with disgust that "the Indians this way, if they had suspected the Marshpee tribe would have been so sick at the knees, would have marched on Snow Shoes . . . to have done the business for them."[4] In New York, Mohawks wrote strident editorial letters to the newspapers and everywhere plastered handbills warning against the purchase or drinking of tea. Indians turned up frequently in political cartoons and in humorous yet pointed proclamations such as the one penned in January 1774 by Tea Party participant Edward Proctor (fig. 1):

[From the] Chief Sachem of the Mohawks . . . and Lord of all their Castles: To all our liege Subjects—Health.

Whereas Tea is an Indian Plant, and of right belongs to the Indians of every land and tribe . . . We do . . . permit and allow any of our liege Subjects to barter for, buy, or procure of any of our said English Allies, Teas of any kind: PROVIDED always each man purchases not less than Ten nor more than One hundred and fourteen Boxes at a Time, and those the property of the East India Company, and provided also that they pour all the Said Tea into the Lakes, Rivers, and ponds, that while our Subjects in their Hunting instead of Slaking their Thirst with Cold Water, as usual, may do it with Tea.[5]

Confronting political and economic incursions against established status quos, eighteenth-century New Englanders often adopted traditional European methods of social protest, resurrecting the blackfaced disguise and the violent (but rarely murderous) crowd reprisals that characterized Old World traditions of misrule. Whether aimed at British officials or colonial landlords, misrule traditions, often performed in Indian dress, remained a vital mode of American political protest for more than a century.[6]

In the middle colonies, other Americans began dressing as Indians for different reasons. While David Dunbar's men were confronting hostile white In-

1. Edward Proctor, Mohawk Tea Proclamation, January 1774. Assuming the Indian identity of Toneteroque, Proctor captured the mix of metaphoric consciousness, carnivalesque inversion, and political outrage that characterized the Boston Tea Party and other revolutionary uses of Indianness. From Francis S. Drake, Tea Leaves: Being a Collection of Letters and Documents Relating to the Shipment of Tea to the American Colonies in the Year 1773 (Boston: A. O. Crane, 1884), clxvii–clxviii.

dians in New Hampshire, the members of the Schuylkill Fishing Company of Pennsylvania may have been preparing Indian costumes for the May first frolics that opened their club's sporting season. According to club lore, its fishing and hunting grounds had once been the territory of Tamenend, a Delaware leader who had granted William Penn access to the river and woods.[7] The Schuylkill club inspired the formation of similar clubs in urban areas of the middle colonies, the Chesapeake, and the seaboard South. Each group gathered on May Day for dinners that featured songs, tobacco, a huge dinner, and prolific toasting with bowls of potent alcoholic punch. May first was proclaimed King Tammany's Day, and, to celebrate the return of spring, revelers sponsored maypoles, dances, vigorous speeches called longtalks, and Indian-costumed parades.[8]

After the passage of the Stamp Act in 1765, increasingly resistant colonists gleefully promoted Tammany from king to "tutular [sic] saint of America" and turned their May Day songs and revels into overtly politicized demonstrations of patriotic Americanness. The Indian saint's supposed motto, Kwanio Che Kee-teru, used formally by the sporting club as early as 1747 (as the inscription on a cannon), became—both in and out of translation—a patriotic slogan of the Tammany societies: "This is my right; I will defend it."[9] The societies created a body of myth to celebrate the recently canonized Tammany and the American continent for which he stood. Long before William Penn's arrival, the American saint had battled with the devil for possession of the land, successfully hunted the most dangerous of animals, nurtured peace in the council chamber, and performed a host of other noble deeds. Growing aged, Tammany refused to burden his family but instead put his lodge to the torch and reclined peacefully inside, perhaps destined to rise again someday. As they imagined and then appropriated this phoenixlike figure, the white members of the societies sought to stake their claim on an essential Indian Americanness.

European antecedents lay closely beneath the surface of these two prerevolutionary traditions of playing Indian. In the middle colonies, bacchanalian parties and patriotic literary fictions recalled the costumed excesses of European holiday festivals. In the North, disguised riot, effigy burnings, and tar-and-featherings evoked Old World misrule traditions. The two traditions—carnival and misrule—are intimately connected and, indeed, often blend seamlessly together. Both sets of rituals are about inverting social distinctions, turning the world upside down, questioning authority.[10]

While recognizing the traditions' common roots, I would like, nonetheless, to treat them separately in order to help clarify the distinctions between New Hampshire and Pennsylvania and between the Old World and the New. What I shall refer to as carnival was associated with specific occasions—holidays and market days, for instance—although the inverted world of carnival consciousness could appear at any time and was a significant element in misrule rituals. What I shall call misrule, although it often occurred in the context of specific holidays, had an aggressive, critical quality that could be mustered at any time to protest transgressions of the social order. Taken together, manipulated by colonists, and transformed by the infusion of Indianness, misrule and carnival offered proto-Americans a platform for imagining and performing an identity of revolution. Such an identity was assembled piece by piece at events like the Exeter riot and the Tammany dinners, and it found its most compelling expression at the Boston Tea Party.[11]

Carnival, the Catholic holiday that ushers in the self-deprivations of Lent, is most visible to Americans as Mardi Gras. But carnival originated in the Middle Ages as a longer, transitional festive *season*. It encompassed the time between the celebrations of Christmas, which were based upon the solar calendar, and the Easter holidays, which marked the meeting of the lunar calendar and the spring equinox. During the carnival season, hearty overconsumption of meat and drink emphasized fertility, wild abundance, and the physical functions of the body. Carnival celebrations traded in humor, disruptive behavior, street theater, processions, disguise, gender reversals, death, regeneration, and the symbolic overturning and inversion of established social orders. In France, for example, at the Christmastime Feast of Fools a choirboy might become a bishop and preside over a burlesqued mass. Mocking paraders might dare to haul an ass through the church. The major sponsors of such festivals were fraternities of young men called Abbeys of Misrule, and they organized themselves around holiday hier-archies of inverted offices: the Prince of Improvidence, the Cardinal of Bad Measure, Bishop Flatpurse, Duke Kickass, and the Grand Patriarch of Syphilitics. In England, holidays featured blackface, transvestism, and costume, the parad-ing of figures in live or effigy form, and the pots-and-pans clamor of "rough music."[12]

By the sixteenth century, urban men's societies—previously defined by youth and marital status—began to cluster around occupational affinities and social distinctions. Increasingly, festival inversions critiqued not only social but also political orders, mocking magistrates and officials and sometimes providing the occasion for armed uprisings. The line between street party and insurrec-tion could blur with alarming rapidity, the semantically linked words *rebel* and *revel* smearing together in the collective mouth of an unruly crowd.[13] Carnival worked transformative magic, however, even in the absence of armed insur-gence. The temporary experience of life as something other-than-what-is infil-trated and permeated the life that was, transforming both.

Carnival, according to the Russian critic Mikhail Bakhtin, represented a sec-ond life, a different consciousness that transcended the everyday. In the festive practices of the common people of Europe, he saw a topsy-turvy, mocking way of being that questioned the rationalized administrative power of the state. As both specific holiday ritual and generalized consciousness, carnival broke down boundaries, demonstrating the commonalities between upper and lower classes, law and custom, food and flesh, past and present, civilized and savage, birth and death. It replaced all forms of rank and hierarchy with a boundless

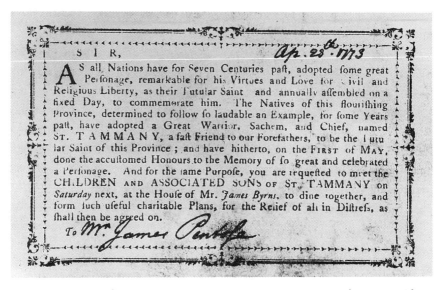

2. *Philadelphia Sons of St. Tammany, Invitation to Tammany Day Dinner, April 28, 1773. The annual dinner combined Old World traditions like May Day celebrations and the designation of saintly national icons with the environmental virtues of the American continent, expressed through mythic songs of hunting, war, and liberty. Courtesy of the Edwin Kilroe Papers, Rare Book and Manuscript Library, Columbia University.*

utopian freedom. Over time, the impact of these different consciousnesses might painstakingly transform the larger structures of a society.[14]

The confusing of boundaries made carnivalesque holidays perfect markers for the simultaneous beginnings and endings of cycles of time—years, mourning periods, planting seasons, periods of denial, rites of passage. Such cycles often ended with the ritual death of a royal figure representing the past year, the older generation, the accumulated evil. This sacrifice required celebration, for only through such an overthrow could the new cycle be born. On May Day, for example, European revelers danced around the maypole—an ancient symbol of the unity of the old sacrificial king and his successor—to celebrate not only the end of one cycle and the beginning of another, but also the oneness of the old year and the new. They frequently burnt the old king and used fire and ash symbolism to evoke the phoenixlike connection between death and new life.[15] Along with the maypole, celebrants held dances, strewed flowers and boughs, wore blackface, and performed mummer's plays, in which costumed actors would break into a gathering, perform a skit, and then take up a collection.

Copious food and drink recalled the abundance of the past and invoked the fertility of the future.

At the same time that this second life awakened participants to future possibilities, however, it reaffirmed the social systems that structured the nonfestive world. The humor in a mocking church parade owed much of its power to the looming presence of a real parade of powerful bishops and clergy. Carnival presented its celebrators a doubled vision of the world: on the one hand, anarchic possibility; on the other, affirmation of the status quo.

American Tammany societies created May Day rites that drew directly from these older European traditions (fig. 2). Endowed with kingly control over American fecundity, the mythic Tammany served as the counterpart of the traditional May fertility king. "It is usual on the morning of [St. Tammany's] day," noted one account of a Chesapeake Bay celebration,

> for the members of the society to erect in some public situation in the city, a "May-pole" and to decorate it in a most tasteful manner, with wild flowers gathered from the adjacent woods, and forming themselves in a ring around it, hand in hand, perform the Indian war dance, with many other customs which they had seen exhibited by the children of the forest. . . . A large company usually assembled during the course of the evening, and when engaged in the midst of a dance, the company were interrupted by the sudden intrusion of a number of the members of "St. Tamina's Society," habited like Indians, who rushing violently into the room, singing the war songs, and giving the whoop, commenced dancing in the style of that people. After which ceremony, they made a collection and retired well satisfied.[16]

The maypole, floralia, and costumed mummers were all familiar European holiday practices, claimed now as the supposed American customs of the "children of the forest."[17] The Tammany societies also celebrated the death of the Indian saint as the overthrow of an aged fertility figure. In Charleston, South Carolina, Tammany followers reenacted his mythic end by literally setting him on fire: "At about 4 o'clock they sat down to a plain and plentiful dinner, and after imbibing a suitable quantity of Indian drink proceeded to the solemnity of burning the Old Chief, who being placed in the Wigwam and having sung the death song, fire was set thereto and the whole immediately consumed. A dance, after the Indian manner, concluded the ceremonies of the day."[18]

When Indian-garbed proto-Americans wound around the maypole, they celebrated not only the departed Tammany, but also his heir apparent—themselves.[19] The rituals worked in countervailing ways. Tammany's death was a metaphor for the "disappearance" of Indian people from the land, the destruction of the old cycle, the dawning of another era in which successor Americans would enjoy their new world. His implied rebirth, on the other hand, suggested that Americans were not successors so much as aboriginal Tammanys themselves. And if the new ruler was literally the same as the old, it was only fitting that the Tammany members share his identity by clothing themselves in Indian garb.[20]

While Tammany rituals enacted the displacement of Indians, they also relied upon reborn Indian Americanness to question the British identity that the empire would have preferred to see among its colonists. John Leacock's comedy *The Fall of British Tyranny; or, American Liberty Triumphant* (1776) captured this mixture of nascent American political identity, spring fertility ritual, and doubled consciousness as it coalesced musically around the carnival theme of abundance:

1   Let Hibernia's sons boast, make Patrick their toast,
          and Scots Andrew's fame spread abroad,
      Potatoes and oats, and Welch leeks for Welch goats,
        Was never St. Tammany's food, my brave boys.

2   In freedom's bright cause, Tamm'ny pled with applause,
          And reason'd most justly from nature;
        For this, this was his song, all the day long;
        Liberty's the right of each creature, brave boys.

3   The strong nervous deer, with amazing career,
           In swiftness he'd fairly run down;
      And, like Sampson wou'd tear wolf, lion, or bear.
      Ne'er was such a saint as our own, my brave boys.

4   On an old stump he sat, without cap or hat,
          When supper was ready to eat,
      Snap, his dog, he stood by, and cast a sheep's eye;
      For ven'son's the king of all meat, my brave boys.

5   Like Isaac of old, and both cast in one mold,
          Tho' a wigwam was Tamm'ny's cottage,

He lov'd sav'ry meat, such that patriarch eat,

Of ven'son and squirrel made pottage, brave boys.[21]

Tammany songs frequently played on the significant differences in food between the Old and New World. Enlightenment notions of environmentalism inclined both Europeans and Americans to the idea that one was, quite literally, what one ate. Leacock's derisive nods to oats, leeks, and potatoes (ironically a New World vegetable) are directed at diets that define the dominated provinces of the British empire—Scotland, Wales, and Ireland. Rejecting such a colonial position, Leacock praises quintessentially American culinary alternatives—venison and squirrel—and links them to freedom, kingship, and patriarchal control. The result of such a diet was Tammany himself, a skillful debater who furnished a natural rationale for liberty, the cornerstone of American political argument.[22]

If food and fertility rarely appeared in political and philosophical pamphlets, they nonetheless carried a hearty political burden. At their annual May feast, Tammany disciples ate, drank, and sang songs like Leacock's in boisterous recognition of the gifts of the American land—gifts, they argued, that encouraged a different kind of social order.[23] The intertwined meanings of American landscape, meaty carnival abundance, and revolutionary egalitarianism came together especially clearly, for example, in the societies' treatment of hunting— the mythic Tammany's most impressive skill and the one around which the groups had originally organized. America's profusion of wildlife stunned early seventeenth-century commentators, who were accustomed to the overhunted lands of the Old World. On his trip to America in 1633, William Wood reported his astonishment at the "millions of millions" of passenger pigeons, the great gray squirrels, of which "one might kill a dozen in an afternoon," and the twenty-pound lobsters and foot-long oysters.[24]

Tammany society songs regaling the kingship of venison and meat celebrated both this environmental distinction and its political consequence—the destruction of Old World social restrictions. Those restrictions appeared most significantly in the form of English hunting laws, which mandated severe penalties for the taking of deer and fish. English constructions of social class dictated that hunting be a gentleman's sport, inaccessible to other classes. In the New World, however, the abundance of game made hunting democratic, allowing every man to imagine himself a patriarch in a gentry of egalitarianism. Through Indianness, Tammany members tied the act of hunting to political and social control over the landscape and an ethos of equality.[25]

In sum, a collection of colonists created a patriotic, self-identifying fertility figure in order to celebrate American abundance and its social and political implications. The celebrations used Tammany as a sacrificial figure, the pivot point in a rite of passage ritual that described a transition from Indian to Euro-American rule. At the same time, the Tammany societies conducted their revelry through carnival forms that carried familiar connotations of revolution, over-throw, and transition. And this sense of rebellion was logically directed at a king, who turned out to be not only Tammany, but also George of England.[26]

The festivals, however, meant little without the figure of the Indian. Through Indianness, colonists articulated a revolutionary identity, drawing on the deeply rooted power of familiar ideologies surrounding Native Americans. As Robert F. Berkhofer, Jr., has pointed out, there have been two different manifestations of the Indian in American history.[27] One group of Indians is material and real—a diverse set of tribes and individuals with whom Europeans have interacted for the past several hundred years. The other set is ideal—a collection of mental images, stereotypes, and imaginings based only loosely on those material people Americans have called Indians.

Indian "Others" have been constructed at the intersection of real and imagined Indians. Colonists (mis)perceived real Indian people through a variety of European cultural lenses. Religion, gender relations, subsistence, technology—these and many other perspectives defined and distorted the ways Europeans saw Indians. These perceptions and misperceptions inevitably included imaginary and symbolic qualities as well, the visible products of the sea of ideology in which humans swim. Dignified nobility and inhuman savagery have, of course, been the most familiar principles for organizing these complicated constellations of perception, imagination, and ideology.

It has become a truism that such images of good and bad Indians reveal more about the people who created them than they do about native people themselves. This suggestion is true, but perhaps it is also limiting. To understand the identities of imagemakers, one has to explore not only the meanings of their images, but also the ways those images were assembled. Eighteenth-century colonists constructed Indian Others along two critical axes. They imagined one axis—the noble savage—in terms of the positive and negative values that could be assigned to Indians and that could then be reflected back upon a Self, either as cultural critique or colonial legitimation. Equally important, they imagined a second axis focused not on Indian good or evil, but upon the relative distance that Indian Others were situated from this Self-in-the-making.

> We construct identity by finding ourselves in relation to an array of people and objects who are not ourselves. Every person and thing is Other to us. We situate some Others quite closely to the Selves we are calling into being; others, we place so far away as to make them utterly inhuman. My sister is Other to me but she is relatively close when compared to an anonymous New Yorker. That New Yorker is not as Other as a French policeman, who is not as Other as a Russian soldier. Our familiar sense of constructed social divisions—race, gender, sexuality, class, ethnicity, religion, region, nationality—helps us categorize, clarify, establish, and empower these relations. In situating ourselves, we define our identities as individuals and as members of various groups.[28]

One of the most powerful lines that can be drawn across the spectrum ranging from sister to nonhuman is that which delineates the nation. Nationalism links land, subsistence, political identity, and group destiny together, creating a clear-cut boundary between insiders and outsiders. National identity was indeed the goal of the protonationalist celebrations sponsored by the Tammany societies, and Indian Others were clearly being included on the inside of the American boundaries the members sought to create. Along with the positives and negatives of the noble savage, then, we need to consider the distinction between Indian Others imagined to be interior—inside the nation or the society—and those who are to be excluded as exterior. The matter can get extremely complicated, for both interior and exterior Others can take on positive or negative qualities, depending on the nature of the identity construction in which they appear.[29]

In eighteenth-century America, colonists were especially sensitized to the lines that delineated their society. For most English colonists, so-called savage Indians defined the boundaries and character of their civilization. Conversely, noble Indians allowed the romantic intellectuals of the Enlightenment to embody a critique of European social decadence. In both cases, the exterior relationship between us and them allowed Europeans to define themselves through comparison with a radically different society.

In the late eighteenth century, however, rebellious American colonists in New England and Pennsylvania did something unique. Increasingly inclined to see themselves in opposition to England rather than to Indians, they inverted interior and exterior to imagine a new boundary line of national identity.

They began to transform exterior, noble savage Others into symbolic figures that could be rhetorically interior to the society they sought to inaugurate. In short, the ground of the oppositions shifted and, with them, national self-definition. As England became a them for colonists, Indians became an us. This inversion carried extraordinary consequences for subsequent American politics and identity.[30]

Focused on defining themselves against the mother country, the Pennsylvania Tammany societies almost eliminated the rhetorical boundaries between Indians and white colonists, creating an Indian hero virtually indistinguishable from the average patriot.[31] Representing absolute individual freedom, yet also political control of the landscape, Tammany verged on being a pure representation of an American Self, reflecting the colonists' increasing need to define themselves as something new and non-British. Tammany created American patriots out of British traitors. Regenerative carnival festivities served as a stage for the public performance of this identity shift. So it was that rebels and revels intersected, as May Day and Tammany joined to produce a revolutionary sensibility well suited to the colonies' complicated sense of developing national identity.

Something different was going on in New England. Puritan New England proved to be far less tolerant of transformed fertility rituals than did Quaker Pennsylvania, passing laws against carnivalesque holiday celebrations like May Day. Carnival had always worked both to question and to reaffirm social orders. The Pennsylvanians emphasized the questioning elements that implied rebellion. By trying to stamp out festive humor and fertility celebrations, New Englanders pushed their rituals in the opposite direction—toward misrule and a single-minded concern with protecting social order. The Puritans created a society of rigorous, detailed, and sometimes intrusive rules. And while they backed their laws with civil courts, citizens might keep one another in line through the public humiliation of misrule rituals. Indeed, the lines between official punishment—ducking or the stocks, for example—and folk sanction often blurred.[32]

The changing uses of misrule appear with special clarity in early eighteenth-century England, where centuries-old traditions of masked social sanction took on more overt revolutionary contours around the problem of deer poaching. Severe penalties and paid informers made it, at least in theory, a dangerous and occasionally terminal offense, and poachers, subject to regulation since at least the fifteenth century, maintained a long tradition of blackening their faces in order to disguise their identities.[33] These poachers were the cultural (and perhaps literal) ancestors of those who would later celebrate Pennsylvania's utopian abundance and egalitarian hunting opportunities.

In 1485, a Royal Act formally codified deer hunting in disguise or at night as a felony. In Windsor and some other royal and manorial forests, however, the law went largely unenforced for more than two hundred years. Instead, the inhabitants of the walks and towns of the forests developed what E. P. Thompson has called "moral economies," complex systems of customary rights and obligations, most of which shared ambiguous, interlocking relations with formalized law—and most of which were made visible only when threatened by formal authority. Under these traditional systems, individuals had subsistence rights to the forests' common turf, grazing land, wood, and game. Gamekeepers turned a blind eye to many offenses, and, on the rare occasions when an individual was prosecuted, the local magistrates frequently refused to hand down jail terms, realizing that a poacher's family would simply end up on the local dole.[34]

Reinforced by centuries of practice and a symbiotic relation between law and custom, the forest residents understood the working system of the forest to be a form of law.[35] Resentment burgeoned when the routine came under gradual attack after England's Civil War and the Restoration of 1660. Newly rich and titled landowners slowly replaced older lords whose fortunes had declined. This new gentry, created by success in the national and international markets, staked economic rather than hereditary claims to the forests. They pushed the Crown for tougher laws and enforcement in the private parkland they now claimed as their own. A series of acts passed in the late seventeenth and early eighteenth centuries aimed to reestablish royal dominance over the forests by offering substantial rewards to informants and mandating transportation to overseas penal colonies for deer poachers. By raising the stakes, however, the government succeeded only in elevating petty blackfaced poaching to a more organized and serious endeavor. Misrule, until now simply a method of enforcing the rhetoric of moral economy, became a more formalized mode of rebellion.[36]

Between 1720 and 1723, groups of so-called Blacks dominated Windsor Forest. Disguised in blackface, they hunted deer in large mounted groups calculated to intimidate gamekeepers. If a king's official seized a dog or a poached deer or levied a fine, a party of Blacks would soon appear at the door and threaten to burn his house unless the penalty was quickly returned. Gamekeepers were often "beset in the heath" and threatened with bodily harm. With local

magistrates still reluctant to sentence offenders and many forest officials intimi-
dated, the Blacks effectively stymied initial attempts to reassert royal control.

Blacking drew much of its power from socially prescriptive misrule rituals. In
France and Britain, the Abbeys of Misrule had protected moral economies
and enforced social custom through noisy charivari parades featuring effigies of adulterers, men beaten by their wives, and other transgressors. English
rough music accompanied the victims of "riding skimmington" or "riding the
stang"—the parading of people or effigies on poles, carts, or donkeys. Such
rituals frequently featured blackface, masking, and ritual burning, but they were
cut from different cloth than those of carnival. Rough music groups acted to
reinforce traditional, customary social orders, not to play on the edges of
revolution.[37]

In Windsor Forest, however, blacking and misrule began to acquire a more
fully developed revolutionary shape as customary rights collided directly with
royal prerogative. The government responded accordingly. In 1723, the English
Parliament, concerned with the threat to royal authority and rumors linking
Black groups with the Jacobites, passed the Black Act, an extreme piece of
legislation suited more to revolutionaries than to forest dwellers protecting
customary rights. It mandated the death penalty for blacking, hunting at night,
and assembling in disguise. Backed by a network of informers and a troop of
soldiers, officials made sweeping arrests of suspected Blacks in Windsor Forest.
Eventually, four Blacks were executed, six were sentenced to transportation
overseas, and several more were indicted.[38]

As David Dunbar had discovered in New Hampshire, Old World misrule
rituals remained in the customary repertoire of many colonists. Periodically
rejuvenated by arriving immigrants, they could be activated and reshaped according to the needs of specific local groups.[39] Southern New Englanders, for
example, had already turned misrule toward the preservation of the customary
status quo. Between 1630 and 1650, the Massachusetts Bay Colony established
social, political, and cultural hegemony over the region. Such dominance required the elimination of the carnivalesque, for its wild unpredictability threatened the ordered world the Puritans desired to build.[40]

By the mid–eighteenth century, officials had stamped out every traditional
festival save one. Maypoles, morris dances, summer kings and queens, autumn
harvest festivals, Christmas, New Year's, and Easter celebrations all disappeared.
Only Pope Day (November 5), an anti-Catholic celebration grafted on to an
ancient complex of winter holidays, remained, a misrule ritual directed against

a rival church. Such civic celebrations as Artillery Day, Election Day, and college Commencement Day offered small, easily contained demonstrations of public festivity.[41]

By repressing specific holidays, the Puritan elites disengaged misrule rituals from their association with festive time. When misrule was directed solely at enforcing customary community standards and was stripped of the elements of holiday celebration, it lost much (but not all) of its revolutionary world-turned-upside-down power. Ironically, what New England misrule lost in terms of carnivalesque revolutionary consciousness, it regained as a channel for defending custom against the incursions of the British state. The ineffectuality of Dunbar's enforcement efforts demonstrates the potential power of this newly focused, rebellious misrule. Indeed, the Tea Party and the American Revolution itself can be seen as the culmination of a long transformation of misrule-based social protest that extends back to Windsor Forest and beyond.

The Indianization of misrule transformed the rituals of protest still further, for it allowed rioters to invent the American customs they so sorely lacked. The idea of custom was as thoroughly embedded in Exeter as it was in Windsor Forest. For both Blacks and loggers, it was the "rhetoric of legitimation for almost any usage, practice, or demanded right."[42] The problem in New Hampshire, of course, lay in locating legitimate customs to defend. English Blacks fought to protect recognized centuries-old traditions. Colonists had no such ancient history to bolster their claim to a vernacular system of social order. The loggers' claim to a local law of custom depended mostly on empty rhetoric and (more significantly) distance from the seat of royal authority. As Dunbar's effort demonstrated, officials could not always count on the latter.

As a rhetorical device, Indianness helped the Mast Tree rioters define custom and imagine themselves a legitimate part of the continent's ancient history. Indians and the land offered the only North American past capable of justifying a claim of traditional custom and a refiguring of the rhetoric of moral economy. Native people had been on the land for centuries, and they embodied a full complement of the necessary traditions. By becoming Indian, New Hampshirites sought to appropriate those laws of custom. White Indians laid claim, not to real Indian practices, of course, but to the idea of native custom—the specifics to be defined not by Indians, but by colonists. These ancient customs were then claimed to supersede royal law, especially as it pertained to the trees of the New Hampshire forest that colonists wanted to harvest and take to market.

By playing Indian, the rioters evoked and invented local understandings about the freedom, naturalness, and individualism of native custom. Conflating Indians and land, the rioters suggested that these qualities lay embedded in the American continent itself and that, as the environment reshaped settlers' personalities, freedom and liberty had made their way into the psychic makeup of white Europeans. As in Philadelphia, playing Indian suggested that a powerful landscape had somehow transformed immigrants, giving them the same status as Indians and obligating them to defend the same customary liberty.

In the 1730s, after decades of conflict with local Indian people, New Hampshire residents hardly valued actual Indians. In donning Indian dress, of course, they were engaging in a dialogue not about Indians, but about themselves and their beliefs, and that dialogue was directed primarily toward colonial and imperial authority. Yet the rioters did differ from the Tammany paraders. The Philadelphians' urban setting tempted them to downplay actual Indians and accompanying images of savagery. Tammany was a noble figure. When the Mast Tree rioters played Indian, they engaged both noble and savage, interior and exterior Indian Others.

As they sympathetically evoked noble American commonalities, the loggers' Indian disguise played simultaneously on the contradictory image of the savage Indian who existed outside the pale of law and civilization. Masked disguise of any sort allowed one to hoot and howl and beat up the king's surveyors. The feeling of moral detachment that came with being masked or in blackface was amplified, however, when the mask was not simply an anonymous blank but rather the sign of an Indian Other who existed outside of social boundaries. If a loyal colonist would not assault the king's men, an Indian savage surely might.

The rioters used disguise to experience and perform the opposed identities of rebel and citizen. Indians were noble and customary, and they existed inside an American society that was not British. But Indians were also savage, existing outside of a British society that included both colonists and officials. Indian disguise allowed individuals to cross the boundaries of law and civilization while simultaneously reaffirming the existence and necessity of those boundaries. Like the carnival revelers in Philadelphia, New Englanders used Indianness to create an identity psychologically attuned to resistance and, eventually, rebellion.

Carnival and misrule thus sprang from European roots and became infused with revolutionary messages through the figure of the Indian. Many of those transfigurations occurred in the blur of half-consciousness that characterizes cultural rituals. In some instances, however, the forms and contents of the rituals were intentionally altered to serve the purposes of resistance. Colonists came to the rebellion with diverse experiences and motivations. Historians have quite profitably viewed the Revolution as a complex interaction among many social groups—artisans and sailors of the "revolutionary crowd," explicitly political radicals, Enlightenment philosophers, middle-class merchants, rural farmers, frontier settlers, women of all classes, occupations, and residences, African Americans, Indians, and others. This diversity also led to differences in the transmission, regeneration, and use of European traditions like carnival and misrule. The challenge for would-be revolutionaries lay in creating points of unity and shared meaning out of this diversity.[43]

In Pennsylvania, the organizers of the Tammany societies' May Day festivals tried to do exactly that, reshaping plebeian traditions in order to unify participants around a more coherent American identity. Unlike Old World carnival, the May Day frolics passed out of control of the area's common farmers and laborers. Indeed, the society's practice of precomposing formal toasts and elaborate songs and then immortalizing them in postcelebration print points to the decline of oral and folk elements in the face of a more formalized, self-conscious understanding of the festival as a medium of political communication and image making. The Philadelphia society counted among its members John Dickinson (lawyer, pamphleteer, politician), Tench Francis (financier), Thomas Mifflin (future state governor), David Rittenhouse (astronomer and member of Congress), Dr. Benjamin Rush, and other men firmly in the forefront of colonial religion, science, law, politics, and publishing.[44] They were well positioned not only to define the general nature of the Indian, but also to construct Smith-Rosenberg's national subjectivity. Middling and elite intellectuals used Tammany to articulate their political concerns. In doing so, they changed the very nature of the carnival celebration, taking it out of the more spontaneous, reveling hands of the common people and explicitly and self-consciously putting its transformative political potential to work.[45]

A similar transformation occurred in New England, as can be seen in the Mast Tree riot. The event's perpetrators may have been simply a group of millworkers drinking in a rival public house and deciding to have some serious fun and eliminate a perceived threat. Given the political rivalries hanging in the balance, however, it seems more likely that members of the Gilman family—allies of Dunbar's antagonist, Governor Belcher—rounded up some local toughs and

gave them direction. At the Mast Tree charivari, misrule entered the political
arena as a self-conscious defense of both custom and the economic and political
interests of colonial elites.[46]

New World transformations, of course, never completely eradicated the
plebeian nature of carnival and misrule. In Boston, colonial crowds retained the
festival qualities that lingered over Pope Day even as Samuel Adams and other
leaders tried to turn its misrule to more overt revolutionary ends. By the early
1760s, charivari parades that had once featured the pope displayed British and
colonial officials hanging and burning in effigy. North and South End gangs
reminiscent of the Abbeys of Misrule did battle while small boys in blackface
ran throughout the throng. And Boston crowds summoned this politicized,
carnivalesque misrule on other occasions.[47] On the day of the first Stamp Act
riot a festive craziness—something akin to that of Pope Day—crackled in the air.
Liberty boys turned puns on the Stamp Act, stamping papers into the ground,
and on the English Lord Bute, epitomized as evil and represented by a boot.

In several Boston riots, in fact, the crowd got carried away, taking the rituals
beyond the political demonstrations envisioned by colonial leaders and into the
realm of disquieting violence. If a ride on a skimmington rail could castrate or
occasionally kill, it lacked the vicious, out-of-control character that elites perceived in the mob beatings of stamp collectors and the violent destruction of the
stamp collector Andrew Oliver's home. The order and discipline that characterized the Tea Party suggest that it was an event plotted and controlled by those
elites, who took pains to avoid involving a crowd that had demonstrated a
collective mind of its own. Indian costume now signified not only a leap across
British legal boundaries, but also discipline and planning in the execution of
crowd activities. While the Indians worked on the tea, a potential mob watched
quietly from the wharf. Misrule, like carnival, had been turned largely away
from the common crowd and pushed toward specific channels of political
activity.

At the Tea Party, these altered rituals traded meanings with a long tradition of
symbolic Indianness. Like the ritual forms themselves, those symbolic meanings could be turned to revolutionary ends. Europeans had used images of
Indians to signify the North American continent since the sixteenth century
(fig. 3). In the British political cartoons of the mid–eighteenth century, however, the Indian became a familiar symbol of the American colonies themselves.
Between 1765 and 1783, the colonies appeared as an Indian in no fewer than

3. *Vespucci Discovering America, ca. 1600, Theodore Galle, after Jan vander Straet.*
Represented as a prone, naked Indian woman confronting a standing, clothed European man, America
was portrayed as sexually available to the colonial desires of white Europeans. Surrounded by the
emblems of Christianity and technology, Vespucci wakes the barbarous Indian princess, who is, by
contrast, surrounded by pagan cannibalism and a collection of slothlike animals. Courtesy of the
Beinecke Rare Book and Manuscript Library, Yale University.

sixty-five political prints—almost four times as frequently as the other main
symbols of America, the snake and the child. British cartoonists used Indians to
symbolize the colonies as alien and uncivilized and therefore needful of (and
deserving) the rule of the empire. At an intersection between noble and savage,
tawny white or colored, the figure of the Indian had enormous iconographic
flexibility. By arming it, clothing it, shifting its gender, or coloring its face,
British cartoonists could depict the colonies as violent, civilized, savage, genteel,
aggressive, subservient, rebellious, or justified. Visualizing the figure as an
Indian Princess, for example, allowed one to evoke female sexuality in picturing
the fertile landscape or to show the colonies as available and vulnerable to the
desires of English men (fig. 4).[48]

Because many American political cartoons were reprinted or redrawn from
British sources, these British conventions frequently came into play in reverse

4. "*The Female Combatants or Who Shall*," January 26, 1776.
Figured as a promiscuous "slut" in relation to British colonial
authority, the Indian princess could also be a potent symbol of liberty
and justified rebellion. Courtesy of the Print Collection,
Lewis Walpole Library, Yale University.

form in the colonies. Although most Americans initially accepted the idea of a
political hierarchy over which the Crown held sway, they reacted violently to
British implications that the colonies themselves were an alien place outside the
boundaries of British society. Colonial papers therefore whitened Indian figures
that had initially had dark skin and clothed bodies that had been naked when
they first appeared in London publications. The Indian Princess sometimes took
on the more chaste demeanor of European female icons.[49]

Colonial propaganda brought symbolic Indians inside the boundaries of
colonial identity, adapting the figures in order to convey revolutionary messages. As conflict between the Crown and the colonies intensified, Indian images began to represent America as vulnerable, abused, and enslaved (fig. 5).

5. "*The Able Doctor, or America Swallowing the Bitter Draught,*" *London Magazine, May 1, 1774. Once the Indian princess came to represent the colonists themselves and not simply the landscape, images of sexualized violence had less to do with imperial conquest and more to do with British repression. With arms and legs pinioned, breasts exposed, dress lifted, and petition in tatters on the ground, America is force-fed by Lord North. In a clear reference to the Tea Party, the Indian princess spews tea back in North's face while France and Spain look on (and Britannia turns away). Courtesy of the Beinecke Rare Book and Manuscript Library, Yale University.*

With the onset of outright war in 1775, the figure of the Indian appeared as not only noble and civilized, but also willful, determined, and strong. Indians appeared on military flags, newspaper mastheads, and numerous handbills. In a clear reference to the Tea Party, later printers would portray the American Congress as a colonist in Indian disguise.[50]

By December of 1773, appealing to the ancient, natural customs of the American continent proved a familiar exercise for such Bostonians as Edward Proctor, the author of the Mohawk tea proclamation. Influenced by both European and American political philosophers, the Boston rebels propounded a social order based on Enlightenment ideals of individual freedom. Using Indian identity, misrule, and carnival inversion, Tea Party revolutionaries crossed the boundaries of civilized law in order to attack specific laws that displeased them and to speak to the British from a quintessentially American position. Their Indian disguises (or claims of disguise) played ambiguously on social boundaries. By being both Indian and not-Indian, repulsive savage and object of colonial desire, representation of social order and disorder, the Tea Party Indians revealed the contingency of social order itself and thus opened the door to the creation of the new.

Bostonians blended rhetoric—in which Indians represented America on handbills and in songs—and ritual—in which printed and oral words could be made material in the streets. By smearing their faces, speaking "ugh"-peppered pidgin English, and throwing tea from merchant ships, colonial rebels brought cultural understandings to life through dramatic performance. Through this "theatricalized rhetoric" they solidified their common understanding of themselves as Americans, their freedom an ancient thing linked intrinsically to the continent, its custom, and its nature.

On an early winter night in 1773, white, male Americans staked a unique and privileged claim to liberty and nationhood. They acted through the channels cut by European traditions of carnival and misrule, traditions that they made uniquely their own through the use of Indian Others. The Tea Party represents the culmination of colonial Indian play—an event in which transformed Old World traditions mingled ritual, festival, social sanction, and political protest in dramatic fashion.

As one of the foundational moments of American identity, the Tea Party stands at the heart of a darkness subsequent Americans have struggled to reveal. In order to understand the legacy of the event, we need to turn to another kind of analysis and consider the vagaries of identity formation itself. How did Indianness help create the contradictory identity of Crèvecoeur's "New American"? Eighteenth-century Britons located themselves as social beings through a collection of oppositions: civilized-savage, gentry-commoner, male-female, immigrant-native.[51] For American colonists, Indians broke down these oppositions, serving as a savage Other while at the same time representing an American Self. Two major venues—language and clothing—reveal with particular clarity the ways in which this sense of doubled possibility came to permeate the very fabric of colonial thought.

Indian play was the concrete expression of a metaphoric sensibility, familiar to would-be rebels through the very words they uttered. Even in translation, native expressions had captured the ear and the fancy of Europeans. Early commentators spoke with awe of Indian speech making and rhetorical talent. Diplomats treating with Indian people adopted elements of native languages out of sheer necessity, and Indian words crossed social and cultural boundaries to become part of a wider colonial American language. Such adoptions included greetings ("sago, sago"), mottoes (Kwanio Che Keeteru), terms of exchange (wampum), gender and sexuality (squaw), rank (sachem), and politics (brightening and breaking the covenant chain; younger and elder brothers) as well as thousands of place-names.[52] The presence of Indian words in prerevolutionary language, however, can be seen as more than simply a borrowing of the exotic or the quaint. As many scholars have argued, in representing reality, language is crucial in framing the *experience* of reality for its users. As Indian words and expressions spread into proto-American discourse, they subtly shifted the ways in which colonists understood themselves and their world.[53]

The most important of these linguistic intruders was metaphor, a language trick that suggests the continual shifting, replacement, and doubling of ideas and identities. Colonists thought that native languages lacked the descriptive power of English and had to rely on the almost continual use of metaphor to describe abstract ideas. Accordingly, they adopted it as a general way of signifying Indianness. At Tammany dinners, for example, pseudo-Indian speakers frequently offered toasts that used strings of metaphor: "May the industry of the beaver, the frugality of the ant, the constancy of the dove, be the perpetual characteristicks of the Sons of St. Tammany." In Boston, Proctor's Mohawk proclamation used a variety of metaphoric linkages to create its pointed humor.[54]

And while the use of metaphor evoked Indians, the idea of Indians might bring the notion of metaphor to mind with equal urgency. The words reinforced each other, and, for Tammany diners and Indian rioters, they suggested a way of thinking in which one could figuratively be what one was not.[55] The metaphoric sensibility associated with Indian talk underpinned the Indian/ colonist doublings of the Tammany society and the Tea Party Indians. It made the shift in identities appear almost natural. After the dinner of 1786, for example, the society "proceeded to the wigwam of his excellency brother Benjamin Franklin who appearing was saluted with 13 huzzas from all the warriors. . . . the brothers [then] retired to their own wigwams to see their squaws and papousees."[56] The linguistic status of "wigwams," "warriors," "squaws," and "papousees" is the same here as that of "huzzas," "brothers," and terms of address like "his excellency." "Wigwam" signified not only an Indian dwelling of bark or woven mats, but also the wood and brick homes of Tammany society Americans. Both meanings were metaphorically true, and both legitimated residents as aboriginal.

Indian disguise allowed Tammany members to give material form to the doubled identities they had found in metaphoric language. Tammany warriors and Tea Party Mohawks transformed metaphor into a theatrical reality, literally becoming what they were not.[57] Colonial Americans understood certain well-known rules for the wearing of clothes. One dressed as what one was, and jockeys and gentlemen, for example, had vastly different constraints on what they were "allowed" to wear. The very existence of these cultural codes, however, gives clothing the power to suggest other identities as well, to tell about its wearer lies that may be something more. Misleading dress possesses a surprising degree of power, conferring upon its wearer a doubled consciousness, the physical equivalent of metaphoric language.[58]

At the first Boston Stamp Act riot on August 14, 1765, gentlemen joined the mobs in supposed commoner disguise—they wore trousers and jackets instead of breeches.[59] Like the unmasked Tea Party Mohawks, this particular form of disguise failed to conceal their faces and their identities. What mattered more was that contemporary commentators recognized the breach of cultural rules that normally governed colonial dress. When gentlemen wore trousers, they were breaking that code and, hence, must have been disguised. In other words, this sort of disguise did not necessarily conceal identity so much as complicate it. As with metaphor, the gentlemen used trousers to double their identity. They visualized themselves not only as gentlemen, but also as members of a nascent artisan republic, bonded solidly with the common people. The internal distinction between colonial gentry and commoners dissolved, laying bare the larger distinctions between England and the colonies.

Playing Indian was a performance of doubled identities—those known through visible faces or context and those suggested by inappropriate clothing. For people who linked Indianness with metaphor and who found so many useful meanings encoded in Indian identity, it was not hard to imagine that both the sign of the disguise and the visible identity of the wearer could be true: a shoemaker in Indian costume was both a shoemaker and an Indian. These identities existed simultaneously, and they were something more than make-believe. They did not represent a "wilderness marriage" synthesis of European and Indian character. Neither were they a schizoid, back and forth confusion of alternating Indian and white identities.[60] White Indians were metaphors come to life, and they allowed colonists to imagine themselves as both British citizens and legitimate Americans protecting aboriginal custom.[61]

On the one hand, linguistic play and Indian disguise let colonists experience a liberating doubled identity. On the other hand, the practice also created a different, less affirmative kind of ambiguity. For if the shoemaker was both shoemaker and Indian Other, he was also neither. Two visible identities could operate simultaneously, but they could also cancel each other out. The shoemaker (and those around him) presumably knew that he was not an Indian. When he donned his costume, however, he was no longer simply a shoemaker either. If Indian play allowed colonists to take on dual, metaphoric identities useful in creating a sense of Americanness, it also carried the threat that they would lose themselves—and their identity—in the netherworld between Briton and Indian.

From the very beginning, the Revolution has been conceived as an enormous societal rite of passage, a ritual characterized by difficult social separation, grueling trial, and triumphal reemergence. The carnival sacrifice of Tammany and the blackfaced defiance of the Tea Party enacted such rituals on smaller, perceptible scales. In such rites of passage, participants are forced through a period of emptiness during which they are neither one thing nor another. Anthropologists have a word for such suspended time—*liminal*. Liminality is like the light at dawn or dusk, when one can speak of neither daylight nor darkness but only of something in between. Liminality implies change—the world will either get brighter or will sink into night—but if one were plopped down, without any context, at the exact moment of dusk or dawn, it would be hard to discern whether day or night was approaching. Liminality is a frozen moment of unpredictable potential in the midst of a process of change, and it is in that sense that it has been used to describe the in-betweenness found in rite of passage rituals. Evocative, creative, and often frightening, it is critical to an individual's (or a society's) final reemergence as something new.[62] "After separation [from one group] and before incorporation [into another]," notes the critic Michael Bristol,

> the liminary participants enter a peculiar and ambiguous social space. "Betwixt and between" the categories of social life, liminality is the experience of the social "other." Neither here nor there, the participant in the liminal experience is, socially speaking, "elsewhere." This confers immunity for otherwise unlawful acts; it provides an alibi and an excuse. It is also, perhaps, the fulfillment of wishes that ordinarily cannot be satisfied, or, in other words, utopia."[63]

The classic models for rites of passage and the liminal experience come from studies of tribal rituals, often couched in terms of the primitive. But like carnival and misrule, liminal ritual has also been subject to historical change. With the advent of new social worlds, liminal experiences have, according to the anthropologist Victor Turner, acquired self-consciousness and intentionality that have made them likely settings for the acting out of rebellious impulses.[64] The historian Peter Shaw has argued that the rituals of the American Revolution—explicitly channeled and constructed to meet the needs of the occasion—were such events, colonists consciously characterizing themselves as rebellious children undergoing a rite of passage.[65] The Tammany society dinners, the Mast Tree riot, and the Boston Tea Party all reflect this linkage between older, liminal rites of passage and the planning and conscious intent of colonial elites.

If this was a ritual of becoming, however, it was never fully completed. As the historian Michael Kammen has observed, the American obsession with the Revolution as a rite of passage suggests the unfinished character of the ritual and a concomitant self-identity that revolves around a perpetual "season of youth."[66] In other words, Americans may have failed to resolve the experience of liminal nonidentity, a failure that left the nation (as D. H. Lawrence observed) unfinished. And it is that unfinished quality that brings us back to a final consideration of Indianness.

Both multiple identities and the "betwixt-and-betweenness" of transformed rite-of-passage rituals existed together, working to create a collective consciousness attuned to revolution and the possibility of new identity. In playing Indian, Americans invoked a range of identities—aborigine, colonist, patriot, citizen— all of which emerged from the categories Indian and Briton. In the process they created a new identity—American—that was both aboriginal and European and yet was also neither. They controlled the center in an intricate, shifting three-way system of self-identification. Although this control was effective in establishing an American identity as both non-English and non-Indian, its continued openness prevented its creators from ever effectively developing a positive, stand-alone identity that did not rely heavily on either a British or an Indian foil. After the Revolution, Americans remained stuck in the middle, lost somewhere between "simultaneous identity" and "no identity."[67]

The uncertainty that continued to haunt Americans can be traced to the contradictory meanings assigned to interior and exterior Indians. Tammany— and other interior Indians—proved crucial in letting one oppose the English and be American. Complete incorporation of this particular form of Indian was impossible, however, as long as its savage twin existed at the edge of expanding national borders. The exterior, savage Other assured Americans of their own civilized nature and, more important, justified the dispossession of real Indians. The presence of actual Indians, persistently struggling to maintain land and sovereignty, necessitated the continued reconstruction of the savage, exterior Other throughout the nineteenth century.

Americans might have taken a different path, choosing to abandon the interior Other and devote their full energy to exterminating the oppositional savage. Tammany's powers of aboriginal legitimation, however, proved too strong. Killing off both real and imagined Indians swung one's identity in an arc that passed uncomfortably close to the Old World. Indianness lay at the heart of American uniqueness. The revolutionaries and the citizens of the early Republic were unable to take either a rhetorical or physical stand, leaving the exterior savage and the interior American locked in a perpetually unresolved state.

Here, then, lies a critical dilemma of American identity: in order to complete their rite of passage, Americans had to displace either the interior or the exterior Indian Other. As long as Indian Others represented not only us, but also them, Americans could not begin to resolve the questions swirling around their own identity vis-à-vis Indians and the British. Yet choosing one or the other would remove an ideological tool that was essential in propping up American identity. There was, quite simply, no way to conceive an American identity without Indians. At the same time, there was no way to make a complete identity while they remained.

As a result, Crèvecoeur's question of American definition, "What, then, is the American, this new man?" has, as Henry Nash Smith observed, been asked and reasked for two hundred years without ever having been satisfactorily answered. The powerful and creative identity embodied and performed at the Tea Party made it clear that Americans were, in fact, something new. It remained far easier, however, to say what Americans were not or what they might become than to articulate what they actually were. Beyond the Tea Party and the Revolution lay a land characterized by uncertain identity and a progressive hope for future clarity, a place that Americans would continue to explore and refigure as they consolidated the new nation.

That's it. If they really looked inward to exterminate, then they wouldn't have tried to exterminate 'Indians.'

two

Fraternal Indians and Republican Identities

> Here are men—pale faces in calico bags. Why do they run
> about, and dishonour the red-man by calling themselves Injins?
> They want the land of this young chief . . . You hear my voice
> for the last time. I shall soon cease to speak. When I reach the
> happy hunting-grounds of the Onondagoes, I will tell the
> warriors I meet there of your visit. Your fathers will
> know that their sons still love justice.
>
> JAMES FENIMORE COOPER
> *The Redskins: Indian and Injin* (1846)

In 1846, James Fenimore Cooper published *The Redskins: Indian and Injin*, a lightly
fictionalized apologia for Hudson River valley landlords plagued by Indian-
disguised tormentors during the New York antirent conflicts of the 1840s. As
the book opens, young Hugh Littlepage returns from a grand tour of Europe to
find his ancestral estate threatened by bands of disgruntled tenants. While some
renters propose legislation that would limit the terms of Littlepage's leases or
even force him to give up his lands, others take a more direct course, donning

calico masks, speaking a gruff, pidgin "Injinspeak," and attacking buildings, fences, and the patroon residents of the Littlepage manor, Ravensnest. After a series of confrontations, Littlepage turns, ironically, to Ravensnest's aging resident Indian, Susquesus (the Upright), to instruct the antirent rioters in the importance of the law. A band of hardy Indian (as opposed to "injin") visitors from the West stands armed and ready to enforce the Littlepage title and quite literally pound home the moral of social stability embedded in what becomes Susquesus's death speech.

Like the Tea Party Mohawks, the Indian-disguised antirent protesters shared the ambiguous doubled identities of insider and outsider, citizen and traitor. The injins insisted upon the continued vitality of Revolution, thereby threatening the social order of the nation. In *The Redskins*, Cooper responded by characterizing them as unreasonable savages who had corrupted new national ideals of political stability and economic continuity. For Cooper and other members of the new order, the injins' rebellious proclivity for murder, arson, cowardice, and bad manners (especially in contrast to the wise Susquesus and his gracious comrades) placed them outside the borders of American society, "skulking from and shirking the duties of civilization." Yet even as Cooper excluded the antirenters, they remained white, part of a racially defined American us that retained its citizenship and would no doubt return to the fold. The injins' forced return to civil society marked, for Cooper, the victory of legal government over the rebellious politics of custom, a necessary shift of focus from Revolution to nationhood.[1]

Indian disguise continued to evoke contradictory identities, but the meanings that clustered around it had shifted substantially since revolutionary times. As he refigured the rebellious injin savages, for example, Cooper also created new senses of the narrative's real Indian people. Susquesus and his friends did not fail to appear as exterior figures, far outside the lines being drawn around American society. But, in *The Redskins*, they were also quintessential Americans. Heirs of Tammany, they had smartly turned their backs on revolution and were now articulating ideas about law, honor, and justice that justified Cooper's conservative interpretation of post-Independence property rights.[2]

Cooper's most significant reimagining of the Indian, however, may have lain in his focus on the nostalgic past rather than the difficult present. By the end of *The Redskins*, the book's problematic characters—real Indians, real antirent rioters, and the conflicting images constructed around them—have all vanished into history. The Indian visitors, who had marched out of an archaic past, return to their homes in the West. Like Tammany, the aged Susquesus willingly departs this world for the happy hunting grounds. The rioters throw away their calico bags and slink home to become simple farmers, leaving the field clear for the formalizing of the inevitable romantic connections among the elite Ravensnest crowd. The Littlepages will propagate, and their ownership will thus extend from the spatial to the temporal realm, from mere landholding to control of the future itself. Indian and injin, on the other hand, both retreat into a nostalgic, antiquarian tale about the region's curious history.

Cooper's novel reflects a cluster of transformations that postrevolutionary Americans worked on Indian Others during the first half of the nineteenth century. As the Revolution gave way to the Republic and, later, to Jacksonian democracy, many people played Indian as a way of imagining new American identities, meaningful in relation to the successful Revolution, the emerging market economy, and the new governments and political parties busy consolidating and distributing power across the landscape. At the same time, the United States began its own expansion into Indian territory, and Americans increasingly told themselves bloody stories of Indian savagery. Noble, interior Indians like Susquesus and Tammany still embodied crucial ideas about Americanness. But as the United States moved from Revolution to nation building, an identity that carried connotations of savagery and of the idea of rebellion—no matter its origins or its multiple meanings—was destined to receive an increasingly chilly welcome.

Citizens of the new United States inaugurated the Republic by struggling over the meanings of the Revolution. Many saw it as a past event, successful and wholly complete. Others could not understand why they did not feel free. The former groups thought it necessary to contain any leftover rebellious impulses, while the latter concluded that still more rebellion might in fact be required. Post-Independence uprisings came quickly, and they often maintained revolutionary traditions of Indian disguise. In October 1791, for example, Hudson valley tenant farmers chased the Columbia County sheriff, Cornelius Hogeboom, from a farm property being auctioned to pay rent that had fallen into arrears. A few days later, when Hogeboom made a second attempt to seize the land, "seventeen men painted and in Indian dress sallied forth from the barn, fired, and marched after them keeping up a constant firing." Sheriff Hogeboom assumed that the men only wished to frighten his party and so let one of the Indians ride up close. The masked man shot and killed him. Rebellion and riot over rents and manorial holdings in the Hudson valley continued for the next fifty years, providing Cooper with literary grist for *The Redskins*.[3]

The Revolution had been the work of both educated elites and the often riot-prone groups of sailors, workers, and small farmers who had borne much of the military burden. In the rebellion's aftermath, intellectual and economic leaders tended to move easily from philosophizing and merchandising to practical governing. Artisans, mechanics, and farmers found the shift from oppositional rebel to sacrificing citizen more difficult. They had fought and died for a freedom largely defined by repetitive assertions that the British Empire had unfairly restricted their personal and societal liberty. Many had rallied around Tammany, using Indian costume to claim unconstrained freedom as an essential American quality, a customary right inherent in the land itself. In the Republic, however, the line between personal freedom and anarchy proved to be extremely fine. Lacking access to the corridors of nascent government power, many people continued to view attempts—like that of Cornelius Hogeboom—to organize society, generate revenue, and rearticulate pre- and post-Revolution property status as hostile encroachments on a personal freedom conceived to be almost boundless.[4]

The Revolution itself gave playing Indian even greater evocative power, for now the practice turned on an established history. In addition to its connotations of aboriginal freedom, Indianness might also evoke the Boston Tea Party, the Philadelphia patriots, and wartime military celebrations. When they donned their costumes, the injins who shot the sheriff sought legitimation in the collective memory of the Revolution while, at the same time, suggesting that the true revolution was yet to come.

This doubling of meaning appeared in Maine, for example, where landlord-tenant conflict produced a sometimes enormous tribe of white Indians. As in many instances of disguised riot, the local tradition predated the Revolution. As early as 1761, a charivari held by a group of angry backcountry settlers in Indian dress had driven one of the area's principal proprietors out the back door of his lodging. Although such activity ceased during the War for Independence, it commenced again in the late 1780s, intensified throughout the 1790s, and exploded in the early 1800s as land title became an increasingly important point of conflict between proprietors and tenants. The historian Alan Taylor has exhaustively catalogued these incidents, making clear that by the end of the first decade of the nineteenth century Indian disguise had become a characteristic feature of backcountry harassments.[5]

A recruiting notice penned by Daniel Brackett, the Maine backcountry's White Indian King, referred to rebellious settlers as English subjects and used the monarchical images of kings and crowns to deny the significance of the Revolution as a liberating experience for the backcountry. In recreating the Revolution's opposition between a distant, royal enemy and aboriginal settlers, Brackett relied on the same interior sense of Indianness prominent in pre-Revolution Tammany celebrations: "And to bring [the settlers] under lordships and slaveourey and as we poor indians did see your situation and did see it was a plan of pollicy and rogurey in great men and unjust: we poor indians did pitty you and was willin to spend our life for you because we all won brother."[6] This layering of meaning—in which Indian costume could evoke the Revolution while denying its significance—testifies to the increasing difficulties that would confront Americans who imagined that they could simply transfer prewar patriotic festivities to the post-Independence Republic.

Nowhere were the shifting and multiple meanings of Indianness as visible as in the Pennsylvania Whiskey Rebellion of the early 1790s. Homemade whiskey occupied a preeminent position in the Pennsylvania backcountry, both as beverage and as commodity. Made with rye, whiskey offered farmers a common currency in the backcountry's barter economy and an easily transported, non-perishable product for more distant markets. When the federal government levied an excise tax on whiskey in 1791, angry Pennsylvanians immediately hearkened back to the Revolution, pointing out the parallels between the whiskey excise and the various taxes levied by the British.[7]

The whiskey protest developed along two lines. A predominantly intellectual group pressed for change through petitions and public gatherings, while a more raucous faction turned to tar-and-feathers-style intimidation of federal officials. In the summer of 1792, twenty men arrayed in Indian warpaint appeared at the backcountry home of William Faulkner, who had rented space to a government tax collector, and began to break down the doors to the house. Let in by a sympathetic soldier, the Indians tore up the home, leaving bullets and shot in every ceiling. Faulkner told the tax collector to find other quarters.[8]

In 1794, the rebels assembled their demands and strategies in the form of a metaphorical "Indian Treaty" that appeared in the *Pittsburgh Gazette*. The treaty, a collection of speeches by the purported heads of the "Six United Nations of White Indians," drew on the old notion of aboriginal Indian custom, the popular memory of the Revolution, and the political strategy of actual Indian people. "Captain Whiskey, an Indian Chief" questioned the inequities of taxing whiskey but not cider or beer and the economic sense of sending a large army to Pennsylvania to collect only three or four thousand dollars a year. "It is a common thing," he said, "for Indians to fight your best armies at the proportion of one to five. Our nations can produce twenty thousand warriors; you may then calculate what your army ought to be." "Captain Alliance" underscored the United States' precarious geopolitical situation and pondered the possibility of the western territories throwing their allegiance to either Spain or England. Finally, "Captain Pacificus" laid down the whiskey rebels' terms: remove the army and the excise tax. The treaty ended with a description of a wampum belt—the traditional method of discussing and ratifying agreements among the region's indigenous groups—inscribed "Plenty of whiskey without excise." The whiskey rebels used the Revolution and its rhetoric of liberty to assert that authority rested with the people, not as a representative state or federal government but in terms that were local and specific.[9]

The rebels turned to Indianness to construct a three-layered rhetoric of protest. The first layer evoked the same, largely imagined, aboriginal legitimation of custom drawn upon by revolutionary colonists. This layer, however, was overlaid by a historical layer, in which the rebels cited the Revolution itself, drawing parallels between the federal government and the English monarchy and between themselves and the Sons of Liberty organizations. Finally, playing Indian allowed the whiskey rebels to portray themselves in terms of the geopolitical strategies of the Indian peoples of the old Northwest. Native village coalitions had consistently sought political advantage by trading on their ability to alter the European balance of power. The Pennsylvanians, with their nods to Spain and England, threatened no less.[10]

Although the meanings of Indian Others depended on the changing social and political struggles of white Americans, they also relied upon the shifting circumstances of real Indians. Because Americans negotiated the import of the metaphor of being Indian through this mixture of real Indians and imagined and ideological ones, shifts either in American ideology or in perception of Indian people altered the significance of Indian dress. And by the late eighteenth century, many Americans had come to view resistant native people as national enemies.

The Seven Years War had been a turning point in the racializing of native people and the development of a full-blown ideology of Indian-hating. In the Pennsylvania backcountry, for example, the Paxton Boys and other Indian-haters demanded the extermination of native people—and they acted on their beliefs, massacring peaceful Conestoga Indians in 1763. At the same time, of course, the citizens of urban Philadelphia were performing a more positive Indianness. Dressing like Tammany gave concrete form to the localized antipathy that Philadelphians sometimes felt for the wild settlers of the backcountry. It also pointed to the fact that, for them, the British, not the Indians, were the most important rival, both militarily and ideologically.[11]

During the War for Independence, however, the backcountry's racialized, savage notion of Indianness began to find a larger audience. Most native people remained neutral, sided with the British, or fought Americans in the backcountry to protect their lands from settlers' incursions. General wartime brutality and complex customs of torture provided American propagandists with ample material for reimagining a negative, alien Indian. In 1777, for example, twenty-four-year-old Jane McCrae, who was being escorted by a party of Loyalist Indians, was killed and apparently scalped in a skirmish with another native group. The American general Horatio Gates spread the story widely in order to whip up sentiment against Indians and their British allies alike. Gory tales of white women murdered, raped, and scalped by Indian people helped shift the symbolic weight of Indianness from the familiar patriot Tammany toward a generic, inhuman, savage Other.[12]

After the Revolution's conclusion, backcountry Americans and speculators—often claiming that British defeat was a defeat of British Indian allies—moved into the Old Northwest. Native people did not see themselves as defeated, and they reacted violently against squatting Americans. Unable to staunch the flow of anarchic immigrants streaming into Kentucky and Ohio, the federal government often ended up reluctantly fighting on their behalf. Indian coalitions proved to be formidable enemies. In 1790, Indian people united to defeat Gen. Josiah Harmar, and they went on to rout Arthur St. Clair's army the following year. The United States spent a large portion of a tight federal budget on these campaigns, which had resulted only in the loss of much of the federal army. With the British weakened, Indians now seemed the most pressing threat to the Republic, and they bore the brunt of American cultural anxiety. At the same time, the stark differences between backcountry and seaboard diminished as the Pittsburgh-Philadelphia corridor, directly linked to the Ohio country, became a central axis for commerce, credit, and capital flows in the new Republic. It became far easier to find common ground between city and backcountry when Indians threatened the interests of both.[13]

After Independence, as the list of Indian problems grew, dressing native to celebrate one's patriotism became a far more complicated endeavor. Indian opposition to American expansion posed a complex political, economic, and military problem, and Indianness was frequently reimagined in negative, racial terms. At the same time, though the Revolution had ended, Indian-garbed rebellions had not. As political and class factionalism became visible in the constitutional debates, economic elites and advocates of federalism confronted political rivals sympathetic to antigovernment injin rebels. The Philadelphia elites had defined themselves, in part, through an Indian patriotism firmly under their control. Now, however, the meanings attached to Tammany were up for grabs. The mythic chief signified real-life savages who threatened the nation, a hostile class that had taken democratic politics too far, and a privileged elite reluctant to share its power.

The disintegration and rapid reorganization of the Philadelphia Tammany society offer a particularly visible instance of the ways in which postrevolutionary Americans used Indian play to contest and organize the politics of the new Republic. Dormant through the war, the Philadelphia Tammany paraders revived their organization in 1783. They became the first in a series of societies—including the better-known New York–based Tammany as well as various orders of Red Men—that would become critical venues for Indian play in the early nineteenth century.

The elite Philadelphia celebrants had always had critics, and they now turned the increasingly popular idea of the savage Indian against the group. The monarchical threat had been subdued, they argued, and all that remained of the Tammany celebrations was a "stupid mummery"—and a dangerous one at that. In 1786, for example, the Seneca leader Cornplanter visited the Philadelphia Saint Tammany society and was feted in full costume by the members. A sarcastic letter to the journal Watson's Annals, ostensibly written by Cornplanter, appeared soon after. It reaffirmed the importance of societal distance between Indians and non-Indians:

> You know kinsman how much pains our white brothers have taken to cause us to renounce our independent and happy mode of life and to exchange it for what they call the pleasures of civilization and religion; but they now think differently. As proof of this preference of our manners and principles to their own, a large body of the citizens of Philadelphia, assembled on the first day of May on the banks of the Schuylkill every year, and then in the dress of Sachems celebrate the name, character, and death of

Utter
Framing

Old King Tammany. This entertainment ends as all such entertainments do with us, in drunkenness and disorder, which are afterward printed in their newspapers in the most agreeable colours, as constituting the utmost festivity and joy. But the principal end of this annual feast is to destroy the force of the Christian religion.[14]

A new focus on savage Indian drunkenness and paganism proved an effective counter to the Tammany groups' older claim to an aboriginal connection between Indians and Americans.

But the Philadelphia society also suffered from internal dissensions that mirrored the social and political shifts taking place in a larger American society. The celebrations of 1783, 1784, and 1785 featured an uneasy mingling of Federalists and anti-Federalists, elites and artisans, native-born and foreign immigrants. Patriotic opposition to Great Britain, a powerful point of unity during the war, could no longer hold such an assembly together in a fractious political climate. Indeed, at the last large celebration, in 1786, "native" Tammany members confronted a "rude" and "knavish" crowd that thought "Common Sense too common" and acted on the assumption by intruding on the festival (fig. 6).[15] Many in the crowd were Irish immigrants (indeed, when a branch of the New York society reemerged in Philadelphia in the 1790s, its explicitly political membership would be contentious, controversial, and heavily Irish). By 1789, the gentlemen had retreated permanently to a small, quiet dinner at the Fish House of the State of Schuylkill, bringing the Tammany organization full circle in the most literal way. The Philadelphians had foundered on the differences between an Indianness conducive to patriotic rebellion and one reshaped to meet the internal and external challenges to the nation.[16]

The year 1789 also marks the rise of the New York Tammany society, an organization far more successful than the Pennsylvania order in remaking Indianness.[17] The New York society came together in 1786 under the leadership of the businessman John Pintard, a New Jersey Tammany society alumnus, and William Mooney, a New York upholsterer who would become the organization's first grand sachem. Their initial Saint Tammany's day celebration in 1787 was a smallish affair. Within two years, however, it had blossomed into a major social event. The society erected marquees along the Hudson River, served dinner, and provided entertainment. With each of thirteen toasts, the guests enjoyed thirteen ordnance salutes in honor of the states. The society members walked in

Philadelphia, April 20th, 1786

BROTHER,

IF you wiſh to celebrate the anniverſary of our Antient Grandfather, St. TAMMANY, on Monday, the 1ſt of May next, you will be furniſhed with a ticket, by applying to Brother Peter January, treaſurer, at the north-weſt corner of Market and Second ſtreets. and depoſiting *Ten Shillings,* by Friday, the 28th inſtant, after which day no tickets will be delivered to any perſon, oh any terms whatever.

Proviſion will be made for none but thoſe who do pay for their tickets by that day.

The celebration to cloſe at ſeven o'clock.

☞ *A buck's tail and the ticket in your hat, a knife and fork in your pocket.*

To Brother ~~Peter A Glentworth~~ № 25

6. Philadelphia Sons of St. Tammany, Invitation to Tammany Day Dinner, April 20, 1786. The final year in which the Tammany Day celebration featured public parading, 1786 was marked by an invitation that set up a series of checks designed to prevent intrusions from the common crowd. Despite such cautions, when the members took to the streets, they found themselves the subjects of ridicule rather than envy. From Francis Von A. Cabeen, "The Society of the Sons of Saint Tammany of Philadelphia," Pennsylvania Magazine of History and Biography 26:4 (1902): 442.

Indian file, wore Indian costumes, painted and smeared their faces, and carried bows, arrows, and long smoking pipes, which they passed around after the twelfth toast as a sign of friendship and peace.[18] Defining itself primarily as a patriotic fraternal order, Pintard's organization acquired almost five hundred new members between 1789 and 1794, the bulk of the membership drawn from the city's plebeian, artisan class with a sprinkling of politicos of the better sort and merchants of middling classes. Unlike the Philadelphia order, the New York society made specific provisions for keeping Irish immigrants powerless and marginalized. This new formula—fraternal, democratic, and nativist—proved popular, and the New York order established branches in Pennsylvania, Rhode Island, Kentucky, and Ohio.[19]

Whereas the Philadelphia society had operated on an informal basis, the New York Tammany society was an early entry in the proliferation of highly organized, secret fraternal groups that attracted millions of nineteenth-century American men to weekly meetings and initiation ceremonies.[20] Historians have pointed to many important functions of these groups. Rituals, costumes, secret handshakes, signs, and codes allowed fraternal members to construct unique insider identities that proved valuable amid the dislocations of a society rapidly embracing modern capitalism. As geographic communities and subsistence economies gave way to the mobile communities of the early industrial social order, fraternal groups, especially the often elite gatherings of Freemasonry, provided key points of unity for nascent class identities.[21] At the same time, philosophies of fraternal brotherhood softened market competition and emphasized a genial human universalism. The organized benevolence systems of many fraternal groups eventually replaced the economic safety net previously offered by craft guilds. By broadening the base of benevolent support from one particular type of production—shoemaking or upholstery, for example—to a whole class of production, the societies created a less vulnerable and more reliable union.

The societies also tempered and channeled the impulsiveness of youth. Young men who might otherwise have been excluded from the political process experienced a measure of authority, both within the group and in its outside activities.[22] Men came for social fellowship as well. New York's Tammany society was one of many groups known for postmeeting drinking and storytelling sessions that lasted until dawn. Fitz-Greene Halleck, one of the so-called bucktail bards, captured the society's sociality in verse:

> There's a barrel of porter at Tammany Hall,
> And the bucktails are swigging it all the night long;
> In the time of my boyhood 'twas pleasant to call
> For a seat and cigar, 'mid the jovial throng.[23]

As gender distinctions came to rest firmly on separateness rather than mutuality, the societies helped define the clubby sociability thought to accompany a distinctly urban masculinity.

Unlike many other fraternal groups, however, the New York Tammany society connected its fraternal identity with a larger, American identity, the members imagining themselves as an avant-garde who had captured the egalitarian essence of American society. In order to have an Indian society that made sense to a broad public, however, Tammany had to deal with the negative emotions associated with images of the Indian savages and overly democratic injin rebels of the backcountry.

The order moved first to dilute the importance of Tammany by turning to Columbus as a crucial figure of American identity. In April 1791, cofounder

Pintard queried Jeremy Belknap about the workings of his Massachusetts Historical Society. Pintard contemplated using Tammany as the cornerstone for a similar organization, one that would feature manuscript collections and a museum. His inquiry left little doubt as to the changing balance between the society's figurehead patrons:

> I wish to hear whether your Antiquarian Society is commencing, or its prospects. An account will be given in some future magazine of our Tammany Society (We have lately uncanonized him). . . . We have got a tolerable collection of Pamphlets, mostly modern, with some History, of which I will also send you some day an abstract. Our society proposes celebrating the completion of the third century of the discovery of America, on the 12th of October, 1792, with some peculiar mark of respect to the memory of Columbus, who is our patron.[24]

One can see hints of Tammany's decanonizing as early as 1788 in a Philadelphia Fourth of July poem:

> The savage tribes their jubilee proclaim,
> And crown Saint Tammany with lasting fame.
> E'en the poor Negro will awhile resign
> His furrows, to adorn Saint Quaco's shrine;
>
> While mimic Saints a transient joy impart,
> That strikes the sense but reaches not the heart,
> Arise Columbia!—nobler themes await
> Th' auspicious day, that sealed thy glorious fate.[25]

After having moved through the obligatory list of saints and their associated nations—Spain with James, France with Denis, Ireland with Patrick—the author separates Tammany from Americans in general, assigns him only to Indians, pairs natives and African slaves, questions the legitimacy of "mimic saints," and finally calls forth Columbia for American sainthood.

In 1789, the New York society, which had initially featured Tammany as its sole namesake, adopted a dual name—the St. Tammany's Society or Independent Order of Liberty. By the end of the year, a formal constitution had shifted the name to Saint Tammany's Society or Columbian Order. In 1790, Columbus appeared in the group's pantheon of toasts as a "secondary patron." The following year, as Pintard noted, the society changed to the more secular Tammany

Society or Columbian Order and began making plans to celebrate the Columbian tercentenary.[26]

The society's rituals and customs reflected the shifting fortunes of its patrons. Philadelphians had made Tammany an American saint and celebrated the fertility of springtime and the future possibilities of a new republic. New Yorkers now decanonized him and turned to a commemorative, autumnal feast day that looked back to Columbus. As part of this legitimating backward glance, Americans began visualizing the Republic in the classical tradition of Greece and Rome. Lacking Parthenian columns and crumbling amphitheaters, however, American tastemakers turned to visible signs of time and history in the landscape: Indians and nature joined as important artifacts of contemplation and commemoration. Tammany went from a figure of possibility to one of history.[27]

As Americans founded towns in New York, Pennsylvania, and Ohio, they endeavored to classicize the landscape by adopting Greek and Roman city names—Troy, Utica, Ithaca, Sparta, Rome, Athens—thus transplanting rhetorically an ancient republican past. Indian names remained on the landscape as well, but their meanings were often transformed in a conflation of Indianness and classicism (Cooper, one might observe, blessed his native hero, Susquesus, with a latinate name, probably an adaptation of Susquehanna). "Indians and fauns and Arcadian shepherds were all essentially of the same breed, sharing the animal life of nature," observes the historian William Vance. John Galt's biography of the artist Benjamin West, published in 1816, is a representative example of this explicit intertwining of classic American and European pasts. At one point, Galt placed the painter in Rome, with a Vatican cardinal attempting to awe him with the ancient statue of Apollo Belvedere, well known in the world of eighteenth-century classicism. "My God, how like it is to a young Mohawk warrior!" Galt had West exclaim. Pointing to the Apollo, West continued, "I have seen them often standing in that very attitude, and pursuing, with an intense eye, the arrow which they had just discharged from the bow."[28]

If Indians cavorted with Roman gods, they also represented a particularly pastoral vision of America's historical landscape. In 1790, for example, Philip Freneau, another Tammany bucktail bard, wrote a poem entitled "The Indian Burying Ground," in which he linked departed Indians, rocks and trees, and the aesthetic and historical contemplation of ruins and the past:

> Here still a lofty rock remains,
> On which the curious eye may trace

(Now wasted, half, by wearing rains) — *NA or European A.?*
The fancies of a ruder race.

Here still an aged elm aspires,
Beneath whose far projecting shade
(And which the shepherd still admires)
The children of the forest played.[29]

The use of Indian and nature to imagine a meaningful history followed the
literary mythologizing that had swirled around the prerevolutionary Tammany.
Now, however, this past was ancient and real rather than self-consciously
mythic, and the stories were histories to be possessed rather than explicit definitions of Self.

Possession over / looking to / Self

Fraternal societies offered prominent venues for performing such usable classic pasts. English and American Freemasons, for example, had built a compelling
(if imaginary) fraternal history centered on Solomon's Temple and the crusader
Knights Templar. Young men could find Robin Hood reenactments at the Ancient
Order of Foresters, "patriarchal encampments" at the Odd Fellows, hooded
ritual sacrifices at the gatherings of the United Ancient Order of Druids, and a
host of other inventive rituals that linked the present with a legitimating past.[30]

In making Tammany a figure of America's ancient republican history, the
society sought a position of authority in American cultural discourse. Sachem
William Pitt Smith, for example, claimed a role as a national tastemaker with his
suggestion that Indian costume should afford the basis for a distinctive American clothing style.[31] At the same time, the order aimed to mute criticisms of its
Indian celebrations by pointing to a historical Tammany rather than a recent
token of rebellion or a reminder of actual Indians.

Even so, the society joined with other Americans in moving away from
Indians and toward Columbus, a symbol of the nation's blossoming national
culture. This larger shift is aptly illustrated by the rise of Columbia, Columbus's
abstracted female counterpart (fig. 7).[32] In the eighteenth and nineteenth centuries, European empires glorified themselves through classicized female figures. Great Britain, for example, venerated Britannia, a Romanesque figure
dressed in robes and cloaked with the symbols of British authority, the crown
and the sword.[33]

Colonial Americans had sometimes been represented by a female figure—the
so-called Indian Princess, who served as a counterpart to Tammany and a sort of

FIRST in WAR,
FIRST in PEACE,
&
FIRST in the HEARTS
OF HIS
COUNTRYMEN.

primitive younger sister to Britannia. The Indian Princess may have been the correct gender to signify the transformation from crude colony to domesticated Arcadia, but, like Tammany, she carried too many negative associations to function effectively as a national icon. Unlike the chaste breast occasionally revealed by a fold in the asexual Britannia's robe, the Indian Princess's frequently naked body symbolized not only fertility and the natural state, but also *availability* (see fig. 3). The sense of availability applied both to the American landscape and to real Indian women, who were often represented as being sexually available to white men. In order to symbolize the colonies' maltreatment by Great Britain, revolutionary-era cartoonists repeatedly pictured the Indian Princess through images suggestive of sexual abuse and rape. The widely reprinted cartoon "The able Doctor, or America Swallowing the Bitter Draught" (see fig. 4), for example, shows several Englishmen restraining the Indian Princess while one lifts her robe in order to expose her. In a colonial context, representing the continent as being available served useful purposes. The message of availability proved contradictory, however, when one wanted to demonstrate not colonial opportunity, but independent nationhood. The associations of primitivism, sexuality, and miscegenation that accompanied the Indian Princess were highly inappropriate to the magisterial figure required by European conventions.[34]

Columbus and Columbia allowed Americans to proclaim their political independence through a non-British, non-Indian figure. Columbia signified the dignity and gentility of civilization in a way that the male Columbus could not, while, at the same time, retaining his history. Swathed in Greco-Roman robes and adorned with latinate mottoes, lines from the Declaration of Independence, and the badges of the Republic—flags, eagles, stars, and colors—the figure represented a new American past while asserting that the United States had taken its place among civilized nations. By 1815, Columbia had become the predominant formal symbol of the nation.

Americans built postrevolutionary identities around such symbols of political distinctiveness and authority. The New York Tammany society, already tied to

7. Artist unknown, Liberty and Washington, ca. 1800–10. By the early nineteenth century, the Indian princess had given way to Liberty or Columbia, magisterial figures more appropriate to European conventions of national iconography. She is surrounded by the critical emblems of the new nation: stars and stripes, an eagle, the liberty cap and pole, and a laurel-wreathed George Washington. The British crown lies trampled under her foot. Courtesy of the New York State Historical Association, Cooperstown.

the historical Columbus and the ancient Tammany, made government itself into a third key symbol of identity. The society staked yet another claim to authority by playing up its connections with American political institutions. New York, the nation's capital from 1788 to 1790, anchored the country's political life, and the Tammany society hovered close at hand. By using its constitution of 1789 (rather than the dinner in 1787) as an origin point, the society connected its birth with that of the new nation, symbolized by the inauguration of George Washington in 1789. The society made its claims temporally, noting that its constitution had been written within a fortnight of Washington's swearing in, and spatially, asserting that the document had been signed within a few blocks of the spot where the inauguration had taken place. The members initiated a threefold calendar system, referencing dates to the Columbian 1492, the 1776 of Independence, and the 1789 founding of the order itself. In a Tammany document, for example, July 1800 would appear as "Season of Fruits, Seventh Moon, Year of Discovery three hundred and eighth; of Independence twenty fourth, and of the Institution the twelfth."[35]

The elements that defined the society—archaic Indianness, Columbian history, pseudo-governmental status—came into clear focus at a meeting between the society and a group of Creek leaders in 1790. Attempting to avert war with the Creeks and to reassert federal power over the state of Georgia, Marinus Willett, a member of the New York Tammany society, had been sent to ask the Creek leader Alexander McGillivray to journey to New York and make a peace treaty with the federal government.[36]

When Willett and the Creek leaders arrived, the Tammany members met them in full costume and flanked the Indians as the two groups marched together through the streets of New York, waving and shouting the society's "Et-Hoh" song at bystanders. They passed Congress, exchanged mutual salutes, and moved on to the Tammany wigwam.[37] That evening the society held a formal welcoming in which they used the figures of Tammany and Columbus to signify Indian-white concord and to lay the groundwork for the treaty negotiations to come. Grand Sachem Dr. William Pitt Smith delivered the welcoming address:

Although the hand of death is cold upon their bodies, yet the spirits of two great Chiefs are supposed to walk backwards and forwards in this great wigwam and to direct us in all our proceeding—Tammany and Columbus. Tradition has brought to us the memory of the first. He was a great and good Indian chief, a strong warrior, a swift hunter, but what is greater than all, he loved his country. We call ourselves his sons. Columbus was a famous traveller and discoverer; [he] was the first white man that ever visited this western world. But history makes it known that because he wished to treat the Indians with kindness, friendship, and justice, he was cruelly used. Brothers—Tammany and Columbus live together in the world of spirits in great harmony, and they teach us to cultivate like friendship and reciprocal good offices with you and all Indians.[38]

The sachem portrayed a new Tammany, constructed not around patriotic rebellion, but around an unquestioning love of the nation. Smith then turned to Columbus, painting him as a kind man victimized by those who would mistreat Indian people. By claiming the Indian Tammany as his father, Smith, in effect, offered up Columbus—a figure of supposed integrity in Indian-white dealings—as a patron to the Creeks. This exchange then moved to the level of government, the two groups trading titles. The Creek leaders (upon whom the society bestowed the monarchical title king) gave Smith the name Tuliva Mico, Chief of the White Town. Smith turned next to McGillivray himself, representing the Creek leader, who was half Scots, as a perfect expression of the concord that came with peaceable Indian-white exchange; not to be left out, the Sons of Saint Andrew held a similar ordination in honor of McGillivray's Scottish ancestry a few nights later.[39]

love of Nation

Even as they claimed ties to real Indian people, the society experienced them as Others, falling easily into the same contradictory doublings of identity that had characterized the Tea Party Mohawks' attempts to negotiate Americanness. Through face paint and costumes, the society claimed aboriginal American identity. The members and the Creeks exchanged names, titles, and patrons; they sang, danced, and drank together as if both groups were part of the same social whole. As would-be treaty negotiators, however, the Tammany members never forgot the societal lines between Creek and white American.

The Tammany society seemed to be feting the Creeks—and they were. But equally important were the messages that William Pitt Smith was sending through the Creeks to members of the government and American society as a whole. The speeches, made to real Creek people who were, in a sense, transparent, informed other *Americans* of the society's patriotism, love of country, and authority as mediators. Ironically, the society's distance from real Indians was matched by a similar distance from the government. The actual treaty negotiations were yet to come, and they would not include the Tammany society.

Yet even if Tammany did not participate in the treaty, the society nonetheless felt it had staked a claim to paragovernmental status and authority. Tammany continued to link its governing structure with that of the nation, naming the United States president the honorary Kitchi Okemaw, or great grand sachem, of the society. The doubled identities of figures like Marinus Willett—Tammany chieftain and presidential envoy—and the occasional presence of government officials at its festivities—including the secretaries of War and State (Henry Knox and Thomas Jefferson), the chief justice of the Supreme Court (John Jay), and the governor of New York (George Clinton), among others—only reaffirmed the connection. Prior to meeting the Creeks, the Tammany society had also hosted the Oneidas, with whom they held a similar faux treaty meeting, and the Cayugas, who danced with the members at their celebration of May 1790.[40] For the Tammany society, claiming congruence with both the federal government and with Indian people, the powerful legitimating role of political and cultural mediator was tailor-made and eagerly accepted. In the process, Tammany aimed to redefine the public practice of dressing Indian. Faced with the reemergence of exterior savage Others and the shifting of once-favored revolutionary Indian play to the far side of American societal boundaries, Tammany remade interior Indianness. Indian costume now signified an American identity based upon republican order rather than revolutionary potential. Parading down Fifth Avenue in paint and fur and feathers demonstrated a peculiar, but useful and powerful form of patriotism.

The society's desire to play a role in government, however, compromised the political neutrality it had created around fraternal fellowship. The group soon found itself the site of impassioned disputes between Federalists and anti-Federalists. By the mid-1790s, many Federalist members, dubious of the society's support of a now-tumultuous French Revolution, had withdrawn.[41] When, in the wake of the Whiskey Rebellion, Washington attacked "self-created societies" in 1794 and again in 1796, membership plummeted still further. According to the Tammany historian/mythmaker Judah Hammond, the Tammany Day festival of 1797 drew only three people. The society's numbers began to rise again soon after this holiday debacle, but the organization's government-linked patriotism had been transformed into a more purely partisan Republican activism.[42]

As the society shifted from patriotism to partisanship, it continued to deemphasize Indianness. And as public opinion turned increasingly negative toward both real Indian people and the politicized Tammany society itself, society leaders intensified this process. In the parades of the early nineteenth century, for example, the society sponsored two floats—one of Tammany, one of Columbus—which they treated as equivalent.[43] As the society became a partisan stronghold, however, its Indian image became a point of attack for Federalist enemies, and Columbus proved an ineffective counterweight. After the July fourth parade of 1809, the *American Citizen and General Advertiser* scolded,

> It is painful to observe the ridicule which is annually thrown upon this glorious event by some semi-barbarians calling themselves the Tammany Society. Instead of commemorating the birth of the nation with that manliness and dignity which the occasion calls for and inspires, we see them with pain and disgust daubing their faces with paint, crowding their heavy heads with feather, making savages in appearance more savage; representing, as they term it, the genius of the nation in the person of some one who has no genius.[44]

Other critics went beyond a purely Indian version of racial savagery, using satirical black dialect to link Indians with uncivilized slaves and to further invert the notion of Tammany as a noble, wise American. The *New York Evening Post* carried accounts of an "African Tammany celebration" in 1809, and the following year the *Rhode Island American* reported, "Las April Fool Day we light de council fire at de wigwam in my house. Well, dan we chuse officer. Toby we make him Gran Sachem. Cudjo we make him farrer in council; Yellow Sam he set up for Sagemall be he no brack enough. Dem we chuse Whish-em-Stirky." The "celebrants" then toasted "Broder Tomm Jefferson, de lass gran sachem of dis country," "Black Sal, his squaw," and "Our broders, de white Indians."[45]

In 1813, angered by reports of Indian border "atrocities" during the War of 1812, other societies refused to parade with the Tammany society, and the members publicly renounced their Indian costumes, ceremonials, and titles and walked in plain clothes. After the war ended, they reintroduced Indian themes in a scaled-down form, but it was a rebirth that mattered little, for the society was in the midst of more significant changes. By 1822, when the New York constitution eliminated property requirements for suffrage, the Tammany society had recognized the increasing power of the Irish Catholic voting bloc and had courted, won over, and been swallowed up by immigrant Irishmen (ironically, the Philadelphia society had become an Irish-based political machine almost immediately, becoming entrenched in that city's politics by the late 1790s). As the New York society's Irish membership focused on acquiring and manipulating political capital, they unofficially replaced both Tammany and Columbus with St. Patrick. In 1825, having gained a form of political authority that no longer required public display, the Tammany society stopped marching in parades. In 1831 they ceased to observe Tammany Day altogether.[46]

The figure of Tammany had come a long way since serving as the festival patron for a Schuylkill River hunting and fishing society. When John Pintard displayed Indian objects in his Tammany Museum and Philip Freneau characterized Indians as "shades" in "endless sleep," they were defining Indian difference around boundaries of *time* rather than racial or societal difference (although these were, of course, critical aspects in the temporal definition). Ancient, classical Indians reproduced the ambiguous contradictions of the Indians that symbolized Americanness during the Revolution. The society continued to appropriate the interior, aboriginal identity of the Indian—now fused to a Greco-Roman history. As an artifact vanished forever in the ancient past, however, Indianness was also exterior, far removed from the American society of the present. Tammany members could visualize Indian contemporaries—the challenging savages on the border—as simply predead Indians who, upon dying, would become historical, locked in a grand narrative of inevitable American progress.

The New York Tammany society lost much of its interest in Indian impersonation as a new ethnic membership garnered an institutional form of political power. Tammany, however, represented only one branch in the Indian society family tree. Other groups—among them the Society of Red Men and its lineal descendant, the Improved Order of Red Men—also remade Indianness to create American identities that resonated more deeply with the cultural anxieties of the new Republic.[47]

Even as the Indian atrocities of the War of 1812 caused New York Tammany to recoil, an older logic simultaneously pointed the Society of Red Men to reprise the Indian as an anti-British figure. These contradictory figurings of Indianness should come as no surprise, for, as we have seen, different social groups used Indian play to advance different agendas and materialize a complex range of identities. During the Revolutionary War, many of the old Saint Tammany societies had stopped meeting, as members scattered and celebratory gatherings seemed unjustified or even dangerous. Many military units took up the springtime celebration, however, and it functioned as an informal military holiday until shortly before the War of 1812, when Secretary of War Henry Dearborn canceled it as overly debauched.[48]

The holiday did not stay submerged for long. When the United States became involved in the War of 1812, a group of Philadelphia men under the command of Capt. James N. Barker rebuilt and occupied Fort Mifflin, located four miles below the city on the Delaware River. Barker was the son of John Barker, a prominent member of the Philadelphia Sons of Saint Tammany. Confined at the fort, Barker, who had written a play about Pocahontas, and a group of young volunteers founded a fraternal order modeled on the first Tammany societies, the early New York organization, and the military associations. The Society of Red Men sprang to life during a two-week period during which its members focused entirely on an immediate British threat to their home. But the Red Men reflected more than opposition to the British. Its members also eschewed the political activism of the still-powerful Philadelphia Tammany society, and they pledged themselves to sociality, patriotism, military comradeship, and, most especially, benevolence. Faced with the uncertainty of wartime, the Society members vowed "to relieve each other in sickness or distress."[49]

In 1816, after the war was over and the negative feelings about Indians had begun to subside, the group reorganized as a full-blown benevolent society, offering relief to members in distress and to orphans and widows of deceased Red Men. Sending recruiters as far south as Charleston and as far north as Albany, they quickly created a chain of organizations that rivaled the New York Tammany group, which had started to lose tribes as its partisan activities generated widespread hostility. Throughout the 1820s, Red Men's lodges prospered across the country. The Philadelphia wigwam boasted almost six hundred members, and missionary Red Men traveled as far as New Orleans to consecrate new groups.[50]

Like the New York society, the Red Men adapted older formulas to meet changing social conditions. Whereas New York Tammany used Indian dress to perform a public, political identity, however, the Red Men found import and identity in private, highly secret "Indian mysteries." Indeed, secrecy helped them avoid the weight of anti-Indian sentiments that plagued the Philadelphia and New York Tammany societies. The members modeled the society after Freemasonry, duplicating its plethora of secret ceremonies, costumes, and hierarchies and adding coded Indian identities. Inductees received Indian names after surviving an initiation ritual that marked the passage from paleface to Red Man. The society's first leader, an engraver, Fort Mifflin volunteer, and former Mason named Francis Shallus, boasted the name Yeougheowanewago, or Split Log. Other names were more imaginative (and less Indian) in nature: Peruvian Bark, Hospitality, Long Pen, Fair Play's Brother.[51]

Indianness, for the Red Men, reflected a doubled identity well suited to the anxieties of the 1820s, when mechanics and artisans began to realize the degree to which wage labor and industrialization threatened their autonomy and competency. Real Indians may well have been the last thing on their collective mind. Play Indians, however, offered reaffirmation. On the one hand, they represented the kind of unfathomable secrets that could make a man feel valuable and important. Fraternal organizations commonly claimed to possess mysterious archaic knowledge, encoded to elude complete human comprehension. The Red Men represented this unknowable knowledge with an enigmatic Indian—a figure from the ancient past that lay traced on the national landscape in the form of thousands of mysterious burial mounds. Even as Indianness was imagined as being temporally and intellectually outside national boundaries, it remained essentially American in nature.

When they gave human form to this imagined Indian in their costumed meetings, the Red Men asserted their uniqueness and importance. Like Tammany, they wished to see themselves as an elite, especially in relation to the often-dangerous transformations occurring in the modernizing republic. On the other hand, the society also promised a stable, reliable community with benevolent structures in place for those whose American dreams came to nought. Interior Indians served as markers of communal bonding, of what Alexis de Tocqueville saw as the American impulse to associate in order to address economic, political, and moral issues.[52] Like the Tammany society, the Red Men found deep meaning in the connections between politics and fraternal and national identity. In the darkened meeting rooms of the Society of Red Men there existed a "second society" in which ordinary men mirrored the country's political and military struggles. The mechanics and artisans who made up the Red Men were finding it increasingly difficult to participate in the formal governing mechanisms of state and nation. They might parade in the streets, but they rarely got elected to office (fig. 8).[53]

Politics remained critical to the Red Men, but it was a politics that mimicked and echoed that of the nation. As the society's leader, for example, Shallus held the title generalissimo, and he was assisted by first and second captain generals, six lieutenant-generals, twenty major-generals, forty brigadier-generals, and so on through an ever-expanding hierarchy of various grades of subordinate commissioned officers. In addition to the military titles, the society offered a wholly different set of Indian ranks: kings, half-kings, sachems, chiefs, old men in council, squaw sachems, and warriors. With literally hundreds of roles to be filled, members quickly acquired a formal rank and a role in the society's gov-

8. *Society of Red Men Meeting Poster, May 9, 1825. Founded during the War of 1812, the society observed military protocols, with headquarters, marching orders, and abundant hierarchies of rank and authority. Members claimed multiple identities, and one might present oneself as the mysterious Lappopetung, the more accessible Black Wampum, a powerful generalissimo, or the rather regular George Knorr. From Charles H. Litchman, George W. Lindsay, and Charles C. Conley,* Official History of the Improved Order of Red Men *(Boston: Fraternal Publishing Co., 1893), 234.*

ernance. And these authorities did indeed govern: constitutions, amendments, bylaws, ritual practices, communiqués were all proposed, debated, voted upon, and proclaimed to the membership.[54]

By acting out the rituals of governance, members gained an emotional stake in the nation's rule and a sense of American political identity. In fact, the group allowed members to claim multiple identities, each of which offered reassurance in the new Republic. Now, in addition to being both a shoemaker and an Indian who signified the patriotism of the past, the Red Man could also be a legislator, a military man, and a judge—important roles in the American polity.

What Red men Cold Do for Work — "Oked!"

Mutualism and benevolence helped members escape the increasingly dangerous market economy which, notwithstanding its rhetoric of egalitarian opportunity, left many in the dust. At the same time, however, one might also enjoy climbing to the top of the Red Man bureaucracy. Young men experienced ritual rites of passage, as their own rebellious inclinations were defused and contained by a structure that reproduced and reinforced the larger political system. Finally, through limited public appearances on Washington's Birthday and Saint Tammany's day, one could demonstrate a special identity *as* a Red Man in relation to the outside world, celebrating one's secret, privileged rites and one's patriotic Americanness at the same time.

Like the Tammany organizations, the Red Men used Indian play to act out a story about their identity as Americans—in this case, a tale of convivial egalitarian brotherhood mixed with the guardianship of unknowable national mysteries. In the end, the stories all circled back to similar meanings. It was important, especially in a young republic seeking collectivity and self-definition, to see oneself as both an egalitarian patriot and a member of a special extra-American elite—to have one's cake—as Crèvecoeur and Lawrence had observed—and to eat it too.

In the early 1830s, the Philadelphia chapter of the Red Men dissolved, taking with it a large part of the organizational structure that had held the national society together. Richard Loudenslager (Old Warrior), the last generalissimo, blamed the society's decay on members of "a certain class, who were so clannish and offensively aggressive that they disgusted the better class of members, who withdrew." Like the earlier societies, the Red Men confronted class and ethnic differences introduced by new immigrants. Unlike the New Yorkers and their Philadelphia offspring, the Red Men quarreled, splintered, and eventually disintegrated. Immigrants, however, accounted for only part of the Red Mens' troubles. Throughout the 1820s, clergymen and women working their way into the public sphere attacked fraternal groups for the immorality of a convivial life marked by excessive drinking.[55] Secret societies also suffered in the anti-Masonic persecutions of the late 1820s. And, as a crowning blow, in 1832 America experienced a widespread cholera epidemic. All types of associations suffered as people, unsure of the cause of the disease but hoping to avoid contagion, stayed home or moved away from the cities.[56]

As the "better class of members" fled the disintegrating Society of Red Men, one of the Baltimore tribes initiated a middle-class revival—the Improved Order of

Red Men (IORM), improved by the addition of temperance to their creed and a rededicated interest in patriotism and American history. The new founders preserved much of the basic structure of Red Man organization and ritual. Members continued to use the order as a place to work out compensatory political identities par excellence. In 1835, with but two tribes in place, the order set up a statewide governing council, thus creating several additional positions of power. After adding a few more tribes in Washington, D.C., in 1845, the order founded a national grand council in 1847 to supervise the affairs of only two localities. With the addition of each bureaucratic level, more IORM members were able to engage in heady debates over the legalities of jurisdiction and the nature of the uniform and the ritual.

Like the other Indian fraternities, the IORM intended to legitimate itself through patriotic connection to the American state. Unlike Tammany, which opted for direct political involvement, or the Red Men, who set up a shadow government, the Improved Order chose, interestingly enough, to trumpet its historical roots in the revolutionary Tammany societies. This proved no easy task. Playing Indian had allowed rebellious Americans to cross and confound boundaries of national identity, and Indian costume would forever maintain that connection. Antirent and tax rebels, although largely confined by the 1830s to the Hudson valley, continued to testify to the powerful revolutionary impulses that persisted in Indian dress. For the IORM, maintaining the link between revolutionary patriotism and Indian costume meant containing this potentially dangerous legacy of rebellion and once again refocusing the interior Indianness that, in various ways, meant America.

The members of the IORM confronted the symbolic legacy of Indianness and the Revolution in ways that mirrored broader patterns of American cultural change and new strategies for dealing with Indian people. By the 1830s, American imaginings of the Indian had coalesced on a common theme: the past. The ongoing physical removal of Indian people from the eastern landscape proved to be the key prerequisite for this particular rethinking. For just as the Indian resistance of the 1790s had been accompanied by an emphasis on savagery, so actual Indian removal led to a friendlier, more nostalgic image, such as that proffered by Cooper in *The Redskins*.

Federal Indian policy was meant to clear eastern territory by forcing Indian people to move to the west side of the Mississippi. From 1813, when the final defeat of Tecumseh at the Battle of the Thames marked the end of Indian attempts to offer a unified, interregional resistance, until the 1830s, when

President Andrew Jackson defied his own Supreme Court and forced the Cherokees to take to what became known as the Trail of Tears, Americans waged war, signed treaties, and used guile and force to relocate hundreds of thousands of Indian people. By the middle of the nineteenth century, most native people had indeed been made to disappear from the eastern landscape.[57]

In conjunction with Indian removal, popular American imagery began to play on earlier symbolic linkages between Indians and the past, and these images eventually produced the full-blown ideology of the vanishing Indian, which proclaimed it foreordained that less advanced societies should disappear in the presence of those more advanced. Propagandists shifted the cause-and-effect of Indian disappearance from Jacksonian policy to Indians themselves, who were simply living out their destiny. "By a law of nature," claimed the Supreme Court justice Joseph Story in 1828, "they seem destined to a slow, but sure extinction. Everywhere, at the approach of the white man, they fade away. We hear the rustling of their footsteps, like that of the withered leaves of autumn, and they are gone for ever. They pass mournfully by us, and they return no more."[58] These vanishing Indians were more highly developed forms of the classic, ruin/rock formation Indians that Freneau had envisioned forty years earlier. But Indians and Indian Others now appeared in a past that was wistful and commemorative rather than mythic and aged. Whereas Freneau placed Indians safely in ancient history, Story positioned them in a past so recent that one could yet hear their rustling footsteps and find their still-warm campfires. The two images mark the distinction between archaism and nostalgia, very different (but equally useful) narratives of the past.

Some of the best examples of the ideological force of the vanishing Indian appeared in the series of Indian plays that gained special popularity in the decade 1828–38. The dying chief Menawa, for example, offered a typical dramatic trope in *The Indian Prophecy* (1828), extending his blessings to the new nation (in the form of George Washington) before departing for the happy hunting grounds: "The Great Spirit protects that man [Washington], and guides his destiny. He will become the Chief of nations, and a people yet unborn, hail him as the Founder of a mighty Empire! Fathers! Menawa comes. (*Menawa sinks slowly into the arms of his attendants, strain of music, curtain falls.*)"[59] Some of the most popular dying Indian figures included Metamora (1829), Pocahontas (1808, 1830), and Logan, whose famous speech—really the founding statement of the "last of the . . ." genre—appeared in everything from popular newspapers and

schoolbooks to Jefferson's *Notes on the State of Virginia* (1785) to Joseph Doddridge's play *Logan: The Last of the Race of Shikellemus, Chief of the Cayuga Nation* (1823):
"There runs not a drop of my blood in the veins of any living creature. Who is
there to mourn for Logan?—Not one."[60]

The Indian death speech brings us full circle to *The Redskins* and the justice-
minded Susquesus, who, after reprimanding the antirent injins, declares, "You
hear my voice for the last time. I shall soon cease to speak."[61] Susquesus and
other vanishing Indians represented sophisticated refigurings of Tammany, who
voluntarily climbed on to his own funeral pyre. In their dying moments, these
Indian figures offered up their lands, their blessings, their traditions, and their
republican history to those who were, in real life, violent, conquering inter-
lopers. Not coincidentally, the first lodges of the Improved Order of Red Men
were named Logan No. 1, Metamora No. 2, Pocahontas No. 3, and Metamora
No. 4. Tribes named for Powhatan, Pocahontas's father, and Uncas, Cooper's
penultimate Mohican, followed shortly after. By insisting that real Indians were
disappearing or had already vanished, the Improved Order was able to narrate
and perform a fraternal Indian history without having to account for the actions
of real Indian people. This history was possible only when Indian removal
policy was widespread and advanced.

The IORM dropped the Red Men's abundant military titles and expanded the
possible Indian-named ranks and metaphoric Indian nomenclature (fig. 9).
Years became great suns, months became moons, minutes became breaths,
money became fathoms, feet, and inches of wampum; the meetings were
marked by the kindling and quenching of the council fire; a disbarred member
was tomahawked; and so on.[62] At meetings, Indian talk prevailed, creating the
same metaphoric atmosphere that the revolutionaries had used to help them
become Indian. The meaning of such metaphoric transformation, however, had
taken on connotations of preservation and commemoration. Now, when the
Red Men donned their florally decorated canvas costumes and met for arcane
rituals in shadowy rooms, their practice of being Indian had little to do with
revolution and crossing boundaries of national identity (fig. 10). It had little to
do with the politics that attracted Tammany members and Red Men. Instead, the
ritual had everything to do with custodial history—the preservation of a vital
part of America's past. The Improved Order painted itself as a gathering of
historians, the worthy keepers of the nation's aboriginal roots. "The value of the
ceremonies of our Order," one Red Man later observed,

Calendar of the I. O. Red Men.

A minute is	a Breath.
An hour is	a Run.
A day is	a Sun.
A night is	a Sleep.
A WEEK is	SEVEN SUNS.
Sunday is	the First Sun.
Monday is	the Second Sun.
Tuesday is	the Third Sun.
Wednesday is	the Fourth Sun.
Thursday is	the Fifth Sun.
Friday is	the Sixth Sun.
Saturday is	the Seventh Sun.
A MONTH is	a MOON.
January is	the Cold Moon.
February is	the Snow Moon.
March is	the Worm Moon.
April is	the Plant Moon.
May is	the Flower Moon.
June is	the Hot Moon.
July is	the Buck Moon.
August is	the Sturgeon Moon.
September is	the Corn Moon.
October is	the Travelling Moon.
November is	the Beaver Moon.
December is	the Hunting Moon.
A YEAR is	a GRAND SUN.
Morning is	the rising of the sun.
Evening is	the setting of the sun.
Mid-day is	the high sun.
Mid-night is	the low sun.
Our friends out of the Order are	the pale faces.
The treasury purse is	the Wampum belt.
The place of meeting is	the Wigwam.
Organizing a meeting is	kindling a Council fire.
A meeting is	a Council.
Closing a meeting is	quenching a Council fire.
A Tribe is	a Subordinate branch of the Order.
A Great Council is	the head of the Order in a State.
Following one's usual business is	following the Hunt.
Wronging one is	crossing the path of each other.
MONEY is	WAMPUM.
A Fathom of Wampum is	$1,50 cents.
A Yard of Wampum is	25 "
Nine Inches of Wampum is	6¼ "

9. Hammonassett Tribe, Improved Order of Red Men,
Nomenclature, 1848. The Improved Order turned away from
the Society of Red Men's military structure and focused instead
on easily accessible Indian metaphors like "sun," "moon," and
"wampum." Courtesy of the Beinecke Rare Book and
Manuscript Library, Yale University.

is their historical accuracy. They seek not merely to imitate, but to preserve. When the time comes that the Indian race is extinct, our Order will occupy a place original and unique, growing more interesting as years pass on, and becoming at once, the interpreter of Indian customs and the repository of Indian traditions. Could a higher destiny await any Organization?[63]

The commemorative renditions of vanished native people extended to the revolutionary Indians at the Boston Tea Party. Making Native Americans historical

10. Improved Order of Red Men Costume, late nineteenth century. The heavy canvas costume, with floral decorations, an American flag motif on the collar, and bucktails hanging in the rear, was an impressive vestment for fraternal ritual. Courtesy of the Department of Anthropology, National Museum of Natural History, Smithsonian Institution.

went hand in hand with a reverential remembering of the Revolution. Jefferson's and Adams's deaths on July 4, 1826, brought home the passing of the revolutionary generation, and the resulting campaign of nostalgia, remembrance, and reenactment faded in and out of public consciousness until midcentury. With this heightened consciousness of the passing of time, the idea of Indian-garbed rebellion—especially as it was being practiced by the New York antirenters—could be locked, along with the Founders and the Revolution itself, in a revered, commemorative past tense. The May Tammany celebration died out in the mid-1840s and was replaced, not only by the familiar commemorations of Washington's Birthday and the Fourth of July, but by celebrations of the Boston Tea Party. In making this shift, Americans replaced carnivalesque, revolution-tinged Indian celebrations with sanctioned holidays in which Indian play transformed the wildness of the Revolution into an obedient patriotism.[64]

The Improved Order found its identity in this turn toward history, seeking connections to both the nostalgic haze of the Revolution and the so-called American traditions of now-departed Indian people. Through commemoration and institutional genealogy, members linked their order with the early Saint Tammany societies. They became antiquarian detectives, tracing documents back through the Society of Red Men to vague reports of military Tammany groups that they could connect to the prerevolutionary Sons of Liberty. At the same time, they turned to the protoethnographic works of Lewis Henry Morgan, Peter DuPonceau, and John Heckewelder in order to capture for themselves the vanished customs they claimed to be preserving in their rituals. In the mid-1850s, Past Grand Sachem Morris Gorham began writing the first of several IORM histories, most of which aimed to make the order a direct descendant of both Indian people and the Tea Party Mohawks.

After the Revolution, different groups of Americans remade Indian Others, creating national and group identities that had meaning in the social and political contexts of the early Republic. In urban areas, fraternal societies placed the interior Indian-as-American into a commemorative past that legitimated governmental authority and downplayed the possibilities of rebellion. At the same time, fraternalists dressed up as exterior Indians to signify their own exotic difference as possessors of secret knowledge, super-patriotism, and the culture of vanished Indians. A very different collection of people in costume—both Indian and non-Indian—made these doubled identities even more contradictory. Across rural America, from Maine to New York to western Pennsylvania, agrarian protesters adapted the Indianness of the Revolution to proclaim their desire for independence from landlords and government. And actual Indian people fought fiercely to hold on to their land.

In *The Redskins*, Cooper's "Indian and Injin" subtitle promises to separate real Indians from the fakes in calico-hooded costume. Instead, Cooper followed the historicizing inclinations of the Tammany society and the IORM—he suggested that both real Indians and agrarian injins who challenged governmental power were illusory and illegitimate. Susquesus and his Indian visitors, who represent actual Indians and a nostalgic construction of the Indian Other, prove to be vanishing relics of the past. The antirent protesters appear as cheap imitations of real Indians and revolutionary patriots, figures with a slightly deviant grip on reality. After humiliating the protesters and force-feeding them Indian instruction, Cooper made them vanish, transmuting riot-prone injins back into subservient tenant farmers. With actual Indians and antirenters gone, Cooper enshrined the images that he had arrayed around them in a safe, consensual past, while the elite Littlepages moved forward into a future.

Yet, the Indians and the injins were, in fact, the figures least amenable to literary vanishing acts. Real Indian people continued to challenge American expansion and steadfastly refused to vanish. Antirenters still turned to the revolutionary meanings that the nation's Founders had implanted in Indian dress in order to challenge the configuration of social and political authority in the Republic. Throughout the 1840s, the injin descendants of the painted farmer who shot Sheriff Cornelius Hogeboom gathered in headdresses and calico to challenge their landlords. The New York manorial system that Cooper defended was, in fact, the institution that eventually disappeared.

While actual Indian people struggled against removal and land loss and calico-hooded farmers plotted resistance, the imaginative urbanites of the Indian fraternities gathered in dark halls to don Indian dress and initiate palefaces into the historical mysteries of Indianness and patriotism. More than a half century before, Bostonians had dressed as Indians to leave their colonial status behind and to define and then become Americans. Now, when the Red Men met in the wigwam in full paint and costume, they journeyed back in time, celebrating not an identity of revolution, but a historical moment—the revered instant in which the Bostonians had dressed Indian to signify a revolutionary identity. And this commemorative act itself created a distinctive patriotic American identity, one changed and contained to meet the requirements of the new Republic.[65] Despite the various manipulations of Indianness, however, these forms of American identity continued to carry with them the threads of doubt, ambiguity, doubledness, and contradiction that had been sewn from the very beginning into the fabric of the nation. Indians (and Indian Others) were not going away, and white American identity quests based on Indianness would confront the inevitable consequences of that fact.

And it still goes on
Today! ugga----

three

Literary Indians and Ethnographic Objects

The moon is dancing in the heavens and the stars are wandering
through space, the courthouse of the sky. The silvery waters of
the Oneida sleep in the distance and the light is frozen upon the
icy beach. Beside this quiet and beauteous inland lake the
Tekarihogea has this day stood and in silent meditation recalled
the days when the forest cast its shade far over its horizon; and
the Indian with his bow and arrow pursued his game to the
waters edge and along its winding banks; when that stillness of
the wood unknown to us was unbroken even by the Indian
hunter, save now and then by the twang of a bow string and
whizzing of an arrow or the whoop indicating victory in the
chase. But now how changed! Alas Soshawah, in these very
places the Yankees are boiling salt. How bad I feel!

LEWIS HENRY MORGAN TO GEORGE S. RILEY
"At the Great Salt Lick," December 12, 1845

After finishing a degree at Union College, reading law for two years, and passing the New York bar in 1842, Lewis Henry Morgan found himself back in his hometown of Aurora, New York, with time on his hands. His legal career on hold as the American economy struggled to recover from the Panic of 1837, Morgan puttered about the family farms, gave occasional temperance lectures, wrote for the popular monthly literary magazine The Knickerbocker, and began to think deeply about American art and literature. With several equally thoughtful young men from Cayuga Lake Academy, his hometown school, Morgan formed the Gordian Knot, a literary fraternity that took as its myth the story of Gordius, king of Phrygia, who tied a knot so complex that only a person worthy of being the master of all Asia could untie it. Alexander the Great simply cut the knot with his sword. The fraternity's secretive rituals bound the members to master an equally difficult task: the writing of a native, American epic that would define national identity and put an end to unflattering comparisons between the United States and Europe.[1]

Like the Tammany societies, the Red Men, and numerous other orders, the Gordian Knot used fraternal bonds as an effective organizing principle. Morgan's group, however, had a loftier purpose: seeking American identity through an exercise in unabashedly high culture. The fraternity sought literary inspiration in the familiar mixture of Greco-Roman classicism and the natural antiquity of the New World. As symbols both of a classic past and of American nature, Indians inevitably found their way to the very heart of the tales told by the Gordian Knot. In self-conscious letters and essays, Morgan and his friends lamented that the ancient poets and philosophers had not experienced the truly noble savagery of America. The society dreamed of the artistic transcendence that such a marriage of genius and landscape might have produced and set out to master it themselves.

For Morgan, this well-worn brand of Greco-Indian Americanism yielded insights that far surpassed the standard rhetoric. As he wandered the landscape of western New York, he found himself vividly imagining Indian people walking in the forests and canoeing on the rivers. He made deep emotional connections between archaic Indians and successor Americans and grew increasingly intent on basing his national literature upon the myths and histories of the supposedly vanished members of the Iroquois confederacy. "We are now upon the very soil over which they exercised dominion," the spellbound Morgan told his confederates. "We have the same natural landmarks, the same lake to which

Morgan sounds like he has respect + understanding for Indians too! Empathy.

they bequeathed their name; the same hills and forests and streams, even the graves of many generations—indeed everything around us speaks of the ancient and departed Cayugas. Poetry still lingers amid the scenery which they enjoyed and prose has sufficient employment in recording the deeds of the past."[2]

Morgan was a persuasive sort—he would later make a small fortune as a lawyer—and by the summer of 1842, the Gordian Knot had turned from its classical orientation toward a more precise, local focus on the Six Nations of the Iroquois: "We finally concluded," he said later, "to cut this knot and change our organization into an Indian society under the name of the 'Cayugas,' as we resided in the ancient territory of this Indian nation and quite near the site of their principal village." The group began meeting at monthly campfires deep in the New York woods. Garbed in Indian costume, they called one another by Indian names and proffered nostalgic, metaphor-drenched poetry and prose as prototypes of a national literature.[3]

It was a familiar fraternal form of playing Indian, directed now to a new purpose—literary inspiration—that in time would utterly recast the meaning of Indian play. Beginning with romantic notions of vanishing Indians, Morgan's New Confederacy (or Grand Order) of the Iroquois eventually turned from nostalgia toward rationalized, objective scientific investigation. Fictional creation gave way to the compiling of factual knowledge, and what had begun as an effort—firmly rooted in the consciousness of the Revolution and the early Republic—to define a literary national identity took on a modern, ethnographic character well suited to the American social elite of the late nineteenth century.[4]

Morgan investigates

In the course of this shift, Morgan moved from identities imagined in the context of patriotic nationalism to identities that were the product of a quest for the authentic and the real. The rebels and fraternalists who had imagined and then appropriated the meanings assigned to Indian Others had often disconnected that process from actual Indian people. Lewis Henry Morgan, on the other hand, wanted not so much to imagine and implant import as to find it. That desire allowed Indian people to play key roles in the changing literary society, but it also raised awkward questions about the nature of Indians and the uneven social relations between native people and white Americans. Dealing with the contradictions between the simultaneous meanings found in real Indians and made through Indian Others pointed Morgan to a new set of crises, which I intend to define with respect to the notion of modernity.

For our purposes, modernity is the long cultural moment in which the positive / negative and close / distant axes of Indian Otherness become inverted. Americans built the nation on contradictory foundations: a highly positive interior brand of Indian Otherness coexisted with exterior savages lurking outside societal boundaries. By the early twentieth century, however, many Americans had become fascinated with a positive *exterior* Indian Other, one who represented authentic reality in the face of urban disorder and alienating mass society. Indians who had assimilated into modern society were now negative Others, and they could only reflect the savagery and degradation of that world back into American eyes. Morgan, by this definition, was by no means wholly modern. Rather, as he edged into a modern milieu, Morgan found himself caught between it and the older paradigm that had been established during the Revolution. His efforts to deal with these contradictions—especially in relation to native people—helped create ethnography, an extraordinary, contradictory way of knowing that has permeated American encounters with Others from that time forward.

Even before the Revolution, literature and art had been critical venues for imagining American identity. In the 1760s, colonists began to prophesy an imminent outbreak of American greatness in high cultural pursuits. "Not only science," proclaimed Ezra Stiles, "but the elegant arts are introducing apace and in a few years we shall have . . . Painting, Sculpture, Statuary, but first of all the greek Architecture in considerable Perfection among us."[5] In 1771, Philip Freneau and Hugh Henry Brackenridge celebrated their graduation from Princeton by writing "The Rising Glory of America," a poem destined for thirty years of reprints in several versions:

> No more of Britain and her kings renown'd,
> Edward's and Henry's thunderbolts of war;
> Her chiefs victorious o'er the Gallic foe;
> Illustrious senators, immortal bards,
> And wise philosophers, of these no more.
> A Theme more new, tho' not less noble, claims
> Our ev'ry thought on this auspicious day;
> The rising glory of this western world,
> Where now the dawning light of science spreads
> Her orient ray, and wakes the muse's song;
> Where freedom holds her sacred standard high.[6]

As the United States became a nation, this prophetic tradition redoubled its power. In 1786, for example, Matthew Carey founded the *Columbian Magazine* to propound and nurture an embryonic national culture destined for greatness.[7]

The widespread faith in imminent cultural excellence did not simply reflect a crude nationalistic chauvinism (although it was indeed that). It was philosophically grounded in the prevalent belief that artistic excellence and political empire traveled together through time on a journey from east to west. The trajectory—from Greece to Rome, from Renaissance Italy to Elizabethan and then Georgian England—now seemed to point inevitably to America. Nationalistic Americans gleefully welcomed the corollary: the country's rise to artistic greatness would be accompanied by Europe's decay. "The muses," as the historian Joseph Ellis has wryly observed, "traveled in a flock; they left one country *en masse* when it began to decline, flew west, then landed in a rising nation-state."[8] And as the ideological contours of the Revolution had taken shape, American intellectuals linked the westward movement of arts and empire with the flowering of their new political ideals—freedom, liberty, and the removal of tyrannical restrictions. Where unfettered freedom held reign, they claimed, the arts would prosper, inspiring the citizenry.[9]

After the Revolution, however (and despite the efforts of Carey's successful magazine), America's art and literature not only failed to inspire—they frequently drew virulent attacks. Ironically, the same political ideals of liberty and egalitarianism could also lead to a critique of art. The rising glory paradigm, many argued, contained the seeds of moral decay and was to be feared. As a free America prospered economically and joined the ranks of mercantile empires, the arts would migrate westward and settle in the New World, scattering new Shakespeares, Popes, and Scotts across the American landscape. Yet even as these literati created a glorious national literature, they would simultaneously call attention to a successful, cultivated class that could afford to patronize arts and leisure. Art, critics feared, was class-bound and intrinsically antiegalitarian.

The Muses, however, seemed to be hesitating on their westward journey. Early America's best painters, Benjamin West and John Singleton Copley, had trained in Europe and could hardly be called native products.[10] And although later critics might praise the works of Charles Brockden Brown, James Fenimore Cooper, Washington Irving, and others, at the time both New and Old World readers refused to accord American writers what one might now consider to be their due. Why was the prophecy of cultural greatness failing to come true? The prolonged absence of Shakespeares and Michelangelos pushed some toward panic, and, as the years rolled by and the Muses neglected their destiny, worried American intellectuals established another literary tradition, one that would haunt much of the nineteenth century—the frustrated call for a distinctive American poet, a unique American art, a characteristic American epic.

In 1838, for example, Ralph Waldo Emerson lamented the stagnation of American letters. American writing, he said, had nothing active or vital about it. Rather, it was little more than a reflex, the faint, almost vestigial "sign of an indestructible instinct." "Perhaps the time is already come," he continued hopefully,

Poetry a Savior?

> when it ought to be, and will be, something else; when the sluggard intellect of this continent will look from under its iron lids and fill the postponed expectation of the world with something better than the exertions of mechanical skill. Our day of dependence, our long apprenticeship to the learning of other lands, draws to a close. . . . Who can doubt that poetry will revive and lead in a new age, as the star in the constellation Harp, which now flames in our zenith, astronomers announce, shall one day be the pole-star for a thousand years?[11]

Like many young educated men, Lewis Henry Morgan, too, worried about the dilatory American arts and the critical role they ought to play in establishing national identity. Educated and largely freed from the mechanical labor that seemed to be America's most successful expression of native talent, Morgan and his friends aimed to revive poetry and put it to the service of the nation.[12] In 1843, Morgan concocted a mythic, usable past for his new Indian fraternity, a distinctly American history that he proffered hopefully as the scene for a national literature. In an address to the membership, Morgan (styling himself Schenandoah) outlined a narrative that transmuted Old World Gordian knot to New World (Indian) American. Drawing liberally on literary imagination, he linked the classical world of Gordius with the Six Nations confederacy, proposed location of the society's nationalist writing:

> Gordius conceived the mighty enterprise of leading his Phrygian children to this western hemisphere. Having gathered the fragments of the knot and left his malediction upon the land, he conducted them through forest, plains and desert, over hill and mountain, to Bherings Straits, thence across to this Western World, thence down to the chain of lakes and finally after many years of wandering, and vicissitudes of every character; they followed on from Lake Superior . . . until they reached the verdant lands of

Lake Champlain where they first found rest from their protracted wanderings. Gordius soon assembled them all in council. He took the severed fragments of the former knot and separated them into six strands. He then divided the people into six divisions named one the Mohawks, another the Oneidas, another the Onondagas, another the Tuscaroras, another the Cayugas, and the last the Senecas. He then tied up the six strands into a new and mystic knot, and giving it to them as an emblem of the confederacy and union which should subsist between them, he named it the Grand Knot of the Iroquois.[13]

[handwritten marginal note:] Iroquois as combind. of 6 tribes

Once he had chronologically linked the Old World Gordius with the New World Iroquois, Morgan had only to connect the two with the new United States in order to establish the historical framework for an epic national history. He did so by splicing together three "Iroquoian" epochs. The first ended with the migration and the establishment of Gordius's original Six Nations knot. The second epoch, in which the Iroquois confederacy grew, prospered, and fell, recently had also come to an end. Relying effortlessly on vanishing Indian doctrine, Morgan asserted that "nothing that may properly be called the Iroquois can now be found among us. Their Indian empire has passed away without leaving a vestige or memorial."[14] In the third epoch, Morgan and his associates in the New Confederacy of the Iroquois would write a national history and literature based on this past. And when they donned Indian clothing and performed ritual initiations in the New York woods, the New Confederacy members lived their mythic connections to Gordius and the vanished Six Nations. The three epochs came together as one.[15]

Just as it had for the various Indian fraternities that had come before, Indian costume played a crucial role in the New Confederacy's ceremonial initiation. It connected the membership with the Iroquois of the previous epochs and signified rebirth and new identity for members. Penned by Morgan in 1844, the initiatory "Inindianation" ritual was primarily a literary exercise, wrapping high-toned language around the standard tropes of fraternal brotherhood. The ceremony commences with the spirits of departed Indian fathers rising from the grave to chide their Indian children for forgetting them. The children protest, blaming the white strangers whom the fathers once welcomed and who destroyed the Iroquois and drove them from their ancestors' graves. A third chorus, by a fiercely painted ghost sachem, unleashes an emotional critique of American Indian policy:

Oh! Pale face we took you weak and helpless to our wigwams and warmed you and fed you and saw you become strong. . . . Could you destroy the children whose Fathers saved your lives? Could there not be room for them and you? Could you not leave them a little piece of land? Oh, that we had left you to perish. A curse upon ye palefaces. May your cattle perish and your corn die in the fields. May your children cry for bread, and there be none to give them. May fire-breath of Arecouski consume your dwellings and your enimies [sic] slay you, and plagues destroy you; till not one be left to weep amid the ashes of your desolation.[16]

The ceremony moves quickly, however, to cleanse the initiate's soul, tempering the curse by pointing to the sheer inevitability of Indian disappearance. "I am the Great Spirit," intones a ceremonial voice "deep and heavy." "The red men are my children. Long ago I saw in the future their destruction, and I was very sad." The spirit tells initiates that the only way to placate the mournful Indian shades is to preserve their memory and customs. The society's sachem then replies that the membership will accept the "delightful task." The ceremony concludes by offering the initiate complete redemption and a new life through mystic rebirth as an Indian child. "Spirit," prays the sachem, "receive us as your children. Let us fill too the place of those who are gone." And, of course, the initiate was granted exactly that privilege, being blessed with a new name, "the place of an ancient Cayuga," and an Indian costume that proclaimed his new identity.[17]

With its critique of America's treatment of native people, the Inindianation ceremony reflected the physical gulf that had opened between midcentury eastern Americans and real Indians. Their land safely secured, Americans were able to downplay the Jacksonian savage and turn to guilt-cleansing criticism of the very policies that had emptied the landscape. Indians appeared not only as pieces of an incorporative American history, but as nostalgic reminders of the good old days and as object lessons in the chastening consequences of progress. The Inindianation ceremony wrenched members' identities, transforming them from Yankees—the actual beneficiaries of American Indian policy—to aboriginal American Selves. It placed Morgan and his companions in a symbolically powerful and emotionally charged position for creating a literature rooted in America's landscape and nature. New names and Indian dress made the membership indigenous in the present, while vanishing Indian rhetoric relegated the people of the second Iroquois epoch to the past.[18]

Like the revolutionary mythmakers, the young men of the New Confederacy insisted that liberty and democracy lay embedded in the nation's landscape and its past. With modest effort, one could uncover that history, tracing national ideals back to the second epoch Iroquois themselves. "The Indian," observed Morgan, unknowingly echoing the sentiments proclaimed by the Tammany societies seventy years earlier, "is also a Republican and this is more truly a fact than may at first appear."[19] If the rebels had made Indians crucial political figures, Morgan's followers argued that inspiration for the elusive American literature might also be found in Indianness, waiting to be recovered and revealed to the world:

> The Indian loves nature with a boundless enthusiasm and the poetry which breathes through Indian eloquence is but an outbreak of the emotions which it creates. What a loss to civilized man that they had no literature to perpetuate those delicate touches; which would have rivaled the most exquisite periods of Cicero or Demosthenes: What a loss that they had no language to preserve those inspirations of the Indian's Muse, which might have equalled the loftiest flights of Homer or the sweetest strains of Euripides.[20]

By claiming to be the mystic descendants of the Iroquois and using costumed rituals to bring the imagined to life, the New Confederacy hoped to gain emotional access to these native muses who would help them proclaim American identity. As membership increased, the New Confederacy established additional council fires, each named after a different member of the original Six Nations. Utica was home to the Oneidas; Syracuse to the Onondagas. The Senecas had four tribes at Waterloo, Canandaigua, Rochester, and Lima; and the Cayugas branched out from Aurora to Auburn, Ithaca, and Owego. The New Confederacy's membership peaked in 1845 and 1846 at about four hundred.[21]

Like many who had come before, however, the Gordian Indians found it easier to postulate an American literature than to create one. Their inspirational literary creations rarely appeared outside of the flowery letters they wrote to one another. Morgan was one of the few to publish a piece of New Confederacy writing, an article in *The Knickerbocker* for September 1844 called "The Vision of Karistagia, A Sachem of Cayuga." In the piece, which overflows with romanticized notions of Indian disappearance, a spirit guide shows Karistagia a vision of the New York landscape as it appears in the 1840s. He then guides the sachem back through time to witness the treacherous ways in which the land and its people have been conquered. The Cayuga rages over "these multiplied wrongs," but his guide cautions that Karistagia's vow of vengeance "availith nothing and [that he] must be content." Although the writing aptly demonstrates Morgan's fascination with landscape and the passing of time, it is an unremarkable piece of vanishing literature, a jeremiad against Indian decline that at the same time explains the displacement of native people as nothing more than cruel and inevitable fate.[22]

While "Karistagia" revealed the limits of the young men's literary imaginations, Morgan had already sensed a way to transcend those limits—the scientific acquisition of factual knowledge. The transition from Gordian to Iroquoian knot had been an interim step, taking the fraternity's membership from purely imaginative classic realms into an Indian epoch characterized by a tangible location and an actual history. Morgan made his evolving preferences clear. "The whole charm and imposing character of our scheme," he noted, "is derived from its Indian characteristics and the previous existence of the six nations which are our type and progenitor: the mirror upon which our order must draw its image. Their deeds upon the warpath, at the council fire and at the festival are the materials with which we must work and an intimate knowledge of them is manifestly important."[23] Previous Indian societies had been content to enact imagined rituals using standard metaphoric language. Morgan came to reject such casual fictionalization, both in ritual and in writing. If the New Confederacy's ceremonies and literature were to inspire, he thought, they must be firmly grounded in accurate history and nothing less. And so, as a way of becoming an American writer, playing Indian began to carry increasing responsibilities toward Indian history and, eventually, toward Indian people themselves.

With the Indian past fading away, the documenting of it became a vital activity, and in the society it took on a strange life of its own. The newly composed Inindianation ceremony tied redemption to the recovery and preservation of the customs of the fathers, and the members responded enthusiastically. Morgan, ever fascinated by landscape, began an effort to reconstruct Iroquoian trails across New York. His fellow Cayuga Isaac N. Hurd traced Iroquois political organization and ceremonies into the nineteenth century. In the council meetings, literary and social exercises took on an increasingly historical cast as members presented reports on a range of research projects. Initially a prerequisite for the writing of literature, the reclaiming of Six Nations history quickly became the society's raison d'être, a crucial exercise in its own right.[24]

As they moved from imaginative literature to research and investigation, the

Indian names	time gct	English names	Residence
Tho-de-ag-ha-oes	April 17, 1844	Abraham Thorne	Scipioville bay Co
Sken-on-dough	" 1842	John H. Adams	Lyons Wayne Co.
Te-wa-tha-ha-se	Sept 1841	George M. Benton	" " "
Ase-san-go	May 15, 1844	Seth Swift	Aurora bay Co.
Lo-a-coo-chee	" 23 "	Wm L. Salisbury	Ledyard "
Ope-chau-ca-nough	" 29 "	William Allen	Auburn "
Gogh-ge	June 7 "	James Avery	Ledyard "
Th Mik to-ter	" "	Richmond Brownell	" "
So-go-ya-wat-tau	" 21 "	John Griffin	Springport "
Eah-nd-hav-an-dos	July 1 "	Wm N. Shepard	Auburn "
Kan-agh-to-ge-a	" "	Theodore Pomeroy	" "
Ho-wah-nau-da	" "	Parsons	" "
Ka-yen-ta-tiv-hou	"	Benj Fordyce Ch	Scipio Centre "
Ta-hu-ha-go	" "	John Dougherty	Aurora "
Ho-na-s-geh-dah	Aug 1 "	West Ogden	Northville "
Io-ga-ne-oh-doh	" 9 "	D. S. Morgan	Aurora "
Go-ne-ah-gu-u-do	" "	Henry McIllvaine	New York City
Nis-mock-wunten	" 30 "	Eldridge Avery	Ithaca Tomp Co.
O-gough-sa-nu-you-te	Sept 6 "	Montgomery Gibbs	Trumansburgh "
Tho-ge-des	" "	Henry Barto	" "
Tha-th-dar-ho	" 27 "	Clinton Camp	" "
O tat iah te	Nov 1 "	James Clark	Springport "

11. New Confederacy of the Iroquois, Schedule of Warriors to August 14, 1845, Wolf Tribe of the Cayuga Nation of the New Confederacy of the Iroquois. Lewis Henry Morgan spurred the membership to adopt complex Iroquois names that required phonetic spelling and were missing the linguistic familiarity of Metamora, Uncas, or Powhatan. Courtesy of the Lewis Henry Morgan Papers, Department of Rare Books and Special Collections, University of Rochester Library.

Indians of the New Confederacy turned to other scholarly disciplines. Just as fiction shaded into history, for example, so too could it drift into linguistics. Members began gathering descriptive words and place-names and personal names from books and treaty documents. Like the Indians of the Improved Order of Red Men, the members of the New Confederacy acquired Indian names at their initiation. As the group delved more deeply into its studies, the character of these names began to change from the standard, non-Iroquois Logan, Osceola, and Uncas to more difficult, untranslated Iroquois names. At his initiation in 1844, for example, Henry McIllvaine was reborn as Go-ne-ah-gu-u-do. The new member Montgomery Gibbs had to remember his name, the tongue-tripping O-gough-sa-nu-you-te (fig. 11).[25]

found like morgan want to be accurate

Whereas Tammany and the Red Men had used translated, metaphoric names for the days and months (see fig. 9), Morgan, who wrote much of the order's constitution, had his companions adopt a host of unfamiliar Seneca words, each spelled with precise orthographic markings. August, for example, was not simply the Sturgeon Moon, but Sr-is-gak-nah. When Morgan discovered that what he thought to be the head leadership title of the confederacy, Tekarihogea, was in fact simply the first name on a list of confederacy leaders, he quickly corrected his error, substituting the more correct Tadodahoh in its place. Similarly, as he came to understand the clan structure of the original confederacy, he changed the organization of the New Confederacy Iroquois to match it more exactly.[26]

Morgan's growing desire to mirror the second epoch confederacy's political and social organization soon led the group from literature, history, and linguistics into what we have come to label ethnography and, in a broader sense, anthropology. When, as the order's Tekarihogea, Morgan instituted the Wolf tribe of the Oneidas in 1844, he urged the new members to move beyond the strictures of the arts: "Seek out and treasure of whatever remains to you of the Oneidas; of the manners, customs and history; of their government, mythology and literature and especially preserve the vestiges and relics of their civilization."[27] The following year, he presented a detailed research plan built upon an efficiency-maximizing division of labor. Tribes, he charged, should devote themselves specifically to the study of their own tribe and area. Each group should exchange and file copies of their work, which they should classify under the headings Government, People, Laws, Religious System, and Historical Events. For each of these categories, Morgan laid out a brief research agenda. By 1846, the group had organized a research committee that proposed sending agents out to interview members of the Huron and Six Nations tribes in Canada and the far west.[28]

The society's shift from literary exercises to systematic ethnographic research changed the ways in which the membership imagined Indianness. The group's initial Indians looked very much like those of the earlier fraternal societies. Interior Indians signified a natural, classic American Self with a long, legitimating history on the continent; exterior Indianness offered an elite custodial identity and a noble outsider position useful for cultural critique.

As New Confederacy members entered the world of fact-finding, however, they found themselves dealing not simply with their own cultural imagination, but with actual Indian people. These people presented the New Confederacy with the same dilemma real Indians had presented the Improved Order of Red Men: how could Indians be vanishing (as they continued to be in New Confederacy narratives) and yet be physically present in western New York? Having few opportunities to interact with Indian people, the urban members of the Improved Order had simply pointed to vanishing ideology, insisting that Indians were no more. As the New Confederacy devoted itself to unearthing hard evidence about Indian people, however, it became increasingly difficult to maintain the Jacksonian fictions of Indian disappearance. The New Confederacy developed a new, more complicated set of rationalizations that would eventually explain away the contradictions of Indianized American identities in the modern terms of ethnography.

Morgan came to realize that real Indian people offered the best hope for reclaiming the history and culture of the Six Nations. He rapidly abandoned the sparse written materials on the Iroquois. William Stone's works on Joseph Brant and Red Jacket told him nothing about the structure of Iroquois society, and neither did B. B. Thatcher's well-known *Indian Biography*. Morgan held out faint hope for Cadwallader Colden's writings but, in the early 1840s, had been unable to lay his hands on them. In 1844, he turned to primary sources, traveling to Albany to examine Iroquois treaties.[29]

While in Albany, Morgan encountered a very real Seneca, Ely S. Parker, a young man serving as translator for a delegation of Seneca political leaders. Both men's worlds immediately became more complicated. The meeting helped propel Morgan into a founding role in American anthropology and Parker to a unique career as an engineer, military officer, and political appointee.[30] As Morgan later recounted to his friends,

> It was my good fortune to encounter one afternoon at a Book Store, a young Indian of genuine extraction. He was about eighteen years of age and of a pleasing and interesting appearance. To sound the war whoop and seize the youth might have been dangerous and to let him pass without a parley would have been inexcusable; accordingly, your humble Prophet assumed a civil attitude and accosted the young warrior in a friendly manner.[31]

Parker, his brothers Nicolas and Levi, and his sister Caroline became Morgan's most valued collaborators over the next eight years. They wrote Morgan letters filled with ethnographic detail, escorted him to ceremonies, and manufactured objects for his collections and those of the New-York Historical Society. In return, Morgan (acting loosely on behalf of the New Confederacy) sponsored Ely and later his sister Caroline and another Tonawanda Seneca, Sarah Spring, as students at his alma mater, the Cayuga Lake Academy. Morgan's major ethnographic work, *The League of the Ho-de-no-sau-nee or Iroquois*, published in 1851, contained illustrations of Nicolas and Caroline Parker, and the book was dedicated to Ely Parker: "To Ha-sa-no-an-da (Ely S. Parker,) an educated Seneca Indian, this work, the materials of which are the fruit of our joint researches, is inscribed: in acknowledgment of the obligations, and in testimony of the friendship of the Author."[32]

The relationships that developed between New Confederacy members and the Parkers and other Seneca people took the group far from the distant abstractions of fictionalized Indianness and into the free-for-all of Indian-American political conflict. Ely Parker had traveled to Albany to continue a long struggle being waged by the Tonawanda Seneca, who, under the terms of an imposed treaty, were scheduled to abandon their reservation by 1846. The New Confederacy's subsequent involvement with the Senecas foreshadowed what has since become something of an anthropological tradition: political activism on behalf of the native peoples who serve as the objects of study.[33]

Indian philanthropy had been part of Morgan's vision of the New Confederacy from the very beginning. In the Gordius address, in which he laid out his plans for the group, Morgan stressed that the order's purpose was not exclusively "social enjoyment or literary advancement or historical knowledge":

No! No! No! But it is to——Befriend the Indian——. Commiserate the sad destiny of the unfortunate, but noble Indian. They flee before the whelming influence of civilization, as the bark before the tempest and when the last tribe shall slumber in the grass, it is to be feared that the stain of blood will be found on the escutcheon of the American republic. This nation must shield their declining day . . . if it would escape an awful retribution for having appropriated the territory of a whole continent of Indians and consigned them to destitution, to misery and to death.[34]

Morgan's encounter with Parker provided a concrete opportunity for the New Confederacy to befriend the Indian. For years the Senecas had resisted the efforts of the Ogden Land Company to relocate the residents of the four Seneca reservations and sell the land to non-Indian settlers. In 1838, the federal government, having failed to interest Seneca leaders in a treaty that would have sold the reservations to the land company, named alternate chiefs, bribed them, got them drunk, and procured the necessary signatures. When evidence of this fraud came to light, the government responded with a "compromise" treaty in 1842. The new treaty called for the residents of the Buffalo Creek and Tonawanda reservations to relocate within four years to the other two reservations, Cattaraugus and Allegheny, which, although overcrowded, would remain under Seneca control.[35]

The Tonawanda people fought the new treaty through a variety of strategies. They refused to allow appraisals of individual improvements, forbade whites entrance to the reservation, filed and prosecuted lawsuits, and petitioned state and federal authorities. Three years of classical education at Yates Academy had made Ely Parker fluent in both the language and the customs of Americans, and he took a leading role in presenting the Tonawanda case. In spite of his time-consuming duties as an interpreter and advocate, however, Parker hoped to continue his education. Morgan helped provide him with the opportunity, recruiting Parker into the New Confederacy and persuading him to attend school in Aurora, where he could be close at hand to answer the society's many questions.

But if Morgan used Parker, Parker was equally astute at putting a willing Morgan and his society to use. He took Morgan to the reservation and vouched for the good intentions of the New Confederacy. After gaining Seneca approval, the group launched a campaign of protest. They sent a Memorial to the Senate, featuring the names of prominent (although suspiciously recent) honorary members Senators Lewis Cass, John Adams Dix, and Ambrose Sevier.[36] Members of the group began a comprehensive petition drive across western New York, and Morgan helped organize a mass meeting that the *Rochester Daily Advertiser* saw as "indubitable evidence of the almost universal sympathy which pervades this community" for the Senecas' cause. Morgan himself took the resulting testimonials to Washington. A New Confederacy member, Charles Porter, began courting the pioneer ethnographer and Indian policy administrator Henry Rowe Schoolcraft for the fight. Parker, who had met Schoolcraft in the summer of 1845 when the author had addressed the New Confederacy's annual council, made his own contact, requesting Schoolcraft's expert testimony on Seneca decision-making processes and the carrying capacity of the two reservations.[37]

When Lewis Henry Morgan donned his Indian costume, he imagined his identity along the same contradictory lines laid down by the Tea Party Indians and the Tammany societies. As he became an interior part of the American landscape, he reserved for himself a position as an elite, outsider critic. Other dilemmas were more contradictory—and more pressing. There was, for example, a disciplinary question. Was Morgan a scientist or a writer? The New Confederacy seemed to point him in both directions. Even more troubling was his relation with Indians and Indianness itself: were native people like Ely Parker vanished or were they neighbors and informants? The New Confederacy and its leader walked a fine line in the years 1845 and 1846. On one side lay the literary, the subjective, the boyish, and the fraternal; on the other, the scientific, the objective, the mature, the disciplined. Indians looked different from each perspective. In a larger sense, Morgan was wavering between the traditions of the Revolution and the inclinations of modernity. He was prisoner of the revolutionary urge to put on costume and become one with an interior American Indian Other. But he was equally inclined to a modernist quest for a supposedly authentic Indian reality always located someplace outside American society. Morgan's varied uncertainties seemed, oddly enough, to crystalize around the question of fraternal secrecy and ceremony.

He wanted desperately to maintain positions in two different camps. Just as he had pushed the society into a systematized, scientific inquiry that engaged real Indians, he argued equally forcefully for the importance of imaginary ritual, secrecy, and costume—the metaphoric tools through which members gained new American identities and positioned themselves for the writing of the national epic.[38] Morgan had no doubts as to the necessity and importance of meeting in Indian costume. "The first thing necessary is a costume, without which you never can organize," he told William Allen (Opecancanough) of the Cayugas. "It is perfectly understood with us that we do not stir a step until our equipment is right. If you do not get costumes the Confederate Nations will hardly admit you at the anniversary."[39] "In relation to costume," he told the Wolf tribe of the Oneidas, "you are aware that every association—Masons, Oddfellows, fire and military companies etc. all wear uniforms. They lend dignity and interest to the organization, and in my way of viewing the subject, an Indian costume is indispensable and one of the most interesting ornaments of the Order. Have the whole equipage—Chief's bow, tomahawk and head dress of feathers."[40] And he was punningly eager to supply the guest speaker Schoolcraft with a costume: "I send this not to make a suggestion in regard to the address but to a dress. All the warriors will be in the costume of their respective Tribes, not only during the initiation which will precede, but also during the Oration. If therefore it would meet with your approval, we should be pleased to have you appear in costume also."[41] Schoolcraft's decision on this matter remains unclear.

Disagreements about the secrecy that accompanied these costumed revels revealed the uncertainty of Lewis Henry Morgan and much of the membership. The issue of secret versus public identity split the society into factions, forcing members to decide in which of the two enterprises—objective study of alien Indians or ritualized acquisition of Indian Americanness—they really believed. Morgan consistently argued against making the existence of the order public. In 1845, for example, he promoted Henry Rowe Schoolcraft as an honorary member (Alhalla) and invited him to give the annual address at the summer council, which was to be held in Aurora, the hometown of the Cayuga Wolf tribe. Pleased at the prospect of having brought such an eminent figure to their town, the majority of the Cayuga membership voted to forego the order's policy of secrecy and open the council and the address to the public.[42] The order's other tribes, however, spoke vehemently against the idea. "Let not the council of Alhalla and the war-song of our Brothers from Lean-ne-wa-gus be open to the ears of the pale-faces," implored the White Deer Senecas of Utica. "Let not the coward pale-face hear the name of the golden link of Brotherhood that binds together the tribes of our confederacy."[43] Morgan asked Schoolcraft's advice: "Do you think it would be advisable to announce the name of the Order to the World? We have thus far kept everything entirely secret, but the time is near at hand when it may be proper to announce as much as that but it would not do to make any explanation or answer any questions concerning it, because the whole would escape. It must be essentially secret to be successful."[44]

One might have thought that Morgan would have agreed with the public faction. He would make no attempt to hide his activities on behalf of the Seneca Indians against the Ogden Land Company the following year. He had certainly been willing to expose his Indian writing, in the form of "The Vision of Karistagia," to a public audience, and he did not hesitate to bring individual nonmembers like Schoolcraft into the society's secrets. A broad, public awareness of the developing ethnographic mission of the society might have generated more knowledge and inquiries, and the presence of Schoolcraft offered an opportunity to go public with dignity and credibility. Ever the promoter, Schoolcraft himself advised making at least his own address open to the public.

Morgan demurred, however, arguing that no matter how high their aims, the public often looked at secret societies with suspicion. Even though the Cayugas might be strong enough to stand up to public disapproval, he observed, the other tribes were not, and he preferred to wait at least one more year before publicly admitting their existence. The disagreement intensified the following year, as several members proposed either a full public council or, at the very least, a torchlight parade in full Indian dress.[45] Morgan again spoke, a bit defensively, in favor of preserving secrecy: "The public has no claims upon us whatever. We are not engaged in pursuits which need justification. We are pursuing proper objects and until public sentiment is attracted towards us in a way as to render an exposition of our organization necessary to its justification, the question of how far we will be open is one of expediency only."[46]

Morgan almost certainly recalled the experience of his father, a devoted Freemason in the heart of anti-Masonic territory during the worst of the anti-Masonic crusades. Indeed, the New Confederacy sometimes met in the abandoned Aurora Masonic lodge that his father had helped build. His hesitation to open the proceedings stemmed in part from a deeply rooted fear of public censure, for if anti-Masonic activity had generally ceased, its leveling impulses lingered. As a privileged group pursuing the sensuality of literature and landscape, a public New Confederacy presented a fine target for those who saw elites—artistic, scientific, or economic—as corrupting the American polity and disrupting the egalitarian ethic. And on the egalitarian side, the savage white anti-rent farmers of the Hudson valley were, at that very moment, using Indian dress to challenge political and economic authority only a few hundred miles away.[47]

More important to Morgan and the serious members, however, was the need to conceal the frivolous way in which they had manifested their intellectual interests. Even in the 1840s, serious scholars worked through historical societies and respected national publications, not fraternal groups. As a would-be scholar, the Morgan of 1845–46 seemed more than a little embarrassed at the thought of the public's knowing about the rituals and costumes of the New Confederacy. To Henry Rowe Schoolcraft, for example, he offered a sheepish apologia for the social and "boyish, if you please," aspects of the society, claiming that the organization needed both imaginative vitality and scholarly seriousness.[48]

Morgan was perhaps realizing that he might have been better served by enjoying secrecy, ritual, and fraternal fellowship as a Freemason or an Odd Fellow, while keeping his Indian studies dignified and scholarly. Poised to enter (and help create) a rationalized intellectual world in which literary imagination had no place, yet drawn by the power of ritual and the inertial hold of his own role in the order, Morgan found it best to keep the existence of the society secret. Secrecy allowed him to avoid confronting the disjuncture between his subjective literary quest for Indianized national identity and his turn toward objective analysis and ethnographic inquiry.

If, in the end, Morgan's deep unease stemmed from revolutionary identities of American nationalism colliding with still-forming identities of American modernity, these paradigmatic contradictions showed up in more visible ways throughout the fraternity. As the New Confederacy moved from fiction to history to ethnography, its members worked out a range of doubled identities. When the order postulated a new approach to American literature, for example, it conjured a familiar interior Indian Other, an egalitarian, republican figure who, like Tammany, captured the land's democratic essence. The members fused their identities and that of their literary America with this Indianness through a ritualized performance of mythic descent and resurrection. At the same time, becoming this egalitarian Indian also gave the society members a sense of elite authority. Like the Red Men and the Improved Order, the New Confederacy became guardians, a special class that represented an egalitarian polity and yet simultaneously transcended it. In this transcendence of American cultural bounds, the interior figure of the Indian Other inevitably became exterior as well.

At the same time, the Indian-garbed New Confederacy writers self-consciously imagined themselves as a different kind of exterior Indian Other, a no-apologies group of educated intellectuals and cultural critics. If playing Indian placed writers outside American cultural boundaries, it also allowed them to promote artistry, nature, and tradition in a society increasingly inclined to mechanical achievement and economic profit. When Morgan wrote George S. Riley (Soshawah) about how bad he felt that the Yankees were boiling water from the once-pristine Great Lick in order to produce salt, his sadness sprang from a complicated mixture of nostalgic romanticism and puritanical guilt.

Morgan's bad feeling was made possible only by his ability to be Indian and thus differentiate himself from the deceitful, profit-oriented Yankee society the salt-boilers represented. Being an Indian outsider not only allowed Morgan to mourn like an Indian, it also protected the very enterprise of romantic, imaginative artistry from those who valued the manufactured and the monetary. Although the order drew its members from a privileged elite, they chose not to differentiate themselves in terms of economic class. Exterior Indianness was a more important line, allowing the members to see the class distinctions that existed between themselves and Yankee salt-boilers as boundaries of cultural difference. Preserving the illusion of economic egalitarianism, Morgan—

especially when he became Schenandoah—disdained the salt-boilers for their profane approach to what should have been a landscape of nostalgia and patriotic aesthetics.

Equal ambivalence dogged the New Confederacy when it moved into the realm of history. The group had turned, on the one hand, from a mythic Greco-Indian past to the reconstruction of a factual history, the lost past of the second epoch Iroquois confederacy. The historical Iroquois were temporal outsiders. On the other hand, the Inindianation ritual existed solely to close the historical gap between the vanished Iroquois and the members of the New Confederacy. According to the Inindianation, people from the second (Iroquois) and third (New Confederacy) epochs had common American ancestors and were therefore kin, ordained through costume and ritual to share the same national identities. When they confronted initiates around late-night campfires, the members of the New Confederacy experienced both the historical distance between first and second epochs and the fusing of those epochs in the heat of ritual emotion.

After Indian removals, Americans often denied the physical and social presence of real Indians, reimagining vanishing Indian savages as now-noble parts of a unified American past. The Improved Order of Red Men, for example, had no interest in querying Indian people about their customs or recruiting them into the society. They desired Indianness, not Indians. Indeed, admitting the existence of living Indians called vanishing ideology into question. Likewise, the presence of real native people revealed serious cracks in the idea that one could solidify a postrevolutionary national identity by assigning troublesome aspects of the Revolution to a commemorative Indian-American past.

Lewis Henry Morgan's plans for a fraternal Indian organization that would be patterned more than imagined suggest that, even as he looked back to the Revolution, he was looking forward to something new. His protomodernist pursuit of authentic Indians, however, proved no less contradictory. Taking Indian disappearance seriously, feeling bad about it, and being in contact with native people pointed Morgan to what later scholars would call salvage ethnography. Salvage ethnography—the capturing of an authentic culture thought to be rapidly and inevitably disappearing—has from the beginning been haunted by fractures of logic. The salvage workers are required to believe in both disappearing culture and the existence of informants knowledgeable enough about that culture to convey worthwhile information. Morgan, for example, could insist that "nothing that may properly be called the Iroquois can now be found among us" while, at the same time, he or his friend Isaac Hurd could attend

Iroquois ceremonies, talk to Iroquois informants, and commission the manufacture of Iroquois material culture.

The New Confederacy did attempt, almost intuitively, to resolve the contradiction between vanishing Indian ideology and an ethnography of preservation. The result was a confusing interplay between notions of individual and culture (although this was not the term Morgan used). Morgan and his friends made a subtle, unspoken change: Indian *people* (in the form of individuals) were not necessarily physically vanishing, but their traditional culture was. Because it was that culture that made them really Indian, Morgan could believe that the actual Iroquois really had disappeared. The people living at Tonawanda and Buffalo Creek were in fact something different.

The only culture allowed to define real Indian people was a traditional culture that came from the past rather than the present. Even as they continued to live and propagate, then, Indian people in the present were necessarily regarded as inauthentic because their culture did not conform to that of the second Iroquois epoch. Real Indian people both had—and had not—disappeared. For pragmatic reasons, Morgan and his protoethnographers saw a select few as being close enough to tradition—their memories were authentic, even if their lives were not.[49]

At the New Confederacy's summer council in 1845, Ely S. Parker strode headlong into this mass of contradictions, making them visible for perhaps the first time. The result was confusion over the very nature of the fraternity. Which mission—fraternal, literary, historical, ethnographic, or philanthropic—defined the society? Should the New Confederacy view Ely Parker as a catalyst for national literature, a scientific curiosity, or a tragic victim in need of assistance? Even more perplexing were the questions raised by Parker's status as flesh and blood rather than image. Was Parker a fraternal brother, an interior part of contemporary American society? His education, social skills, and participation in the New Confederacy seemed to suggest as much. But one could also see him as exterior, a relic of the second epoch. His role as an ethnographic informant suggested that the latter definition was also true.[50]

The New Confederacy followed familiar American patterns, imagining Indians as both close and distant, assigning values (primarily positive) to them, and then assuming those identities through costume and ritual. Parker's presence required the society to come to terms with a third variable. Real Indian people could themselves be both inside and outside of American society. They could be defined closely as subjects—people with whom one could share empathy—or as remote objects—things outside social boundaries, to be investigated like flora or fauna. Whereas the revolutionaries at the Boston Tea Party got along just fine without an Indian in sight, Morgan's protomodern Indian play would rest on the assumption that real Indians existed and were, for a variety of reasons, worth knowing.

As the summer council of 1846 approached, members of the New Confederacy once again began wrangling about making the society public. Attendance at some local meetings dwindled, and members of both public and private persuasions began sending in their regrets. Morgan's term as Tadodahoh was complete, and the group at Owego began lobbying on behalf of their candidate, a hanger-on named Hamilton Morgan. Morgan lost the election, but it was becoming clear that the organization was having difficulty coming to terms with the contradictions embedded in its costumed rituals. Lewis Henry Morgan had proved exceptional in being able to deal with these difficulties, and, without him in the Tadodahoh's seat, the New Confederacy began to disintegrate quickly. Membership declined, and in the fall of 1846 the society revised its constitution in order to make honorable dismissal a more streamlined process. The tribe in Waterloo shattered, the more dedicated members painfully experiencing the disappearance of the third epoch of the Iroquois at first hand.[51]

Morgan had queried the *American Whig Review* about publishing a series of "Iroquois letters" and in September 1846 received a positive response from the editor George Colton. His correspondence with members of the New Confederacy began to dwindle, and he turned his energy instead to lengthy ethnographic exchanges with Ely and Nicolas Parker. When he stopped attending meetings in the winter of 1847, the New Confederacy's demise was almost total. From a youthful and romantic literary beginning, Morgan had made his first steps toward a more mature, ordered, ethnographic project. In 1851, seeking to complete his Indian work before being married, he assembled the material into *The League of the Ho-de-no-sau-nee* and bade farewell to Indian studies for several years.[52]

Lewis Henry Morgan had transformed the Gordian Knot into an Indian society dedicated to creating a deeply rooted, authentic American literature by making the landscape and its earlier inhabitants its subjects. Playing Indian, he and his companions in the New Confederacy of the Iroquois placed themselves imaginatively and symbolically in the position of these interior Indian subjects, enfolding them into a mythic-historical construction of American identity. But it soon became apparent that Morgan was equally attuned to system building and rationalist methodology. As he sought what he assumed to be the authentic in imaginative literary exercises, he conducted a parallel search that relied upon a rigorous history and ethnography of the Iroquois. Morgan's later anthropological work (from the 1850s through his death in 1881) moved away from the interior literary experience he had gained playing Indian in the New Confederacy and focused instead on scientific paradigms that viewed both Indian people and Indian pasts as objects—figures and histories of significant difference that were thus suitable for a detached analysis.[53] The anthropological discipline that eventually grew to maturity around figures like Morgan gradually institutionalized this subject-object dichotomy, which insisted that authentic Indian people were not just Others, but exterior Others.[54]

In the latter half of the nineteenth century, ethnography became an increasingly powerful and influential method, and many Americans came to see Indian people through it. Emerging academic departments and private philanthropists joined the Smithsonian Institution (founded in 1846, four years after the New Confederacy) and the Bureau of American Ethnology in sending parties west to record the mysterious primitive practices of indigenous people. In practice, anthropology proved to be a problematic science at best, and its adherents bolstered their intellectual authority by insisting on its objective character. The insistence on ethnographic objectivity helped reinforce the perception that its primary research object—Indian people—existed far beyond the pale of American society.[55]

If it was cocksure in its scientific claims, American anthropology nonetheless continued to dance along a faultline of ambivalence. The discipline came eventually to turn upon a new (but related) contradiction. Participant observation—an insider approach that relied on empathy, subjectivity, and close contact with one's subjects—existed in continual tension with the analytical system building of objective, outsider comparative anthropology. Like Indian-American patriotism and vanishing Indian ideology, ethnography offered powerful—and powerfully conflicted—ways of seeing, conceptualizing, and interacting with both Indian people and other Americans.[56]

As the American colonies prepared for revolution, cultural shapers had turned to the Indian, an imagined figure based upon real native people who existed outside the lines of colonial society. Tea Party Mohawks and Tammany celebrants constructed a sympathetic ideological image, brought it inside their social and cultural boundaries, and claimed a kinship with it. After establishing the nation, fraternalists and agrarian protesters wrestled with the Indian many times, shifting the figure back and forth across social borders in a series of redefinitions always compromised by the contradictory presence of real Indian people.

Lewis Henry Morgan's own particular form of wrestling proved especially conflicted. By placing actual Indian people as well as imagined Indians into a disjunctive past, Morgan pointed toward a sea change in the ways Americans imagined their identities using Indianness. In the late nineteenth and early twentieth centuries, Americans' fascination with playing Indian would shift from the tradition founded during the Revolution—in which Indians represented quintessential American identities—to a new, modernist tradition characterized by an obsessive desire for authentic Indians far outside the temporal bounds of modern society. Ethnography could point one toward such authenticity, and early twentieth-century Americans swirled that together with tourism and a new primitivism in order to address deep-seated social and cultural anxieties. The result was yet another reinvention and dramatic appropriation of Indianness, this one no less uncertain and ambiguous and, in its ambiguity, no less indicative of the continual problems in defining American character.[57]

four

Natural Indians and Identities of Modernity

Mr. Dan Beard	Mr. Ernest Thompson Seton
Christian	Pagan
Whiteman	Indian
American	Englishman
Democratic Government	Monarchy
"That the American Flag is beautiful"	"That it is the ugliest among nations
"That it is the best of governments"	"That it is the rottenest on earth"
"That the pioneers were clean and moral men"	"That the American pioneers were scalawags and low types"

DANIEL CARTER BEARD

personal memo comparing himself with Seton (ca. 1915)

On December 5, 1915, the Canadian author Ernest Thompson Seton, one of the cofounders of the Boy Scouts of America, announced his resignation from the organization, claiming that the group had adopted militarist policies to which he was opposed: "The study of trees, flowers, and nature is giving way to wig-wagging, drills, and other activities of a military nature, thus destroying the symbolism of the organization."[1] The Boy Scouts responded that Seton had, in fact, been dropped by the organization for insufficient Americanism. "He is not an American citizen," proclaimed a counter–press release. "He not only re-sented suggestions and requests made by many of his friends in the scout movement that he become an American citizen, but went further and objected to the Boy Scout Handbook including a chapter on Patriotism." One of Seton's rivals in the scouting bureaucracy, Daniel Carter Beard, prepared a list of Seton's patriotic inadequacies, using his own life to illustrate more appropriate quali-ties. Seton's shortcomings included his British origins, a universalist spirituality, a series of alleged heretical statements and political positions, and—as the cru-cial signifier of these accumulated evils—his affinity for Indians.[2]

Beard's pejorative use of Indianness struck at the heart of Seton's world, for the Canadian had long argued that Indians offered patriotic role models for American youth. The two men saw themselves grappling with the same basic problem: how to create modern American character in children (especially boys), perceived by many at the turn of the twentieth century to be imperiled by an effeminate, postfrontier urbanism. If they agreed on the problem, however, the men's solutions differed radically. Beard turned to a familiar pioneer ideal, while Seton propounded a particularly modern form of Indian Americanness.[3]

For Seton, patriotism meant a hardy yet sensitive, out-of-doors character, best developed by immersing children in "woodcraft." Woodcraft taught children to appreciate and value nature, and its essence resided in Indianness. "Indian teachings in the fields of art, handicraft, woodcraft, agriculture, social life, health, and joy," suggested Seton, "need no argument beyond presentation; they speak for themselves. The Red Man is the apostle of outdoor life, his example and precept are what young America needs today above any other ethical teaching of which I have knowledge."[4]

In 1901, Seton, by then a well-known illustrator, author, and naturalist, created a youth development organization he called the Woodcraft Indians. Seeking to tame a group of local vandals, he invited them to camp out at his estate. After regaling the boys with Indian tales, he organized them into a make-believe tribe, the Sinaways, led them through nature study games, and put them to work making Indian costumes (fig. 12). The experiment worked beautifully, and, after being serialized in *Ladies Home Journal* during 1902, the so-called Seton Indian program spread rapidly. Seton went on to transform the material into a

12. Ernest Thompson Seton's original Sinaway Tribe at Standing Rock Village, Wyndygoul, Connecticut, 1903. *As developmental savages, children slipped easily into the primitivism that so often marked the path to a better kind of modernity. Seton's Sinaway experiment would be carried on by generations of Woodcraft Indians, Boy Scouts, Camp Fire Girls, and hobbyists. Courtesy of the Seton Memorial Library, Cimarron, New Mexico.*

popular autobiographical novel, *Two Little Savages,* which served as a dictionary of woodcraft and nature study activities.[5]

Uncle Dan Beard, on the other hand, thought that patriotism developed from celebrating a particularly white American history. Children, he argued, learned Americanness not through programmatic encounters with American nature, but by recreating the lives of the pioneer scouts who had tamed the wild American frontier (fig. 13). In 1905, Beard formed the Sons of Daniel Boone, an organization that encouraged boys to act out such a pioneer experience. The boy president of a Beard stockade claimed the title Daniel Boone; the secretary, Davy Crockett; the treasurer, Kit Carson; and so on. In their imaginative play, of course, the boys in Beard's stockades frequently pitted themselves against the Indian characters that Seton had used in organizing his tribes. Watching their

13. Daniel Carter Beard, ca. 1938. Beard moved
easily from the leather buckskins he wore as leader of
the Sons of Daniel Boone to the military-cut uniform of
the Boy Scouts. Although patterned on Lord Robert
Baden-Powell's military program for youth training,
American scouting never lost touch with its
"Indian" roots. Author's personal collection.

favorite icons locked in mortal, character-building youth conflict, the two men, genial acquaintances in other settings, could hardly help but disagree.[6]

Like the Tea Party Mohawks and the Indian fraternal societies, Beard and Seton attached great importance to playacting and costuming. They saw Indians and pioneers not simply as historical role models, but as points of entry into a magically transfiguring mimetic play for children. Although the stories each man championed were quite different, Indians figured prominently in both, appearing in positive and negative forms as well as interior and exterior ones. As Indianness changed over time, it revealed shifts in American cultural anxieties, the material situations of real Indian people, and the very ways Americans conceived national identities. At the turn of the twentieth century, the envisioning of such identities required an encounter with a new set of problems—those arising from the challenge of imagining an identity that was centered not so much on Europe and the legacy of the Revolution as on the angst that accompanied the crowded cities and assembly lines of modernity.[7]

If Lewis Henry Morgan lived on the cusp of modernity, Ernest Thompson Seton was quintessentially modern, wracked, like many intellectuals, by the anxieties generated by late nineteenth-century urban industrial capitalism. "Our system has broken down," he claimed. "Our civilization is a failure. Whenever pushed to its logical conclusion, it makes one millionaire and a million paupers. There is no complete happiness under its blight." In recent American history, Seton perceived deep transformations that had shattered an older world and installed a troubled new American society in its place. During the Civil War, the standardized railroads and industrial factories of the North had inexorably ground down the rural, agricultural South. The lessons of the war were not lost on America's leaders, and they launched enthusiastically into what Alan Trachtenberg has called "the incorporation of America."[8] Incorporation—the linking of diverse social and economic units under rationalized control—occurred not only in American business, but also in territorial politics, as Americans exerted military control over the recalcitrant South, the Indian peoples of the West, and eventually the overseas colonies in the Pacific. It affected social relations, as people of different races, ethnicities, and national origins "melted" together in the growing industrial working class. Incorporation reflected a cultural shift, one that allowed and encouraged the objectification of products and people alike. The grain in a Chicago elevator, for example, ceased to be strictly grain—it became instead an abstract commodity that functioned as an interchangeable piece in a larger system.[9] So, too, with individuals, many of whom began (like Seton) to question progress when they saw their fellow citizens defined as cogs in industrial machines rather than as independent yeomen.

At the same time the nation adopted rationalized, technological organization, however, it played host to a disorienting sense of caprice and lost rootedness. The soldier who once could see his enemy aiming at him now died blissfully ignorant, blown apart by a gun fired from miles away. In the mine and the mill, machines maimed and claimed lives randomly. In fin de siècle America, intellectuals began to worry about how easy it was to lose track of individual and social identities, which seemed to fragment the instant they collided with the corporation, the factory, and the city.

The uncertainty about identity strikes one as sadly ironic, for, from one perspective, postbellum Americans had finally put together the pieces of the coherent American identity they had been seeking since the Revolution. Such writers as Herman Melville, Walt Whitman, and Mark Twain succeeded in creating the original American literature that had so concerned the young Lewis Henry Morgan. The Homestead Act of 1862 seemed to legitimate Thomas Jefferson's dream of a nation of self-sufficient, landowning individuals. Post–Civil War reconciliation efforts emphasized American commonality (the Improved Order of Red Men blossomed, as secret societies became favorite sites for renewing national fraternity).[10]

This American identity, however, sprang largely from the traditions of the Revolution. Modernity, Seton sensed, had rendered the older paradigms obsolete at the moment of their greatest power. Expressions of unified American identity that came out of the revolutionary tradition were undermined by corporate monopolies, cutthroat competition, strikes and populist and reform movements. The result was a set of self-conscious attempts to salvage what was being increasingly pointed to as an older, better, but unfortunately disappearing America.

At the same time that Americans such as Seton feared the alienating effects of the machine and the system, others, such as Dan Beard, welcomed a new, streamlined techno-America. Beard sought to construct a national identity around visions of a bright, progressive future and the good life to be offered by technological advance. Ironically, the two positions frequently overlapped. Beard's futurist brand of modernism took its vigor from a nostalgic frontier past; Seton's turn to archaic Indianness served incorporative, progressive impulses. Primitivism and progress defined the dialectic of the modern, and they both reflected the intuition that America had experienced a radical break in its history.

The historian Frederick Jackson Turner's address "The Significance of the Frontier in American History" (1893) is perhaps the most commonly cited marker of this disjuncture.[11] Turner claimed that a distinctively American era had ended, and he proposed 1890 as a critical temporal boundary. On one side of this boundary lay the familiar progressive pioneering narrative embraced by Beard; on the other, the uncertainty and anxiety of modern urban industrialism that so concerned Seton. Earlier Americans—Tea Party Indians, antebellum fraternalists and literary nationalists—had all focused on developing an identity that was explicitly American vis-à-vis Europe. In fin de siècle America, Europe did not seem to matter quite so much. A more important point of identity opposition was the empty sense of self generated by the historical chasm that served as a signpost of the modern. Many intellectuals and critics perceived and characterized this radical break in terms of an older authenticity and a contemporary sense of inauthenticity. Indeed, for Seton, Beard, and many others, American identity was increasingly tied to a search for an authentic social identity, one that had real meaning in the face of the anxious displacements of modernity.

The authentic, as numerous scholars have pointed out, is a culturally constructed category created in opposition to a perceived state of inauthenticity. The authentic serves as a way to imagine and idealize the real, the traditional, and the organic in opposition to the less satisfying qualities of everyday life. The ways people construct authenticity depend upon both the traumas that define the maligned inauthentic and upon the received heritage that has defined the authentic in the past. Because those seeking authenticity have already defined their own state as inauthentic, they easily locate authenticity in the figure of an Other. This Other can be coded in terms of time (nostalgia or archaism), place (the small town), or culture (Indianness). The quest for such an authentic Other is a characteristically modern phenomenon, one that has often been played out in the contradictions surrounding America's long and ambivalent engagement with Indianness.[12]

The frontier's demise hit hardest among those worried about the character development of immigrants and the next generation of American children. How would the nation fare if its future leaders lacked the fortitude of those shaped authentically by America's powerful natural environment? Envisioning a grim set of scenarios, people like Beard and Seton set out to reimagine the frontier experience through scouting, wilderness, and nature study. Even if one could no longer pursue a rugged individualist destiny on the frontier, a rustic week of Indian camping in a national park or a scouting expedition in the country might prove reasonable substitutes.[13]

Members of the upper classes had the resources to act on the problems of modernity first. As early as 1880, a Dartmouth College student, Ernest Balch, began to consider "the miserable condition of boys belonging to well-to-do families in summer hotels, considered from the point of view of their right development." The following year he founded America's first boys' camp—Camp Chocorua, set on an island in a New Hampshire lake. Balch offered to mold a modern American manhood through vigorous athletics and wilderness experience, and upper-class parents responded by sending their children—especially their boys—to summer camps in New Hampshire, Vermont, Massachusetts, Maine, and New York.[14] There, they escaped the effeminacy of the modern city and experienced character-building physical challenges. Camp Harvard, for example, founded in 1882 on Balch's model, planned to "furnish boys with a rational and healthy outdoor life during the summer months, where they can learn to swim, row, fish, do some tramping and mountain-climbing, and engage in other manly sports; form and cultivate good habits, and build up their bodily strength."[15]

Camps also emphasized contact with the natural world—the wilderness that now substituted for the frontier. "Who has not felt the pleasures of life in the forest?" asked one camper. "It is quite impossible to put them into words, or to make one who has never experienced them understand what they are. There is a sense of freedom and freshness every hour. A round of simple, natural toils and amusements fills up each day. The ear soon becomes attuned to the surround-ings, and it begins to hear a gentle sound, like the dropping of ceaseless rain. It is the pattering of the minute particles falling from spruce and pine and hem-lock."[16] Nature study often displayed this primitivist cast, emphasizing holistic experience over the fragmentation of the city and insisting that to feel nature one had to journey back in time to a simpler life, grasp the experience, and then return, richer but unable to articulate what this pseudomystical encounter had been all about. At camp, one felt that work and school lost their artificial, industrial character; here, labor was devoted to the simple, natural tasks of insuring one's own subsistence.

Yet, although these camp activities appeared patently antimodern, they in-variably pointed back to the modern city. Camps frequently set up miniature economies, campers earning money for chores, subcontracting their work to others, forming companies to handle such contracts, hiring, firing, banking, and loaning money across the camp network. And when the campers returned home, "healthily bronzed and as hardy as only life in the open air can make boys," they expected (and were expected) to be better prepared for the pres-sures of school and society.[17] Antimodern campers played the primitive authen-tic against modernity's inauthenticity in order to devise a better modern. The antimodern primitivism that would later appear in Seton's Woodcraft program worked in a similar way. So did Dan Beard's progressivism, which relied upon the evocation of a mythicized authentic in the playacted form of Boone- and Crockett-styled scouts. The two positions—modernism and antimodernism—were, in effect, two sides of the same coin.[18]

Beard's and Seton's ideas diverged, however, when they came to the question of Indianness. Beard tended to shunt Indians into a mythic frontier past. Seton put them to far more complicated uses as manifestations of a modern/antimodern identity. As we've seen, changes in American society and in relations with real Indian people altered the twin axes of positive and negative, interior and exterior in American imaginings of Indianness. Seton's and Beard's ideas about playing Indian demonstrate just how dramatic the shifts created by modernity could be.

At the turn of the twentieth century, Ernest Thompson Seton followed the path blazed by Lewis Henry Morgan, remaking Indian Others in ways diametrically opposed to the Others that had come out of the American Revolution. For the revolutionary generation and its successors, the creating of national identity was wrapped up in imagining and then appropriating an interior Indian Other, a figure situated within American societal boundaries. Indians represented images, emotions, and ideologies that signified Americanness. By imagining Indian Others as a kind of us rather than a them, one could more easily gain access to those Indian/American qualities and make them one's own. The resulting identity was compromised, however, by a political and imperial American identity that also required aggressive, exterior Indian Others who justified the violent acquisition of Indian land.

Now, these constructions flip-flopped. Seton placed exterior Indians outside the temporal (and societal) boundaries of modernity. There, they represented positive qualities—authenticity and natural purity—that might be expropriated, not for critique (as in the case of the traditional noble savage) but as the underpinning for a new, specifically modern American identity. Interior Indians, those within American social boundaries, increasingly represented the negative, savage qualities of modernity from which Seton wished to escape. This reversal can be traced not only to American cultural currents, but also to the changed material situations of real Indian people. It is important, before I untangle these constructions, to trace briefly the historical journey of indigenous people in the nineteenth century.

As the century opened, President Thomas Jefferson assumed that Indian people could and would assimilate into American society, and he created policies designed to make assimilation a reality. Some groups, most notably the Cherokee and other members of the so-called Five Civilized Tribes, did appropriate certain American characteristics, most notably, American-styled political structures, literacy, and legal knowledge. In Andrew Jackson's America, however, many people believed that Indians were destined to die off—to vanish in the face of a superior race. Jackson's own rhetoric was more characteristically separatist: Indian people could best progress if they were removed from their lands and kept segregated from whites. In a series of treaties, negotiators acquired the lands of eastern Indian people, forcing them to relocate to Indian Territory on the west side of the Mississippi.[19] After the Civil War, as Lakotas, Comanches, Apaches, Miwoks, and many other Western tribes fought final battles to preserve Indian land, many Americans came to view them as savages who, if they refused to disappear, deserved extermination. The popular press often linked Indian people with the "inferior" east and south European immigrants peopling the urban slums and low-wage factories.[20]

In the years following George Armstrong Custer's devastating defeat in 1876 at the hands of the Lakotas, Cheyennes, and Arapahos, a mechanized, train-riding, machine-gunning military rapidly subdued native people, forcing them to reservations; U.S. policy turned once again to the idea of assimilation through landowning and farming. Although they would need assistance and protection, the line went, Indian people could in fact be brought into the fold of American society.[21] In 1887, Congress passed the Dawes Allotment Act, whose purpose was to turn Indian people into Jeffersonian farmers by breaking up communal landholdings and allotting parcels to individual owners. The "surplus" reservation land was then sold to non-Indian homesteaders, who would help Indian people become similar to them by being neighborly role models. By articulating assimilation as official American Indian policy, the government insisted that real Indians were now to exist within American national boundaries—they were to disappear as discrete social groups and exist only as individuals.

By the twentieth century, the last shift in perception of and policy toward real Indian people helped invert the definition of Indian Others. Revolutionary era constructions of the interior Indian Other had almost completely emphasized positive qualities—Americanness, a claim to landscape, and individual liberty. Even savagery, coded as martial prowess, could be a positive value when attached to an American Self. Exterior Others had been imagined in terms of the constant tension between Rousseauan nobility and a degraded primitive.

Now, the noble savage—still offering cultural criticism and justifying imperial conquest—could be found most comfortably residing inside American national boundaries. The absorbed Indians wearing white man's clothes represented the ambivalent success of American imperialism. Becoming one with the empire, they justified the noble rhetoric of the white man's burden, which bespoke concern for converted savages. At the same time, however, some twentieth-century critics used the same figures to illustrate the new savagery of the modern. Coded as drinking, tramping, and laziness, Americanized Indians were powerful examples of the corrosive evil of modern society.

If noble savage Indians now found themselves inside American society, the Indianness most desired by white Americans also reversed, moving from interior Americanness to exterior authenticity. Ernest Thompson Seton, for example, saw many of the negative qualities now embodied by interior savage Indians in the very different light of the exterior, antimodern authentic—laziness became freedom from labor, tramping became a carefree lifestyle, and refusal to leave the reservation now meant a folk rootedness to rural place. Although its complex meanings had shifted, Indianness remained a crucial tool with which to reimagine and dispute a contradictory American identity.

Yet, amidst the wilderness of meanings, certain paths carried more traffic than others. Seton's Indians, for example, proved more successful than Beard's pioneers. Any number of reasons might explain this greater popularity—larger circulation of the Indian program in *Ladies Home Journal*, the appealing novelistic format of *Two Little Savages*, Seton's better organizational skills, his personal charisma. But the success of Seton's Indian program, intuitively geared to a contradictory modernist consciousness, also illustrates the cultural weight of antimodern anxiety. Dan Beard's program ignored the purported lesson of Frederick Jackson Turner—there had been a fundamental break between frontier past and modern present. His progressive pioneer model suggested that modern Americans could remake their identities in the same old ways. Seton sensed something new—in the context of such a historical rupture, dialogue with radical temporal and racial oppositions offered a position of cultural power. To reaffirm modern identity, Americans needed to experience that which was *not* modern. Just as one visited nature in order to be able to live in the city and enjoyed leisure in order to work more effectively, one turned to the past in order to understand the present and future. To be modern, one acted out a heuristic encounter with the primitive. Indian Others, constructed firmly outside American society and temporality, represented this break not only historically, but also racially, socially, and developmentally.

Perhaps no discipline was better suited to aid in the constructing of such a favorable exterior Indian figure than the developing field of ethnography. When Lewis Henry Morgan began to view native people as objects of investigation, he inaugurated a tradition that helped shift Indians far outside national boundaries. The salvaging of disappearing native cultures required imagining them in a precontact "ethnographic present" always temporally outside of modernity. A key mechanism of this temporal dislocation was the notion of progressive cultural evolution: human societies progressed through stages—hunter/gatherer, pastoralist, agriculturalist, trader, manufacturer. Indian people necessarily existed in a different stage and thus, in relation to modern white Americans, in a different temporal zone.[22]

Ethnography's contradictory sense of the Indian as someone who existed in both past and present proved a key element in (anti)modern ambiguity. It was sadly obvious that Beard's pioneers were truly a fantasy of the past. But real Indians still existed, and Indian pueblos were in fact rapidly becoming attractive destination points of travelers in the American Southwest, where tourists, like ethnographers, sought to touch an authentic past by touching a contemporary Indian person.[23] As ethnography gained greater popular legitimacy in the last decades of the nineteenth century, its primitivist impulses infiltrated American culture, making Seton's Indians seem a more authentic means of raising children than Beard's pioneers.

At the early boys' camps, the contradictions inherent in using antimodern nature study to prepare children for modernity dovetailed with the accumulated ambiguities surrounding a primitivist construction of the Indian Other. Whereas the parents of modern campers feared that they (and their children) were becoming cynical and artificial, Indians appeared childlike and natural. Whereas moderns lived a high-density, mass-mediated, urban life, Indians were rural and face to face. One of the primary indicators of a healthy summer camp experience was a good tan. A brown face, of course, demonstrated one's contact with the out-of-doors and nature, but it also signified a step back into a premodern time zone, a new self that was kin to the authentic Indians of Seton, Morgan, and the ethnographers.

The connections between Indians and children already had a long history, the two being paired rhetorically as natural, simple, naive, preliterate, and devoid of self-consciousness. It was no accident that romantic literature often referred to Indians as children of nature and that they were denoted as childlike wards in their political relations with the U.S. government. Children, in turn, could be conceptualized as noble savages with equal ease.[24] In 1904, the psychologist G. Stanley Hall endowed this conflation with scientific rigor, viewing the Indian-child connection through the lens of evolutionary biology. In his influential book *Adolescence*, Hall linked the stages of childhood development with the progressive evolution of human society from savagery to civilization. "The child revels in savagery," Hall explained, "and if its tribal, predatory, hunting, fishing, fighting, roving, idle playing proclivities could be indulged in the country and under conditions that now, alas! seem hopelessly ideal, they could conceivably be so organized and directed as to be far more truly humanistic and liberal than all that the best modern school can provide." According to Hall and other recapitulation theorists, children had to experience each evolutionary stage before progressing to the next level. As little savages, they needed to escape the "modern conditions [that] have kidnapped and transported [them]." "Books and reading," Hall continued, "are distasteful, for the very soul and body cry out for a more active, objective life, and to know nature and man at first hand."[25] Education, he claimed, should channel children through the evolutionary sequence in order to prepare them for the civilized life of the modern world.

Ernest Thompson Seton firmly believed in Hall's theory. Writing for *Outlook* magazine in 1910, for example, he heavy-handedly conflated youth and savagery: "I know something of savages—of boys, I mean; it is precisely the same." Seton was an especially youth-oriented antimodernist, worried about the decline of America's next generation from "robust, manly, self-reliant boyhood" into a lot of "flat chested cigarette smokers, with shaky nerves and doubtful vitality." His Indians embodied the ambivalence one might expect to find in a group that forsook the modern for the primitive past in order to train to be modern. Seton emphasized escape, vacation, self-government, relaxation, presocial status: "Most boys love to play Indian. They want to know about all the interesting things the Indians did that are possible for them to do. It adds great pleasure to the lives of such boys when they know that they can go right out in the holidays and camp in the woods just as the Indians did and make all their own weapons in Indian style as well as rule themselves after the manner of a band of Redmen."[26] But whereas revolutionary notions of Indian self-rule had emphasized a semianarchic individualism and had approved of violent means to achieve that end, Seton's tribe taught the importance of social controls. His first law illustrates the ways in which modernity had completely inverted the meaning of the Indian Other. "Don't rebel," Seton admonished. "Rebellion against a decision of the council is punishable by expulsion. Absolute obedience is always enforced." In Seton's organization, rebelling was the quickest way to "un-Indianize" oneself. If his demand for obedience served modern social orders and corporate hierarchies, his subsequent commandments—prohibitions against starting wildfires, harming songbirds, breaking game laws, cheating, and keeping a messy camp—recognized Turner's historical periodization: the free frontier was gone and America was now a land of limits.[27]

Like the Red Men and other fraternal societies, Seton's Woodcraft Indians offered institutionally supported identities through offices and tribal badges. Seton established a hierarchy of chiefs that filled judicial (War Chiefs), secretarial (Chief of the Painted Robe), treasury (Wampum Chief), and administrative (Chief of the Council Fire) functions. Each brave set out to earn awards of distinction called Coups and Grand Coups after the practice of Plains warriors, who proved their valor by "counting coups"—coups were a collection of honors that ranged from touching a dead enemy's body to touching a live opponent and then riding away without killing him. By demonstrating woodcraft knowledge and physical prowess, boys earned their coups and moved through the hierarchy. As they did so, they were allowed to add, subtract, and color various parts—beard, horns, shield—on a buffalo broach that demonstrated their progress. Each boy also had a scalp of horsehair, which could be wagered against another's in competition.[28] Like the boys engaged in their banking exercises at Camp Chocorua, Seton's Indians simultaneously lived out a primitivist fantasy and prepared themselves for a very modern world through competition and hierarchy building.

By the close of the century's first decade, Seton's Indian programs had become firmly ensconced in summer camps, making up the core curriculum at places like Camp Minnewawa, Camp Mirimichi, and Camp Pokanoket, among others. And although the camps continued to cater to middle- and upper-class children, Seton began to consider a broader program, imagining urban rooftop campouts as a way to instill woodcraft character in the city-bound children of the lower classes. Before he could fully pursue this effort, however, Seton found himself being drawn into the rapidly coalescing scouting movement.[29]

Daniel Carter Beard was equally determined to participate in youth reform. Uninterested in leading children through G. Stanley Hall's developmental stages, Beard preferred a hearty dose of the history and morals of previous generations of frontier Americans. He saw Indians not as nature lovers, but as scalping savages and degraded modern failures.[30] Beard's pioneer organization emphasized American technical ingenuity and inventiveness rather than conservation and nature study, and his writings for children, published in *Recreation*, *Woman's Home Companion*, and *Pictorial Review*, were full of quirky projects that tended to function better on paper than they did in three dimensions. Beard loved lashing, knot tying, semaphore code, and the like. His was an industrial sort of child development, overtly geared to a linear, progressive historical understanding of American character.[31]

If Seton wanted children to be young Indians, and Beard, budding techno-pioneers, boy scouting's English founder, Lord Robert Baden-Powell, imagined boys as young army officers. British boy scouting challenged Seton's and Beard's programs, seeking to incorporate them both. Seton found the military model distasteful, but he was fascinated with his own English heritage (although Canadian, Seton had been born in England) and curious about Baden-Powell's organization. Not surprisingly, Beard plunged into the new movement with relative enthusiasm. Baden-Powell and Seton exchanged visits, Baden-Powell reportedly visiting one of Seton's camps in 1905 and Seton making a lecture tour of England in 1906, during which he and the Englishman shared lunch, traded manuals, and amiably discussed youth reform. When Baden-Powell's first scouting handbook came out, however, Seton was outraged at what he considered to be significant plagiarism: "My ideas [were] taken, all my games appropriated, disguised with new names, the essentials of my plan utilized, and not a word of acknowledgement to me, or explanation why I should be left out of a movement that I began."[32]

In spite of his annoyance, Seton had compelling reasons to continue working with Baden-Powell's program as it crossed the Atlantic. First, the initial scouting groups founded in the United States had done well and seemed destined to attract more boys. Seton found these groups distastefully militaristic. The boys practiced aggressive drills, carried guns, and occasionally shot one another by accident. Baden-Powell's less emphatic organization appeared to be the least of all scouting evils. Second, the Americans who backed Baden-Powell's program had wealth and resources and obviously intended to make scouting a dangerous rival to the Woodcraft Indians. Finally, given the multiplicity of interpretations attached to Indianness, Seton had started to hear the complaint that Indians were poor role models for children.[33] He decided, for the moment, to join the movement and work from within. In 1910, the two leaders brought their programs into the nascent American boy scouting movement, Seton hoping to replace the militarism and uniformed conformity he saw in British scouting with hearty doses of Indian and nature lore.

Other factions in the organization, however, preferred Baden-Powell's military vision, and both Seton and Beard found themselves being edged toward the margins. Given the ceremonial title Chief Scout (Beard was National Scout

Commissioner), Seton took on the task of writing the first scouting manual. In the book, he tried to synthesize his Indian and nature study interests with the military values of Baden-Powell. He ran into problems, however, with the new executive secretary, James E. West, who cut large portions from the book and added new essays—including one on patriotism—written by other authors. An embittered Seton continued to publish his Woodcraft manual, the *Birchbark Roll*, and to write for other youth magazines. In 1912, however, when the Boy Scouts launched their own magazine, *Boys' Life*, Seton became a regular contributor and consistently filled his column with Indian and nature studies. This rapprochement proved to be brief, as the saber-rattling atmospherics leading up to the war allowed Beard and other rivals to raise the issue of Seton's supposedly derelict patriotism and to oust him from the organization.[34]

Although Seton had argued successfully for almost fifteen years that Indianness represented a crucial component of modern American identity, the nativist refigurings of national Self generated by World War I gave Beard an opening to reassert the patriotic character of his buckskin scouts. The war turned questions of American identity away from the temporal anxieties of modernity and refocused them on national and societal differences, especially in relation to the European countries. Yet, if it now became important to assert ancestral commonalities with Great Britain and revolutionary ties to France, it was, at the same time, equally important for Americans to reassert their national uniqueness. Beard's pioneers provided a time-honored icon of progressive, civilizing America, an icon that folded easily into scouting's military framework. At the same time, Beard turned to long-standing symbolic linkages among Indians, nature, and the feminine to undermine Seton further. His masculine can-do and scouting's Be Prepared proved to be more evocative pieces of wartime rhetoric than Seton's suddenly dovish Indianesque nature study.

As antimodern Indians lost cultural power, so, too, did Ernest Thompson Seton, and Beard was able to force the issue of patriotic citizenship with increasing authority. "When you go to camp this summer," Beard wrote, in a shot clearly aimed in Seton's direction, "see that you are under a patriotic American camp director. He may possibly be of foreign birth or parentage, but he MUST BE A PATRIOTIC AMERICAN. No others have the right to guide and instruct American youth in these trying times."[35] Indians—patriotic in Seton's estimation—were being reimagined as the antithesis of American patriotism, a term that was itself being contested and redefined. Only an Indian or a traitor, suggested Beard, would claim that the noble American pioneers were scalawags and low types. As they outmaneuvered Seton rhetorically and politically, Beard and West consolidated the Boy Scout narrative around scouts, pioneers, patriotism, and service rather than Indians and nature study. And so, in 1915, Seton and boy scouting parted company.

But if Beard and West won with the Boy Scouts, Seton emerged victorious in defining youth training for girls. Beard's and West's genial acquiescence in an Indian model for girls illustrates the importance of preexisting symbolic links between Indians and women, and the different ways in which Indians could be constructed in order to address the uncertainties surrounding changing gender roles. For a long time, the Boy Scouts' twin organization for girls was not the like-named Girl Scouts, but rather the Camp Fire Girls, who played Indian with the zeal Seton would have liked to have implanted in boy scouting. The cast of characters involved in the origins of Camp Fire overlapped and closely paralleled that associated with scouting. Beard and Seton played roles, and their programs were championed by Seton's wife, Grace Gallatin Seton, and Beard's sister Lina Beard, both of whom worked hard to infuse Indian and pioneer lore into the Camp Fire Girls program.[36]

Camp Fire's primary founders, Luther and Charlotte Gulick, had likewise been involved in the formation of the Boy Scouts. The Gulicks were educators and social reformers who counted G. Stanley Hall, Seton, Beard, and many others among their close friends. When the Gulicks moved to expand a small family and friends summer camp program in the late 1800s, they adapted Seton's Indian lore program, giving it a gender-specific feel. Mrs. Gulick coined the Indian-sounding word Wo-He-Lo—an acronym for the Camp Fire tenets of Work, Health, and Love—as the name of the camp and the program that went with it. In 1910, the Gulicks had seventeen Wo-He-Lo maidens in camp singing songs, learning crafts, sporting in the water, and making ceremonial Indian costumes.[37]

Like Hall, the Gulicks believed that adolescence was a rebirth, and they emphasized the transformative aspects of Indian play. Girls chose Indian names culled from the lexicons of various native languages. They made their own ceremonial dresses and bead headbands, learning both domestic skill and an authentic, unmediated Indian-style labor. Campers decorated each dress with personal symbols that illustrated their individual characters (fig. 14). Like Seton's Indians, they earned coups and grand coups for various accomplishments. With

14. Priscilla Wolfe in Camp Fire Costume, ca. 1910 (Emmanual Wolfe, photographer). Through beads and badges, Camp Fire leaders sought to channel girls away from the labor market and into a symbolic economy based on the work of the home. Dresses were personal, and each one expressed the wearer's own vision of her character and destiny. Courtesy of the Nebraska State Historical Society.

white woman in costume

dedicated to her "Indian Identity"

it's creative it's like black minstrel 40's

each achievement, they moved toward the next level and a new identity: wood-gatherer, firemaker, torchbearer. This basic structure remained with the organization as it professionalized in 1912 with the assistance of the Boy Scouts.[38]

The Indian activities of the Camp Fire Girls focused sharply on reconstructing middle-class notions of gender. If camping and boy scouting were about restoring masculinity to postfrontier city boys, Camp Fire was about reaffirming female difference in terms of domesticity and service. Camp Fire Girls, for example, "were not to wear feathers in their headbands; that was for braves." In one organizational meeting, Gulick laid the matter out plainly: "The bearing and rearing of children has always been the first duty of most women, and that must always continue to be. This involves service, constant service, self-forgetfulness, and always service. I suggest that the fire be taken as the symbol of the girl's movement, the domestic fire—not the wild fire—and that from the first the very meaning of the fire be explained to her in poetry and dance."[39] Camp Fire Girls were to learn the true import of womanhood, defined as knowing the value of domestic work and appreciating art, beauty, and healthy natural living. In theory, this meant changing modern attitudes toward women's work:

> Because of the development of the machine, cooperative labor takes on much of machine-like form, and work thus becomes drudgery. So monotonous is the daily work in the shop, school or home, that some inner vision is needed to show the real beauty that is back of daily work. This we have tried to indicate by the use of poetic form, beautiful color, and the use of symbolism to show inner meanings—by emblems, badges, and music; to take drudgery and make of it a game.[40]

In practice, it involved learning to make ten standard soups, recognizing three kinds of baby cries, sleeping with windows wide open for two months between October and April, keeping a daily account book for one month, and so on.

By devising a set of seven hundred honors and badges and recognizing progress through the identities of woodgatherer, firemaker, and torchbearer, Camp Fire Girls created a symbolic economy for female work that had no formal recompense. Camp Fire encouraged girls not to move out of the home (where they were not compensated for their labor) and into the workforce (where they were) by inculcating a belief in the nonmonetary rewards of domesticity and the essentially domestic destiny of women. It should come as no surprise to find that Indianness played a crucial role in these lessons (fig. 15).

Indian role models demonstrated the difference between natural domestic

15. *Camp Fire Girls letterhead, 1928. Camp Fire combined vigorous outdoor exercise with traditionally feminine practices of nature study, gardening, and childrearing and teaching. Canoeing in an Indian headband dovetailed perfectly with the need to "cook and bake and keep a pleasant house." Courtesy of Camp Fire Boys and Girls.*

labor and unnatural work outside the home. They claimed a transcendent existence as expressions of the universal female activities of childraising and homemaking. Unlike Beard's or Seton's Indians, Camp Fire constructions existed outside narratives of national history and social evolution, floating instead in a primal, ahistorical void. Recalling his first encounter with Indianness in the Gulick home, for example, the Indian affairs reformer John Collier noted this appreciation for universal Indian forms, especially in the context of adolescent rebirth: "A living contact with Indian symbolism and Indian culture is not a mere contact with Indians. It is a contact with universal life—with life at its fountain source of world-old, world-wide and world-foreseeing adolescent consciousness." According to Collier, Gulick claimed that "here in the United States, there is one population that has not lost the heavenly secret of adolescence. That population is the tribal Indians."[41] As signifiers of the universal, Indians evoked the primal secrets of adolescence and womanly domestic virtue.

Although interior and exterior Indian Others had been retooled to meet modern needs, playing Indian as Woodcrafter or Camp Fire Girl evoked the same contradictory identities that had characterized the Tea Party Mohawks and their nineteenth-century successors. White faces meant something, as did Indian costumes, and if both faces and costumes carried meanings, they also canceled each other out. Positive and negative values assigned to interior or exterior

Others (or both) clashed, giving the entire practice a characteristic ambivalence. The American youth in the Camp Fire program were both Indian and white, but they were also neither. As with Boston's Tea Party Indians, these contradictions played themselves out as core uncertainties about national identity.

The antimoderns, however, made the situation even more complex when they imagined a radical break in history and posited a desirable Indian on the far side of societal, racial, and temporal boundaries. To understand the activities of Woodcraft Indians, Scouts, and Camp Fire Girls in relation to these new contradictions, we need to look at their efforts to gain *access* to the authentic. Whereas the American revolutionaries had transgressed easily breached interior boundaries, the Woodcrafters sought entrance into a world that got its power from its radical difference.

The mutually constitutive nature of modern / antimodern practices—becoming an Indian-child in order eventually to become a clerk, banker, broker, or housewife and mother—typified the many touristic escapes that defined modern life. Through purchase and travel, upper- and middle-class Americans made a series of moves back and forth from the city to the country, from work to leisure, from industrial production to handcrafted souvenirs, from the anonymous crowd to the ethnic community, from the insincere contemporary to a more authentic primitive past. Like all these boundary-crossing movements, however, Indianized quests for authenticity rested upon a contradictory foundation. In order to be authentic, Indians had to be located outside modern American societal boundaries. Because they were outside those boundaries, however, it became more difficult to get at them, to lay claim to the characteristics Indians had come to represent. In fact, when one did transgress boundaries, the very presence of a modern person contaminated the authenticity of the primitive. The dilemma of modernity, then, differed completely from that of the Revolution. It centered on finding ways to preserve the integrity of the boundaries that marked exterior and authentic Indians, while gaining access to organic Indian purity in order to make it one's own. Just as the Tea Party Mohawks were both aboriginal Americans and British colonists, Seton's Indians attempted to be two things at once—modern and primitive—while avoiding, if possible, the not-quite-sufficient back and forth of the tourist.

Three interlocked ways of thinking helped justify the Woodcraft Indians' claim to be able to access an inaccessible authentic: first, the childhood savagery propounded by recapitulation theorists; second, the scientific precision required by ethnography; finally, the doubled identity produced by costumed mimicry. As I noted, Hall and his followers thought that children, placed in a special presocietal category, had limitless access to the primitive authentic. Unformed to social convention and still primitive themselves, children experienced no societal boundaries at all. They flitted easily between the as-yet-unpossessed culture of their parents and the more familiar nature of the savage. Parents had the satisfaction of knowing that their children were in touch with the "authentic," and some, no doubt, desired vicarious experience through their offspring.[42]

Since Lewis Henry Morgan's time, ethnography had glossed over a characteristically modernist contradiction—living informants who were simultaneously archaic—by continually exhibiting "proof" of a scientific journey into the world of the authentic Other. Ethnography's claim to scientific legitimacy lay in an accumulation of details that proved the transgression of temporal and cultural boundaries and a subsequent return with objective knowledge. This need to capture authentic Indian culture through detail characterized most of the ethnographic enterprises of the late nineteenth century, which included on-site investigations by a variety of figures—Adolph Bandelier, Franz Boas, Edgar Hewitt, and others.[43] The trajectory of the ethnographic expedition—from the modern metropole to a primitive hinterland where social evolutionary time moved more slowly, and back to home institutions with tangible proof of an encounter outside of modern time—paralleled the modern/antimodern journeys advocated by camping, nature study, and Indian play enthusiasts.

Seton, who did indeed have experience with native people, established himself as a cultural intermediary, a go-between with an ethnographic kind of access to native societies. Like other primitivists, he also drew authenticating detail from the scientific reports of anthropologists. Consulting Frances Densmore, James Owen Dorsey, Frederick Webb Hodge, Charles F. Lummis, Natalie Curtis, and other ethnographers and writers allowed Seton to put his Indian enterprise on the same scientific footing as its recapitulation theory framework. And Seton himself continued to interact with the scientific community, receiving deserved recognition for his research on birds and mammals and his comprehensive study of Plains Indian sign language.[44] He took pains to be seen not simply as an urban social reformer, but also as a scientist/ethnographer—a role that implied an expert ability to gain entrance to the primitive authentic.

Hall's recapitulation theory and Morgan's ethnography afforded intellectual support for a third form of access, that sought through the familiar magic of disguise and ritual. We've seen a range of examples in which the wearing of

Indian clothing has suggested alternative identities. But, as Seton and Turner sensed, the world had indeed changed. Putting on native costume and imitating Indian life in the woods may have worked differently for moderns than for the Tea Party Mohawks a century before. At first glance, the act of mimicking would seem a timeless sort of performance. One observes, rehearses perhaps, and then imitates. But, as we have seen with the transformations of carnival in Pennsylvania and misrule ritual in Boston, such apparently ahistorical actions are in fact often subject to historical change. The cultural critic Walter Benjamin has suggested that modernity altered acts of imitation through, on the one hand, technology-driven changes in perception and, on the other, the practice of primitivism itself.[45]

The interplay between primitive and contemporary was, as we've seen, a defining characteristic of modernity. Primitivists enjoyed contemplating the mystical power of ancient ceremonies, many of which (they hoped) allowed humans to create meaning by miming the natural world. John Collier, for example, who had been primed at Luther and Charlotte Gulick's home, experienced a primitivist epiphany while watching Taos Indians "become" deer during their winter festival: "The Red Deer Dance began. There, in the plaza of the Pueblo, a forthgiving religious (as we white people know it) and cosmical (as we white people do not know) ceremony by men and women, old and young, transported all the Indians, and us, the few spectators, into a region of existence where thousands of years bloomed coldly in the hearts and brains of simple, hardworking humans."[46]

Primitives, imagined as being in close contact with nature, were thought to be able to mime the natural world more accurately than moderns. In their rites, celebrants did more than merely imitate in an offhand way. Their archaic mimetic skills were powerful and allowed them to become something Other—animals, gods, natural forces. Primitivist Indian play, grounded in ethnographic detail, resuscitated archaic imitational skills that were the special province of children. Children imitated the meanings locked into Indianness, one of which was the idea that a person could make significant connections with the world by mimicking it. The logic was circular and hardly conscious, but it helped undergird a new notion of mimesis.[47]

Mimetic abilities had also been changed by technological innovations. In post–Civil War America, moderns encountered their world anew through such mimetic mediums as photography, film, and sound recording, all of which altered one's perceptions of the world. The camera let one control time and

16. *Eadweard Muybridge, Motion Study from Animal Locomotion, 1887. New optical technologies like rapid motion photography and, later, film transformed the perceptual abilities of modern Americans. Heightened perceptual skills, in turn, changed both the ways moderns mimed and the ways they thought about mimesis.* From Eadweard Muybridge, Animal Locomotion: An Electro-Photographic Investigation of Consecutive Phases of Animal Movements, vol. 2, pl. 616 (Philadelphia, 1887). *Courtesy of the Beinecke Rare Book and Manuscript Library, Yale University.*

break a flash of motion into exact, frame-by-frame movements. Eadweard Muybridge's motion studies of the 1870s, for example, allowed artists to represent, for the first time, the movements of a galloping horse. Those movements included positions invisible to the naked eye—all four legs off the ground, legs interlocked like a crab, legs bending in odd ways (fig. 16). Sound and film both promised entry into the new perceptual world Benjamin called "the optical unconscious." When the camera allowed such perceptual precision, the ways in which people imitated things and each other took on new precision and power of their own.[48]

During the late nineteenth and early twentieth centuries, photographers, illustrators, and artists (the latter often using photographs) spread across the American West, recording Indian life and making those images available to a general public. The efforts of people like Edward S. Curtis, Adam Clark Vroman, Walter McClintock, and Laura Gilpin drew inspiration from both salvage eth-

17. Frank Hamilton Cushing in Zuni Garb, 1900.
Cushing's "gone native" mimicking of the Zunis carried
the linkage between ethnographic inquiry and mimetic
modernist escapism to its furthest extreme. From
Land of Sunshine 13 (June 1900): 9.

nography and modernist primitivism. Indeed, ethnography increasingly relied upon the perceptual innovations of film. The discipline had its own mimetic celebrity as well. "White Indian" Frank Hamilton Cushing, who had moved from anthropology to Indian play while doing fieldwork at Zuni, insisted upon exactitude in his costume and in his New York apartment, decorated to simulate a Zuni kiva (fig. 17).[49]

Modern / antimodern Indian play occurred at the confluence of these three interconnected bodies of thought. The ethnographer saw Indians as primal, distant Others; their premodern character could, nonetheless, be possessed intellectually through ethnographic detail and perceptually through the photograph.

The psychologist thought that children existed in a primitive stage of development. They shared ontological affinities with Indians and, as individuals, carried out developmental play by mimicking and thereby experiencing "the dawn of the race." Undergirding these notions was a technological transformation of perception that was reinforced by primitivism and ethnography. This perceptual change had given new power and meaning to mimesis and imitation. Taken together, these notions suggested powerful doubled identities that granted one access to an authenticity that became legitimate only when one could not gain access.

If metaphor was the underpinning for the contradictory costumed identities of the Revolution, moderns relied more heavily on mimesis. Mimetic action reinforced a sense of difference, important when one wished to cross out of modernity. Recognizing that one is becoming *Other* asserts a boundary line between one's always-forming Self and an Other that is most certainly not the Self. On the other hand, as a way of *becoming* Other, mimesis seems to insist that Self and Other are, in fact, the same. Mimesis was not simply the copying of something Other. Rather, modernist Indians imitated and appropriated the Other viscerally through the medium of their bodies. "One tries out the very shape of a perception in one's own body," notes the anthropologist Michael Taussig. "The musculature of the body is physiologically connected to percepts; and even ideational activity, not only perception, involves such embodying."[50] The channeling of mimetic contact with an Other through one's body forced it into concrete social, political, and cultural realities, where it helped define individual and group identities. The tanned faces of Indian campers acted as symbols, to be sure, but they had a powerful material reality as well. Influenced by these kinds of cultural currents, Seton and many others decided that sending their children to live Indian-style in the woods was an intelligent, modern decision.

The Tea Party Mohawks had left behind an uncertain American identity because their Indian dressing had evoked contradictory Indian Others—the exterior savage who required conquest, the exterior philosophe who put forth a platform for cultural critique, the interior American who legitimated national identity vis-à-vis Britain. While these meanings continued to resonate through American culture, modernist constructions inverted them. The Indian that Americans desired no longer resided completely within national identity. Now, that desire rested in some distant time and place in the form of a pure authentic Indian who meant hope for modern society. These complex layers of history, meaning, and

18. Ernest Thompson Seton Family as Indians, 1921, family Christmas card. Seton recognized the limitations placed on his ability to be Indian, but his long practice of Indian play did in fact transform his sense of self and the way he represented himself and his family to others. From Daniel Carter Beard Papers, Manuscript Division, Library of Congress.

reality were confusing enough on their own terms, but they grew even more tumultuous when actual Indian people participated in the dialogue.

Mimetic Indian play conferred a particular kind of authentic reality on Ernest Thompson Seton in his headdress and breechcloth. It was a contingent reality, however, one that differed from that of being an actual Indian. Seton's experience of himself as an Indian was surely a factor in the way he lived his life—it was real—but he knew well the difference between Indian and non-Indian (fig. 18). Seton and the Gulicks made sure, in fact, that their contacts with real Indians—publicized as a necessary part of their legitimation—took place outside the aegis of scouting, Woodcraft, and Camp Fire. Bringing real Indians directly into Woodcraft activities would have undermined the founders' authority as mediators who knew—and who could transmit—hard-to-get authentic Indian culture.

Some lower-echelon leaders had not made the same investment in playing Indian as Seton and the Gulicks, and they imported actual native people to bring unmediated authenticity to their charges. Indian people had their own reasons for participating in scouting and Camp Fire Girl play, and several welcomed the chance to participate. Carrie Eastburn, for example, was a prominent Camp Fire Girl leader in Sloatsburg, New York. She served on the Camp Fire board of directors in the 1920s, was good friends with neighbor and Camp Fire supporter Dan Beard, and led a string of daughters through the Camp Fire Girl program. Between 1929 and 1931, she recruited Ella Deloria, a Dakota linguist working for Franz Boas at Columbia University, to teach her Camp Fire Indians native songs, dances, and philosophies. Deloria was a frequent guest at the Eastburn home, where she advanced her own cultural mission—constructing positive images of Indians around the primitivist foundation laid by the Camp Fire Girls.[51] Just as the Camp Fire Girls used a universal Indianness to reproduce specific ideals of middle-class womanhood, so too did Deloria seek access to American cultural institutions in order to reshape popular conceptions of Indianness. Like Ely S. Parker, she tried to use the American practice of playing Indian to Indian advantage.

But how exactly did Deloria define a positive image of Indians? The very notion of positive image implies an Indian self-definition intimately entangled in non-Indian values and beliefs. Ella Deloria, like many twentieth-century Indian people, was quite conscious of her bicultural identity. The positive female images she reflected back at the Camp Fire Girls undoubtedly drew not only from her knowledge of Dakota kinship, but from the middle-class American gender standards advocated by the Episcopal church mission in which she had grown up and attended school.[52]

The historian Frederick Hoxie has characterized members of Deloria's generation of Indian people as pragmatic—claiming connection to the appealing antimodernity of the old ways, yet also bold, literate, and astute in seeing the benefits of explaining traditional pasts in terms of modern concerns.[53] In other words, Ernest Thompson Seton was not alone in seeing potential power in mediating between modern and primitive. Indian figures like Deloria, Arthur C. Parker, Charles Alexander Eastman, and many others also wanted to become bridge figures, using antimodern primitivism to defend native cultures against the negative stereotypes left over from colonial conquest. The interaction between Indians and non-Indians over the question of Indian Others proved extraordinarily complex, with material and ideal exchanges almost too subtle to grasp. A look at two other Indian mediators can help reveal some of these complexities. Like Deloria, Arthur C. Parker and Charles Eastman are difficult to situate culturally. And, like her, they both chose youth development programs as arenas in which they might construct and exercise Indian cultural authority.

After being raised by traditional Dakota people until he was fifteen, Charles Eastman attended a series of American schools—Beloit, Knox, and Dartmouth

Colleges and Boston University Medical School, from which he received his M.D. degree in 1890.[54] In 1902, Eastman published *Indian Boyhood*, the first in a string of ten books. Although Eastman's writing was often ambivalent, he was inclined to promote a positive, antimodernist understanding of Indian cultures. He wrote frequently for youth magazines, narrating a virtuous construction of traditional Indian life in *Boys' World*, *The Churchman*, *Youth's Companion*, *St. Nicholas*, and the scouting magazine, *Boy's Life*. In 1914, he compiled much of this writing in *Indian Scout Talks: A Guide for Boy Scouts and Camp Fire Girls*. There, Eastman argued that youth should aim to live in harmony with nature, a task that involved being "true in thought, free in action and clean in body, mind, and spirit." Eastman saw only one way to learn these lessons. "We will follow the Indian method," he said, "for the American Indian is the only man I know who accepts natural things as lessons in themselves, direct from the great Giver of Life." He then proceeded through a comprehensive treatment of scouting woodcraft and nature study: signs, tracking, picture writing, camping techniques, Indian names, games, and sports. Eastman used the Dakota language in listing names, and he cited a selection of rituals from his own boyhood: "Indian ceremonies are always in demand, and I shall give you several which have been specially adapted to your use from the ancient rites of the Sioux nation."[55]

Arguing that Indians offered the best example of youthful virtue, Eastman endeavored to carve out a positive role for native people in twentieth-century America. Real interior Indians—not Others, but people, like himself, in full contact with American society—possessed the authentic knowledge that Americans needed. Eastman sought to take the primitivist value attached to exterior antimodern Indian Others and reattach it to real, modern Native Americans. Like Deloria, however, Eastman, in applying primitivism to cultural politics, moved farther away from Dakota traditions and toward a complex, multiple-mirror, bicultural mimesis. When Eastman donned an Indian headdress, he was connecting himself to his Dakota roots. But he was also—perhaps more compellingly—imitating non-Indian imitations of Indians. As he reflected an American image back at American youth, he simultaneously challenged and redirected other, negative stereotypes about Indians. But Eastman's Indian mimicry invariably transformed his construction of his own identity—both as a Dakota and as an American. He lived out a hybrid life, distinct in its Indianness but also cross-cultural and assimilatory. By channeling both a Dakota past and an American-constructed Indian Other through his material body—from mind to pen to paper to book to Boy Scout—Eastman made it ever more difficult to pinpoint the cultural locations of Dakotas and Americans, reality and mimetic reality, authenticity and inauthenticity.

Like many other Indian people, including Deloria, Francis LaFlesche, Edward Dozier, and D'Arcy McNickle, Arthur C. Parker, the grandnephew of Morgan's collaborator Ely S. Parker, aspired to a career in anthropology.[56] In the late nineteenth century, as the dominance of museums in anthropological work began to fade in the face of rapidly professionalizing university departments, Parker chose to continue working at the American Museum in New York under Frederick Putnam rather than pursue an academic credential with Franz Boas at Columbia. And though he went on to have a successful career as the New York State archeologist and director of the Rochester Institute of Science, Parker found himself somewhat marginalized as an anthropological professional. He poured much of his energy into the Society of American Indians, one of the first inter-Indian political and cultural lobbying organizations. From the beginning, however, Parker proved willing to play with primitivist notions of Indianness, linking them to premodern leisure, child raising, and the escape to the past that helped define modernity.

In 1910, for example, Parker wove these issues into a short article with a long headline: "Lure of the Woods: Joys of Camp Life on an Indian Reservation: Put your troubles in your pipe: Be an Indian, forget Work, Go Back to Nature and True Happiness." "Are you hot?" Parker asked perspiring July readers:

> Be an Indian and keep cool. Are you tired of work and sick of the city? What's the answer? Simply be an Indian—cut out the work and take the first trail for the timber. Nobody knows how to enjoy the big outdoors like an uncontaminated redskin and no one better likes a prolonged vacation. Take your cue from the kids on the street. The boys know no greater delight than to play Indian and even the girls dress up like Red Wings and Mineehahas. It's nature to be an Indian in this country, so the scientists say, and the sooner imported Americans understand this the sooner the race will improve.[57]

Parker understood that most Americans viewed Indians as symbols. Unlike many symbols, however, Indians were also real people who could think, speak, imitate, act, and thus manipulate their own symbolic meanings. Like Eastman, Parker did not hesitate to don a literary headdress in order to challenge and redirect American constructions of Indianness. After evoking stereotypes of laziness, leisure, and modernist corruption, for example, Parker turned to

American anxieties about immigration and racial (read national) declension and improvement. He subtly painted "imported Americans" as ignorant and artificial and used the dubious notion of eugenic science to claim a privileged status for Indians as true natural Americans. If imported people (and America itself) were to improve, they needed to recognize the vital place of uncontaminated Indians in the American melting pot.[58] Parker, along with the Arapaho minister Sherman Coolidge and other Indian progressives, commonly evoked, mimicked, and redirected standard Indian symbolism in order to provide rationales for Indian societies, under attack in the early twentieth century by educators, missionaries, government bureaucrats, and land-hungry con artists.

When he moved to Rochester in 1924, Parker became involved with the local scouting program, within which he helped found the Moundbuilders, an organization for older scouts with "social, educational, and fraternal purposes."[59] In the 1940s, Parker helped oversee a program that trained Indian youth as camp counselors for non-Indian Indian lore camps. In June 1940, the *Rochester Democrat and Chronicle* reported that the Indian Training Counselors Course had produced a new crop of "young Indian braves and girls ready to take positions as counselors with various camps throughout the state to teach Indian lore to all classes of boys and girls. Some will go to Boy Scout, 4-H, military, private, and other types of camps wherever boys and girls desire to learn more about Indian crafts and camping."[60] Like Eastman, Parker sought to place real Indians—in this case Indian camp counselors—in positions in which they could claim the cultural authority vested in antimodern primitivism and use it, at the very least, for economic purposes, and potentially to alter American attitudes toward Indian people.

In the early twentieth century, Indian people participated in the making of Indian Others as never before. Yet the fact that native people turned to playing Indian—miming Indianness back at Americans in order to redefine it—indicates how little cultural capital Indian people possessed at the time. Such exercises were fraught not only with ambiguity, but with danger. Mimetic imitations could alter political, cultural, and personal identities in unanticipated ways. One gets the sense, for example, that Arthur C. Parker's tongue was something less than firmly placed in his cheek when he advised Americans to "be Indians." Likewise, Charles Eastman was as capable of mourning the corruption of Indian people as he was of promoting Indian authenticity. To what extent had acting like Indian Others formed a part of their identities around the very images they attempted to change?[61]

On an intercultural level, did non-Indian readers focus on subtle pleas for understanding or on the familiar Indian stereotypes that Parker, Eastman, and Deloria attempted to refigure? Frequently, ideas signified by Indianness were so deeply ingrained in the American cultural psyche and so ideologically powerful, they proved almost impervious to assault. Although they might alter Indian stereotypes, native people playing Indian might also reaffirm them for a stubborn white audience, making Indianness an even more powerful construct and creating a circular, reinforcing catch-22 of meaning that would prove difficult to circumvent.

While some Indian people used antimodern primitivism to assert the crucial Americanizing role of real Indians in a melting pot society, Ernest Thompson Seton's departure from Scouting in 1915 signaled an opposite tendency—a new era in boy scouting in which leaders attempted to redefine Indianness as something less than 100 percent Americanness. Ironically, at the very moment of Seton's ouster, Philadelphia scouts were in the process of reintroducing Indian characteristics as a sign of scouting excellence. E. Urner Goodman and Carroll A. Edson, the directors of the Philadelphia council's summer camp, created an honor society for exemplary scouts based on a loose interpretation of *Hiawatha* and *Last of the Mohicans*. Called Wimachtendiench Wingolauchsik Witahemui, or the Order of the Arrow, the organization gathered around summer camp bonfires in ritual Indian costume to tap out and induct new members.[62] By the late 1920s and early 1930s, Order of the Arrow chapters had spread across the country and turned many scouting groups back toward the Indianness that West and Beard had strived to eliminate.

As time passed, even Dan Beard softened. When, in 1936, he attempted to found a pioneer club for adults called the Buckskin Men of America, Companions of Dan Beard, he agreed that "outstanding American Indians" might be included on the list of great Buckskin Men. For a group of would-be buckskin scouts, the club adopted curious and ironic rituals. They met in a Plains Indian tipi pitched in Beard's backyard and began with a ritual Indian pipe ceremony using preciously preserved tobacco given Beard by his friend Mark Twain. Forsaking the Bible, the group then swore on an Indian scalp to be true, faithful, honorable, and steadfast.[63]

Beard's ritual included all the crucial and contradictory markers one might expect to find when the figure of the Indian was used to make claims about identity. Buckskins and the freshly canonized Mark Twain signified Beard's frontieresque form of Americanness. The tipi, pipe ceremony, and vows of honor and steadfastness evoked a primitivist exterior Indian Other, vanished from the modern world but still accessible through ritual and its accompanying objects. The scalp spoke of imperial triumph over Indian savages, while the concession to include Indians as buckskinners revealed the interior figure of the assimilated Indian-American.

Even as Indianness was being contested in the early twentieth century, then, it continued to reemerge—often keeping odd company in unlikely quarters. If it seems strange to find Indians haunting the buckskin territory of Dan Beard and the honor society of the Indian-free Boy Scouts, it is also completely consistent with a long thread of American practices. Amidst the steel skyscrapers of the alienating modern city, the Indian continued to lie in wait, always materializing when citizens gathered to proclaim American—and now modern—identities.

five

Hobby Indians, Authenticity, and Race
in Cold War America

Two things that most hobbyists have in common are the
owning of a costume and a liking for attending powwows (The
word "powwow" indicates a gathering of hobbyists—usually
for a weekend—during which they wear Indian costumes, sing
and dance Indian, and trade).

WILLIAM K. POWERS

Here Is Your Hobby: Indian Dancing and Costumes (1966)

When the Indian lore hobbyists of the Wushte-nong society promoted their
annual Ann Arbor powwows, they made sure that prospective participants knew
they would be bumping elbows with real Indians. "White groups," noted an
announcement promoting the event in 1961, "will want to take advantage of
this opportunity to dance with Indian singers." At the powwow, one could
expect to find native people of different tribes mingling with costumed non-
Indians interested in the recreation of detailed craftwork and the performance
of Indian dance and song. To guarantee attendees real Indian flavor, the Wushte-
nongs imported carloads of Sauk and Fox singers and dancers from Oklahoma,

recruited Sioux people from the Dakota reservations, hired Comanche dance champion Charlie Chibitty as a special guest star, and, as usual, asked those taking part to "invite any other Indians you know to attend."[1]

By the early 1960s, one could find an almost continuous "powwow highway" of hobbyist gatherings stretching across summertime America. The hobbyist could begin with the Wushte-nongs in late May, travel west to Wisconsin's Wa-Be-Ski-Wa white Indian Fair in early June, catch the Eastern States powwow the next weekend in Maryland, take a week off before the Chank-Tun-Un-Gi powwow near Indianapolis, and so on throughout the summer, winding up the season with the Hotnoweh powwow in western New York the last week of August.[2] In almost every instance, powwow organizers followed the Wushte-nongs in recruiting actual Indian singers, dancers, and crafts vendors.

The white hobbyists' powwow highway paralleled an Indian circuit of inter-tribal gatherings that had developed in the early twentieth century from older dance and meeting traditions.[3] Some Indian people alternated between the two powwow circuits, visiting hobbyist gatherings to sell crafts and to sing songs for cash and their own events to see friends and relatives in the larger Indian community. Many serious hobbyists engaged in a similar kind of cultural criss-crossing. They sang and danced in full regalia not only at white powwows, where they were surrounded by fellow hobbyists, but also at Indian events, where they joined Indian people in the dance circle. Unlike such early antimodernists as Ernest Thompson Seton and Arthur C. Parker, who had set themselves apart as cultural mediators, individuals who bridged implacable social, racial, and temporal gulfs between Indians and modern non-Indians, the new hobbyists placed a premium on unmediated personal contact with native people.

In the Cold War United States, the more direct kind of Indian play addressed anxieties focused on a perceived lack of personal identity. As we have seen, playing Indian has been central to efforts to imagine and materialize distinctive American identities. Indianness helped enable the American Revolution, and it aided in solidifying and expressing new national ideals. At the turn of the twentieth century, Indian play helped preserve a sense of frontier toughness, communal warmth, and connection to the continent often figured around the idea of the authentic. While the revolutionary tradition dominated the nineteenth century, it is this modernist search for authenticity that has reverberated throughout the twentieth, and it took on new contours in the years following World War II.

If the early twentieth century marked a subtle pulsing away from revolutionary nationalism and toward antimodern authenticity in the use of Indian Others, that new quest was still collective and nationalist in nature. And just as
notions of nationhood and authenticity blurred together for Seton, so too did
worries about the threats to both collective and personal identities blur for many
Americans as they lurched toward midcentury. When the reformer John Collier
fled New York City and California for his epiphany at Taos pueblo in 1920, for
example, he summed up the close relation between the personal and the social:
"There were [at Taos] solitary vigils which carried the individual out into
the cosmos, and there were communal rituals [of] grave, tranquil, yet earth-
shaking intensity. Only the Indians, among the peoples of this hemisphere at
least, were still the possessors and users of the fundamental secret of human
life—the secret of building great personality through the instrumentality of
social institutions."[4] And indeed, Collier devoted a long career to social activism
on behalf of Indian people, seeing an infusion of Indianness as a solution to
America's collective worries and to the anxiety of its individuals. Still, for all its
social character, antimodern worry took on an increasingly personal cast as the
twentieth century unfolded.

By the 1950s, detachment, alienation, and anomie had become popular
culture buzzwords for the members of what the sociologist David Riesman
notoriously termed "the lonely crowd."[5] Riesman's bestseller of the same name
suggested that the United States, which had once been a nation of "inner-
directed" individuals with autonomous goals and ethics, was becoming a gray
nation of conformists. Now, "other-directed" folk—those "whose conformity
is insured by their tendency to be sensitized to the expectations and preferences
of others"—were pointing the country toward decline. Riesman was one of a
large cohort of writers who feared the effects of a two-fisted combination of
atomic shock and postwar materialism. William Whyte warned of the dangers
posed by "the Organization Man," and Sloan Wilson painted a disheartening
picture of the colorless "Man in the Gray Flannel Suit."[6]

The sense of national community that seemed so self-evident during the
Great Depression and World War II had declined, many feared, into a shallow
conformism that turned individuals into automatons. For ironically, if the war
had united Americans, it had also confirmed every antimodern anxiety about
the meaninglessness of the individual Self. We were all subject, mourned Norman Mailer, to a death that would be "unknown, unhonored, and unremarked,
a death which could not follow with dignity as a possible consequence to seri-

ous actions we had chosen, but rather a death by *deus ex machina* in a gas chamber or a radioactive city . . . and so our psyche was subjected to the intolerable anxiety that death being causeless, life was causeless as well, and time deprived of cause and effect had come to a stop." "From the end of the 1940s to almost the end of the 1950s," the historian Warren Susman has suggested, "the problem was fundamentally defined as that of personal identity."[7]

These critiques—which spoke almost exclusively to the newly expanding white middle class—came at a time when their readers (and subjects) enjoyed unprecedented material prosperity. As they flipped burgers on the backyard grill and drove big new cars to work in the city, psychologically informed suburbanites sourly wondered whether meaningful personal roles were possible in this contradictory new world. A glance around the cultural landscape revealed, on the one hand, high living standards, happy nuclear families, shiny advertising, proud patriotism, and a feeling of national consensus boosted by powerful social and political institutions. On the other hand, one also found a dark sense of alienation, middle-class citizens constantly suspecting a dry rot beneath their cheerful veneer. If America looked to some like a land of liberty and sunshine, for others it was a world of McCarthyite paranoia, deep racial tension, and hysteria in the face of rock and roll, comic books, and teen delinquency. And it was not just that these two emotional modes patterned postwar life. Many Americans perceived—and quietly obsessed about—the unresolvable disjuncture between them. The enormous distance between happily mythic and popular-critical ways of seeing oneself forced many Americans to think, not necessarily about reevaluating their lives, but about what it would *mean* to reevaluate their lives. Such difficult imperatives have rarely been welcomed or embraced. They are fertile ground for the contradictory kinds of consciousness so well represented by playing Indian.[8]

Ernest Thompson Seton, John Collier, and their peers had felt a particularly social sense of unease. They worried about the fate of America as a collective and responded by trying to teach individuals to be socially responsive by putting them through exercises in primitivist communalism. Now, postwar Americans turned their anxious eyes toward individuals and their quests for meaningful lives. These quests for meaning took a variety of forms, but they often involved personal searches for authentic experience. Artists like Jackson Pollock explored the deepest parts of their psyches through spontaneous painting. Beats like Jack Kerouac and Neal Cassady made the road and movement itself authentic, crossing the boundaries of states, classes, cultures, and consciousnesses.

Blues, jazz, folk, and rock and roll pointed one toward potentially authentic experiences with race, class, ethnicity, and region.[9] And if most white Americans could not afford the time to be free and inner-directed beat poets, they followed along vicariously, and they looked for their own sources of individual identity in toned-down touristic encounters and a range of hobbies and leisure pursuits.

For whites of all classes, the quests for personal substance and identity often involved forays into racial Otherness. Among the many boundaries that separated "inauthentic" Selves from Others imagined to be real and pure, race was perhaps the most visible and the most interesting. Mailer's antidote to a postwar world of meaninglessness, for example, lay in the appropriations of white hipsters, who "drifted out at night looking for action with a black man's code to fit their facts." Drugs, music, art, literature, liberating crime—all of these featured, in the white imagination and sometimes in practice, covert connections to the more authentically rooted culture of Black America. But blackness was not all. In California, white Americans materialized another kind of romantic past when they dressed as Indians and Mexican settlers in staging the town of Hemet's yearly *Ramona* pageant.[10] And a diverse set of hobbyists sought authenticity and identity in America's original signifier of unique selfhood—the Indian.

Although such racial crossings have been a part of American life since the seventeenth century, these particular exercises came at a time when many Americans were rethinking their understandings of racial diversity and cross-cultural encounter. Triggered in part by a war in which people of color had caught a glimpse of freedom and opportunity, Americans of all classes and colors struggled to address the contradictions between the nation's rhetoric of social equality and its history of race-based oppression. The trajectories of African Americans, Indians, and Latinos were similar: returning from national service, minority veterans refused to reassume their second-class status. Many attended college on the GI Bill; others went directly into political organizing. By the mid-1950s, their presence in the courts and the streets had made whites acutely aware of "the race problem."[11]

The conjoined issues of race and social opportunity, on the one hand, and authenticity and meaning, on the other, converged in a widespread reworking of notions of color and culture. Many Americans began playing with the categories into which people seemed so naturally to fall, wondering how those boundaries could (or could not) be bridged, and becoming dimly curious about what it meant to make some part of somebody else—music, speech, authenticity—some part of you. This larger context is essential to understanding why non-Indians turned to a new kind of Indianness, one that, for the first time, actually seemed to require a significant number of real Indians.

In 1950, the magazine *Scientific American* asked a group of leading academics to assess the state of their respective fields at midcentury. Surveying the achievements of anthropology, Alfred L. Kroeber celebrated the victory of the concept of culture over the idea of biological race as a principle for categorizing societies:

> The most significant accomplishment of anthropology in the first half of the twentieth century has been the extension and clarification of the concept of culture. The outstanding consequence of this conceptual extension has been the toppling of the doctrine of racism. . . . We have learned that social achievements and superiorities rest overwhelmingly on cultural conditioning. . . . Anthropologists now agree that each culture must be examined in terms of its own structure and values, instead of being rated by the standards of some other civilization exalted as absolute.[12]

Although Kroeber was probably correct about the rise of cultural relativism, he was almost certainly wrong about its toppling of racialist thinking. If cultural relativism had toppled anything, it was an older idea of culture defined by social Darwinism and the very specific configuration of race that went along with it.

For Edward Tylor, who introduced the idea to anthropology in 1870, the word *culture* had been singular rather than plural. There was one culture, and the world's various societies represented stages in an evolutionary hierarchy that featured white, Western society at its pinnacle and any number of so-called primitive societies below.[13] In order to account for the wide distribution of societies along this scale, theorists of the Tylorean school invoked the biological idea of race. Racial character or temperament, they thought, determined the values, beliefs, and practices of a society. These qualities were believed to be genetic and inheritable in the same manner as physical characteristics. The character of Indian people, for example, was innate, and it channeled Indians almost inevitably toward lower-level subsistence practices like hunting or farming. The problems many Indians experienced as their societies came under American domination could be assumed to result from racial tendencies that made living in a civilized society difficult.[14]

In the late nineteenth and early twentieth centuries, the anthropologist Franz Boas and his students (of whom Kroeber was one) challenged this view. The

Boasian group gradually redefined culture, shifting its meanings away from social Darwinism and toward cultural relativism and racial equivalence. In 1946, Kroeber defined culture as "the patterns of form, style, and significance" that embodied a society's overt and implicit values. Culture, he said, was passed from generation to generation through individuals. Despite its dependence on individuals, however, culture was impersonal and anonymous.[15] By World War II, this new definition of culture had become entrenched in universities. In more intuitive forms, it began to enter the popular mainstream, while at the same time underpinning the postwar critiques of racism offered by people of color. The war and the propaganda surrounding it helped solidify the rise of cultural relativism over social Darwinism. Nazi Germany emphasized Darwinian hierarchies defined by biological race. The Allies, on the other hand, were supposed to represent tolerance and equality, even across racial lines. Thus, when the British scholar Raymond Williams returned to Cambridge after the war, he found that he was hearing the word of victory—culture—with much greater frequency than he had only a few years before.[16] Its toppling of racism became a prominent postwar narrative on both sides of the Atlantic.

Proponents of cultural relativism and racial equality proved to be overly optimistic. Even as behavioral, relativist ideas of culture became common intellectual currency, many Americans simultaneously insisted on racial and biological essentialism or they rejected relativism altogether. The large audience for books like Ruth Benedict's *Patterns of Culture* and *Race and Racism*, Ashley Montagu's *Man's Most Dangerous Myth: The Fallacy of Race*, and, especially, Gunnar Myrdal's *American Dilemma* testified to both the prevalence of the ideal of cultural relativism and the staying power of racialist thinking. Many midcentury white Americans used—and appeared to accept—the unifying rhetoric of cultural relativism and racial equivalence. But their practice often did not reflect that rhetoric. As Susman has written, "The people believed in the democratic creed, but when it came to treating blacks equally, they did not really believe in the democratic creed."[17] Whether or not one denounced racism, race itself continued to offer Americans familiar markers of difference that coded African Americans, Indians, and others as either inferior or authentic (or frequently both).

These interlocked crises of race and authenticity were essentially modernist in nature and, if they owed their newfound visibility to a World War II fought in the name of community and freedom, they often blurred back across the decades to the late nineteenth and early twentieth centuries. Within the Indian lore groups criss-crossing the two powwow highways, for example, one found a mix of modern / antimodern and postwar approaches to race and authenticity.[18] One group, bearing the informal label of object hobbyists, favored the replication of old Indian artifacts and costumes. They were generally uninterested in dancing and singing with native people, seeing Indians in classic antimodern terms as exterior figures. Racially different and temporally separate, Indians were objects of desire, but only as they existed outside of American society and modernity itself. Another faction—people hobbyists—enjoyed the intercultural contact and boundary crossing they found at contemporary powwows. Emphasizing cultural boundary blurring, the people hobbyists constructed interior, us versions of the Indian Other, well inside contemporary America. These interior Indians might have been cultural kin to the interior Others constructed by the Tea Party Mohawks and the Tammany societies, but for a crucial social distinction: Unlike earlier groups, the people hobbyists had to reconcile their cultural imaginations with the real Indian people they wanted to see dancing next to them in the powwow circle.

This tension between imagination and social encounter reflects a history that can be traced back to Ernest Thompson Seton's time. Until the postwar period, antimodern primitivism dominated the hobby, and its object-obsessed adherents focused on the preservation of an allegedly disappearing native culture and the exacting reproductions that object hobbyists called artifakery. This older generation traced its roots to the Woodcraft Indians, Boy Scouts, and Campfire Girls of the early twentieth century. Many hobbyists had grown up in such organizations, become fascinated with Indianness, and now spent their adult leisure time learning Indian crafts, duplicating costumes, and meeting to compare notes and to powwow. They tended to be male—although the hobbyist population became increasingly gender-diverse throughout the 1950s and 1960s—and typically middle and lower-middle class.[19]

Some Boy Scout groups, most notably the Koshare troop of La Junta, Colorado, made Indian lore the very foundation of their programs and slowly drifted away from scouting (fig. 19). Founded in 1933, the Koshares replaced scouting's military hierarchy with Indian terms: papoose, brave, and chief for the various ranks, and Navajo and Sioux tribes for the traditional patrols.[20] They dedicated themselves to the public performance of Indian dances and the perpetuation of what they called vanishing Indian cultures. In striving to keep Indian culture alive, the scouts created a museum that housed both Indian objects and the Koshares' own detailed replications of Indian material culture.

19. *Indian Pageant War Dance, 1915. A pageant involving girls and boys from the Boulder Training Academy. Like many early Boy Scout groups, Ralph Hubbard's troop, which performed in Europe in 1920, revolved around Indian costume and ceremonialism. Many hobbyists became acquainted with Indian lore in similar situations. Photograph by Edwin Tangen. Courtesy of the Carnegie Branch Library for Local History, Boulder Historical Society Collection.*

Revenue from the highly theatrical dance performances funded the group's museum and its sophisticated costumes. During the 1930s and 1940s, scouting tried to bring such groups back into the fold, ordering them to scale back their emphasis on Indian lore. Many troops compromised, but others—like the Koshares, who remain vital today—maintained their interests independently, creating small but self-perpetuating hobbyist organizations.[21]

A similar impulse to preserve vanishing Indian culture inspired other hobbyist groups outside the direct aegis of scouting. The Smokis of Prescott, Arizona, for example, emerged yearly from their kiva to perform a version of the Hopi Snake Dance.[22] Founded in 1921 by the town's Chamber of Commerce, the Smokis performed their annual ritual for seventy years, until pressure from Hopi people caused them to stop. The Smokis originally intended to create an annual tourist event, but they soon began to develop a deeper interest in preserving Indian culture. Located on Prescott's main street, their kiva museum houses an impressive artifact collection and racks of Smoki dance costumes. The group became one of Prescott's primary venues for working out not only modern identities, but also local and personal ones. The Chamber of Commerce organization gradually metamorphosed into an exclusive secret society replete with Indian names and identities and identifying tattoos in the form of small "rattlesnake bites" on the hand. Yet while the Smokis played Indian on a regular basis, they felt strongly about not being mistaken for real Indians. Although their name—Smoki—was originally chosen to evoke Moki, an alternate name for the Hopi people, the group started shifting the pronunciation from a short to a long i, becoming the "Smoke-eyes," a change that helped to emphasize their difference from the real Hopis, who have never viewed their masquerade as anything but insulting.

Object and people hobbyists looked to Indianness for very different kinds of identity, and this led them to different understandings of racial boundaries and the locations of authenticity. The object hobbyists envisioned an antimodern, exterior Indian Other, one that logically fit into the cluster of ideas that accompanied social Darwinism. Indians were easily differentiated along racial lines, but the object hobbyists more often marked Indians as temporal Others, reflections of a primitive stage of cultural existence outside modernity. When actual Indian people did not match this primitivist ideal, object hobbyists tended to dismiss them as tragic, degraded figures, interior Others who had been rendered inauthentic through contact with modern society.

For object hobbyists, the redemptive value of Indians lay not in actual people, but in the artifacts they had once produced in a more authentic stage of existence. To meet the criteria of cultural primitivism, authentic objects should be (or should look) Indian made, the older and more traditional their materials and manufacture, the better.[23] Confining themselves to periods before the twentieth century, material culture hobbyists searched for or replicated authentic materials—real Venetian glass trade beads, bison skins tanned by using the animal's brain, bone and shell wampum, and old-style wool cloth and velveteen. A small industry supplied serious hobbyists with materials, photographs, and technical advice. The *American Indian Hobbyist*, a periodical founded in 1954, became a clearinghouse for information, traders, and dealers. It ran advertisements for genuine eagle feathers and old artifacts and how-to columns illustrating the making of war clubs and hairpieces (fig. 20).[24]

This particular construction of the authentic had a long, reassuring history,

PLUME TRADING & SALES

SINCE 1927

Specializing in American Indian Crafts and
Supplies. All types of Authentic Indiancraft
kits for Hobbyists, Boy Scouts and Cub Scouts.

Catalogue .. Send 25¢ Refundable with your first order of $2.50 or more.

P.O. BOX 585, MONROE, NEW YORK

Classified ...

Hobbyists, historians, students, anthropologists, linguists! "Sioux Language, Grammar, Vocabulary." Accurate, result of 15 years research on Sioux. $2.00 per copy. Frederick Goshe, 153 Harrison, Valparaiso, Indiana.

CREE & CARRIER Indian tanned and beaded: Gloves, Gauntlets, coats, moccasins. COLLECTORS ONLY: NEW Haida and Kwakiutl Masks, $35.00 - $125.00 send 10¢ for price list. Wm. Guy Spittal, RR #2 Ohsweken, Six Nations Res., Ontario, Canada.

Crowbelt, 75 rare feathers, plus 10-layer bustle--genuine trade cloth trailers, $125.00. Otterhide breastplate with four rows metal-back mirrors, $40.00. New Jersey Indian Homecoming Powwow, 50 Lincoln Ave., Totowa Borough, N. J.

Classified ads - Ten cents per word Minimum of 10 words; maximum, 50. Your name and address are included free.

When patronizing our advertisers, please mention POWWOW TRAILS.

Special Group Rates- For 10 or more subscriptions mailed to one address, the cost is only $2.50 per subscription.

20. *Advertisements page,* Powwow Trails, *1964. Serious hobbyists established a hobby economy that peaked during powwow season and sustained itself during the rest of the year through classified advertising. Products were highly specific, and words like "authentic," "genuine," "rare," "accurate," and "Indian tanned and beaded" marked the ideology that underpinned the trade. From* Powwow Trails *1 (September 1964): n.p.*

but many young hobbyists found it insufficient. It failed to address a contemporary reality in which cultures and times seemed not separate, but in constant collision. Neither did it offer the unmediated experiences that now signified a more personal kind of authentic. These people hobbyists drew on a long legacy of their own, best known through the intercultural work of the revered hobbyist Ralph Hubbard (fig. 21). A Montana rancher, schoolteacher, and writer, Hubbard assembled Indian dance groups and took them on tours throughout the West. His own costume was authentic, and he joined the performances without missing a step. His *American Indian Crafts* (1935) extended a detailed course of study for children and Indian lore enthusiasts. Hubbard later became involved in scouting and other hobby venues, building some of the first bridges between Indian people and white Indian lore aficionados.[25]

Soon after it began publication, the *American Indian Hobbyist* began courting the emerging group of people hobbyists who had turned from the duplication of museum-quality artifakes to music and especially dance, activities that could not be effectively duplicated by combing museums and studying ethnographies. Although published sources for music and dance did exist, they were often inadequate, and hobbyists trying to catch a song or the intricacies of a dance turned to Indian people for instruction.[26] William K. Powers, for example,

21. Ralph Hubbard in Indian Costume, 1922. A Boy Scout leader, Indian dancer, writer, promoter, and hobbyist icon, Ralph Hubbard personified the hobby's diverse origins. Photograph by Edwin Tangen. Courtesy of the Carnegie Branch Library for Local History, Boulder Historical Society Collection.

began making yearly trips to South Dakota's Pine Ridge reservation in 1948, studying and performing Lakota music and dance. Between 1960 and 1962, he presented his findings in a series of detailed articles in *American Indian Tradition* (successor to the *Hobbyist*). James Howard started dancing at age twelve and eventually made the rounds of most tribes on the Plains and western woodlands. Parlaying his interests into a career in anthropology, Howard published numerous scholarly articles while continuing to follow the powwow circuits. He would later claim to have participated in the Sun Dance, the most sacred of Plains Indian rituals, and to have led the peyote ceremonies so essential to the Native American Church.[27]

As real Indian people rather than museum artifacts became central to their interests, people hobbyists reconsidered the familiar trajectory of Indian history. Since the early nineteenth century, Americans had frequently insisted that Indians were disappearing—either dying out as a result of social Darwinian inadequacies or melting into American society as detribalized individuals. As the body of knowledge that contemporary Indians had to offer became important, hobbyists began portraying Indian cultures not in terms of declension and unreachable temporal distances (as Lewis Henry Morgan had done for Ely S. Parker and the Senecas, for example), but through a narrative that accorded authenticity to real Indians. Powers summed up this new historical interpretation: "Although the American Indian has resigned himself to wearing Whiteman clothing, working in Whiteman factories, and attending Whiteman schools, he has not forgotten the traditions of his forefathers. During the last twenty years, the Indian has become more interested in his own culture than ever before."[28] Powers argued that Indians were assimilating, becoming equal participants in American society and economy, while at the same time renewing cultural differences built around a native past. The new narrative accompanied a reformulation of the authentic that was consistent with the cluster of ideas by then joined to culture.

Viewed simply as members of one among many equivalent cultures, living Indians could be considered as authentic as dead ones, according to people hobbyists. Authenticity lay not in the archaic object, but in the contemporary Indian person dancing and singing at the powwow. In constructing their dance outfits, for example, the new hobbyists tended to ignore historical styles in favor of the costumes worn by the Indian people with whom they danced. As they crossed the permeable boundaries of culture, people hobbyists found that the problem that had dogged Ernest Thompson Seton and the antimodernists—

access to Indian authenticity—had disappeared. Under the older, racialist regime, truly becoming Indian meant passing—devoting one's entire life to acting out a fraud. White mediators like Seton had belonged to a select clique that established idiosyncratic ways of crossing into Indianness. Now, however, it seemed that the line between white and Indian did not have to be a rigid biological border. Being Indian was most of all a matter of behavior—replicating, in Kroeber's words, "patterns of form, style, and significance."[29] If authentic Indian culture was, as Kroeber claimed, learned behavior, then individual non-Indians could also learn it, grasp hold of the authentic, and thus consolidate a unique personal identity.

In this free-form world, hobbyists tended to forget that there might be problems associated with crossing the line that separated Indians from non-Indians. In the late nineteenth century, the mimetic anthropologist Frank Hamilton Cushing had been viewed (perhaps justifiably) with suspicion by the scientific community for his deep immersion in Zuni society. The newer atmosphere of cultural relativism, however, subsumed the racial taboos invoked against Cushing for literally becoming Other. In fact, anthropology—through the heroic figure of the participant-observer—now supplied a quintessential example of such cross-cultural boundary hopping. James Howard, whose intimate connections with native people echoed those of Cushing, met with a more positive reception from anthropologists seventy years later.[30]

Unlike the unreachably authentic Indians of the early twentieth century, many postwar constructions of ethnic and racial Others emphasized close, interior qualities that encouraged white appropriation and self-discovery. A range of ideas suggested that social boundary crossing was primarily a question of behavior. Anthropology provided a model for such transgression. Music, dance, and literature afforded personal paths of entry into other cultures. In the postwar United States, these notions transcended the hobby, as Americans constructed a variety of extraordinarily accessible Others. Carey McWilliams, for example, identified himself closely with California Latinos (North from Mexico). In New York, Warren Miller found a literary voice representing African-American ghetto life (The Cool World), and, of course, Mailer sang the black virtues of the hip (The White Negro). John Howard Griffin went further, dying his skin black for a literary tour of the South (Black Like Me). William Whyte associated himself with Italian immigrants (Street Corner Society), and Herbert Gans, after defining suburban Americans as Others, moved into Levittown for a spell of participant-observation (The Levittowners).[31] Americans in the hobbyist tradition followed suit, locating authenticity in an accessible Indian Other and seeking personal experience and identity by sponsoring and attending powwows. Indianness, with its multilayered history of evocative symbolisms, offered a rich palette of additional meanings—nature, patriotic rebellion, freedom, and Americanness itself. Indeed, these distinctive meanings gave Indian play a slightly different character than other kinds of appropriations. For hobbyists, many of whom inclined more to conservative American tradition than to beat rebellion, crossing into Indianness evoked primal, national truth as much as it did racial exoticism.

Yet these were engagements not only with authentic identity, but with racial anxiety. People hobbyists knew that Indians occupied the same time and place as themselves. Although that proximity gave hobbyists a new way to play Indian and to gain access to a racially defined authentic, it also threatened the sense of difference that defined Indian Others. For if culture was behavioralist in nature, what happened when Indians (or Latinos or African or Asian Americans) altered their behavior, trading in acts marked as both racially distinctive and authentic for those unmarked and therefore white? In the absence of firm lines around blackness and redness, the very notion of being white became unstable.[32]

In fact, during the 1950s, the sense of exotic difference that lay at the heart of Indian authenticity grew increasingly tenuous. The shared national traumas of economic depression and world war tended to reinforce ideas—among Indians and non-Indians alike—of American cultural unity and homogeneity. Large proportions of the native population had fought in the war. As a result, many non-Indians came to view Indian people as either assimilated or imminently assimilable. The Bureau of Indian Affairs, committed to an urban version of Indian assimilation, inaugurated a termination policy whose aim was to eliminate all tribal political and social structures in order to turn Indian individuals loose into American society. One of the keys to terminating the tribes was relocation—a policy that transplanted Indian people from reservations to urban areas and furnished job training and employment counseling. Relocation helped create inter-Indian communities in almost every major city in the United States. These communities frequently held Indian powwows that were open to both white urban and suburban hobbyists.[33]

The Indian who sang and drummed at the weekend powwow might return to an urban factory job on Monday, making him close cultural kin to the white worker who changed into Indian clothes on Friday night for a weekend of singing and dancing. As the cultural boundaries between Indians and non-

Indians seemed to blur and break down outside the powwow grounds, it became harder for hobbyists to imagine Indians as something Other. It was not easy to see Indians as antimodern and organic when you both rode the same bus to an urban job; difficult to find them more authentic when the lines between your respective cultures seemed to fade in and out of view. By the 1960s, some hobbyists had found hobbyist partners and married, producing "a generation of children who grew up in an atmosphere in which it was difficult to separate non-Indian from Indian culture."[34] Whereas the antimodernists imagined an Indian so distant as to be unreachable, the new hobbyists confronted an Indian figure so close as to be dangerously indistinguishable from themselves.

Within the open borders of cultural relativism, however, one also found re-affirmations of Indian difference that were racialist in nature. Perhaps the most important was Indian blood quantum—a genetic measure of one's degree of Indianness. Blood allowed white hobbyists to differentiate Indians, and thereby the authentic, from themselves.[35] But while blood renewed the hobbyists' au-thentic, it also proved a tricky concept to negotiate, for it commingled racial essentialism with the behavior that helped define a culture. Was a so-called mixed-blood dance champion more or less authentic than a full-blood with less polished skills? If push came to shove, which one should be invited to the powwow? Culturalist criteria helped people hobbyists rank relative levels of Indian blood quantum. One such factor was place—did an Indian person live on or off the reservation? Another was attitude toward white society—traditionals, who favored the old ways, were better than progressives, who had made moves toward assimilation. As hobbyists imagined an accessible Indian culture, they also refigured racial difference around at least three variables—genetic quan-tum, geographical residence, and cultural attitude. The highest possible degree of authenticity inhered in the traditional, reservation-based full-blood. The least authentic figure was the progressive, urban, low-quantum mixed-blood—ironically, the figure often available to urban hobbyists. In the end, regardless of behavioral patterns, an Indian still had to be an Indian.

Attendees at hobbyist powwows clearly valued real Indian singers, especially those hired from reservations. William K. Powers published a list of reservation singers in his hobbyist newsletter, Powwow Trails, as well as guidelines for con-tracts, transportation, lodging, etiquette, and proper compensation for perfor-mance and taping.[36] This preference for reservation singers may have indicated a variation in performance—they might simply have been better singers—but it also signified the celebration of the reservation as a marker of authenticity and racial difference. Being a temporary visitor from the reservation rather than a permanent expatriate meant that an Indian person was still involved in an Indian community defined, in a subtle nod to an antimodernist past, as more authentic than those forming in inter-Indian urban centers.

The reservation signified the racialized authenticity of Indian people. To many hobbyists, it also looked like the ultimate powwow—a huge, contradictory cultural playground that featured both boundary crossing and authentic difference. Nowhere was the vital role of the reservation in generating authenticity more apparent than in the profiles of white hobbyists published in *Powwow Trails*. Each profile described a rite of passage: the grand reservation tour and eventual acceptance by reservation people. Frank Turley, who joined the staff of *Powwow Trails* in 1966, was the consummate Indian powwow tourist. He made the transition from Scout to hobbyist in 1949 at age thirteen and made his first reservation visit the following year. In 1954, he toured reservation powwows in Oklahoma and New Mexico. After two years in the army, he visited reservations in Nebraska, South Dakota, and Montana. In 1960, he moved to Albuquerque and began "Pueblo hopping." By mid-decade, he had ended up in Oregon, "dancing with the Yakimas at the Pendleton Roundup." Larry Morgan, who had been a hobbyist since the mid-1950s, finally made his trip in 1966, shortly before assuming the editorship of the *Trails* newsletter. He attended powwows at "Rosebud, Spring Creek, Red Leaf, Parmalee, Porcupine, Wounded Knee, Pine Ridge, Mission, and Eagle Butte. At Rosebud he participated in a Yuwipi meeting." Admittance into a Yuwipi ceremony, in which a medicine person is wrapped in robes and tied, only to appear among the participants unbound after a period of darkness, marked Morgan's rite of passage. Dennis Lessard enjoyed almost complete immersion, playing a part in ceremonies, being given an Indian name, and living "with a full-blooded Sioux family for four months."[37] The reservation—and the authenticity and racial position it helped define—had become a fetish and a legitimating tool within hobbyist circles.

As it did to Ely S. Parker, Arthur C. Parker, and Charles Eastman, Indian play offered often-conflicted forms of empowerment to some native people. Because hobbyists craved authenticity and because they located it in Indian ancestry, Indian powwow-goers found themselves able to voice opinions and be taken seriously. Such empowerment stood in marked contrast to past experience, when those constructing Indian Others could, if they wished, ignore real Indian people. At the powwows, non-Indians in effect ceded a degree of cultural power to Indians. That cession stemmed from a complex and contradictory set of ideas about assimilation, equality, and consensus on the one hand, and, on the other, a racial difference that was both desirable and frightening. Even as they ceded power, however, white hobbyists maintained—in a classic formulation of Cold War liberalism—control over the ability to give it away.

Nonetheless, the cession had consequences for real Indians, who now exerted at least a small amount of true control over the exchange. Many native people, for example, did not appreciate being the subjects of a hobby, something akin to model trains or old coins, and they protested. *American Indian Hobbyist*, the founding journal of Indian lore devotees, responded in 1961 by changing its name to *American Indian Tradition*. "The name change," an editorial explained, "was made at the request of many of our Indian readers."[38]

Indians frequently put white hobbyists on the defensive. Both Indian people and hobby leaders cultivated hobbyists' sensitivity and deference, attitudes infrequently displayed toward Indian people at the time. This was especially true as more hobbyists began to attend Indian powwows. *American Indian Tradition*, for example, reprimanded some of its readership after being confronted once too often by Indian people demanding, "Why don't [hobbyists] do things the Indian way?":

> About all we could reply was that some hobbyists do try to do things right. But as we look around we realize that there are many individuals and groups who don't even try. They know about three more facts and a lot more fiction about Indians than the audiences for whom they perform; and beyond that, they feel that improvising is the key to success. . . . This attitude may be appropriate for modern dance, but it has nothing to do with Indians.

The editors went on to lambast "girls clad in white (or black or tan) nighties whose only real interest is in the male dancers," and the men of the "Indian Dance Team who will put on any kind of show or ceremonial to please any audience, anywhere." Again and again, editorials in *Tradition* and *Powwow Trails* enjoined dancers not to enter the dance floor at Indian powwows unless invited. "Conduct yourselves as model guests," implored *Tradition*. "Don't be overly forward or demanding, don't try to impress anyone, and watch and listen so that you don't violate Indian etiquette in the area in which you visit."[39] *Powwow Trails* inaugurated a column called "When the People Gather" devoted almost exclusively to spelling out etiquette guidelines.

The desire to conform to Indian cultural practices led in turn to a degree of social power for Indian people, demonstrated perhaps most appropriately by white-Indian conflicts over racial integration. Many hobbyists reserved their cultural relativism and tolerance exclusively for Indian people, maintaining racist stances toward other groups. According to Powers, many hobbyists shared a "tacit philosophy" that "it was appropriate for Whites to dress and paint up but that 'others' looked 'strange' posing as Indians." And how could it not? Americans had a long history of imagining and claiming an Indianness that was about being indigenous, free, white, and male. Their understandings of African-American identity, however, circled around contrasting notions—importation, enslavement, and a sometimes-feminized blackness. Indianness was the province of whites, but not blacks. By the early 1960s, however, the logics of integration and of Indian play had led some African Americans and Puerto Ricans to participate in powwows. White organizers tried to make the events by invitation only, but native singers were able to insist that Indian celebrations should not be occasions for discrimination. Hobbyist powwows remained (or became) integrated, if only in minute proportions.[40]

Indian people also coveted the economic opportunities presented by the hobbyist powwows. Not only did singers receive wages for their performance, but as part of the attempt to promote Indian etiquette, they were often "given-away-to," that is, members of the audience offered them money or goods in order to demonstrate their generosity. Singers also received pay for informal tape recordings made by hobbyists seeking to learn songs and, on occasion, had the opportunity to make professional recordings for small folk music record companies.[41] Some Indian people were sought out as contest judges, and champion dancers might be hired as special powwow guests.

Ironically, the opportunity to sing, dance, and teach Indian tradition may have helped some Indian people consolidate a native sense of self.[42] If the 1950s were a self-conscious age of alienation for whites, they were that and much more for Indian people. After the paternal, but generally friendly policies of the New Deal, the new federal termination policy aimed aggressively to devalue Indian cultures. Urban wage labor opportunities—a much-criticized feature of relocation, but also a draw for many Indians—seemed to represent an even deeper threat to unique Indian identities. Indeed, many native people, in talking later about the 1950s, used the anthropological trope of disappearing culture.[43] Yet the high value that some hobbyists placed on Indian cultures may have helped to fortify Indian identities in the face of the perceived loss of older traditions. As hobbyists fabricated Indianness in terms of authenticity, Indian people, in fact, "became" more authentic. In the early twentieth century, Arthur C. Parker and Charles Eastman had mimed white-created Indian Others back at white Americans in order to subtly alter perceptions of Indian people. Now, many Indians found it more valuable to imitate their own elders. Mirror-image exchanges between Indians and hobbyists exhibited a new tendency to point Indian people toward native cultures rather than toward non-Indian stereotypes.[44]

For their part, the hobbyists' explorations of racial difference offered unique, if contradictory, social identities. Few hobbyists actually went native. That was not the point. Indian play, delineated temporally and spatially by the weekend powwow, the scout meeting, and the downstairs workroom, carried much of its sense beyond these temporary confines. Dressing and dancing Indian at a pow-wow with real, live Indians was a wildly uncommon experience that helped constitute the individual identities of men like Turley, Morgan, and Lessard. Standing around the watercooler at the office or pausing between frames at the bowling alley, hobbyists would have exotic tales to tell, stories that differentiated them from other-directed coworkers and leisure partners.

But if hobbyists pursued self-realization, they did so with an equally troublesome kind of Other-direction, one that forced them to rely either on Indians or fellow hobbyists for validation. In neither case did they escape the rigorous social conformity of which Riesman had warned. Indeed, following the rigid patterns laid out for costumes and dance steps and learning songs note-for-note hardly left much room for displays of heroic individual creativity. And yet, crossing the divide of Indian Otherness—and doing it in the company of Indians—surely meant something. Like the revolutionary who was both shoemaker and Indian chief, hobbyists were simultaneously nonconformists and people who worked doubly hard to comply with two cultural codes. As Indians, they were not only members of two well-defined communities, but also unique, self-directed individuals—confident actors in an organic world of tradition and successful denizens of modernity. These dual identities were possible because hobbyists imagined Indian Others as authentic, yet accessible—culturally close and racially distant.

Real native people called both cultural closeness and racial distance into question. Playing Indian had always been subject to the ideological contradictions between nobility and savagery and the identity confusions of interior and exterior. But unlike previous Indian players, the people hobbyists meant to meet large numbers of Indians on social ground that was both native and inter-cultural, and this contact could not help but create new sets of contradictory dynamics for both Indians and non-Indians.

If hobbyists found authenticity and some part of their identities on the reservation, for example, Indian people sometimes found it in the cities, at the gatherings of local hobbyists. Relocated urban Indians often entered the hobby-ist orbit, where they sometimes began acting more Indian than they had pre-viously. The hobbyists' Indian Other had, in fact, become a point at which Indian and non-Indian identities might be mutually constituted. "Indians who never sang or danced on the reservation," claims William Powers, "did so when they became involved with whites from the cities."[45] New York's Medicine Drum Dancers celebrated in 1964 when they recruited a Lakota from Rosebud. A New York X-ray technician, George Soldier was an "excellent singer" who had previously sung with a Washington, D.C., hobbyist club.[46] Soldier's Indian-ness made him special and unique to hobbyists. But that Indianness may itself have been the product of his relation with the Medicine Drum hobbyists. On the streets of New York and Washington, Soldier undoubtedly faced discrimination. At the powwow, he found, at worst, a semblance of deference and, at best, an affirmation of his personal and social identity as an Indian person.

Such ironies cropped up all over the powwow grounds, appearing most visibly, perhaps, in the craft stalls, where authenticity—for both object and people hobbyists—could be bought and sold in material forms. If the hobby involved an escape from an industrial world to authentic handcraftsmanship and unmediated labor, that escape relied upon the establishment of a hobby economy in which racially defined Indians served as both laborers and market mediators. Hobby leaders clearly felt an obligation to promote Indian hiring at powwows and to support Indian craftspeople, especially against the threat posed by cheap foreign knockoffs. Powers argued that "to promote good arts and crafts and thereby help the economy of the American Indian grow, it stands to reason that foreign-made beadwork be weeded out of all craft exhibits."[47] He advised hobbyist powwow committees to enjoin white traders from selling anything but Indian-made goods. It would seem, then, that good crafts con-sisted of Indian-made objects produced from native materials. The restricting of the market to such goods, authentic by standards of both blood and cultural production (although lacking the age and tradition required by object hobby-ists), would benefit contemporary Indians, who were the only ones capable of creating such authentic products. But then Powers narrowed his definition of

Indianness to blood quantum alone, noting, "There are some American Indian [run] shops which sell foreign-made beadwork. If the beadwork is clearly labelled as being foreign, there is no problem. Indians can make more profit selling foreign beadwork than they can their own."[48] This strategy made economic sense, but it contradicted hobbyists' own emphasis on Indian cultural production, favoring instead the idea of a racial authenticity that could be attached to objects through economic exchange.

The historian Howard Lamar tells a story about shaking the hand of a woman who had shaken the hand of a man who had shaken the hand of a man who had shaken the hand of George Washington. "I'm only four handshakes away from the first president," Lamar jokes, albeit with something of a sense of wonder at this personalization of time and history. Indianness, defined by blood for pragmatic, economic purposes, carried the same magical qualities of transmission. If the item was authentic according to the new hobbyists' guidelines—Indian-made with traditional handcraft methods of production—then it was acceptable for non-Indians to sell it. The back pages of *American Indian Tradition* carried dozens of advertisements for Indian goods that passed through non-Indian traders. Such objects carried even greater weight and authenticity if they were sold by an Indian, of course, but non-Indians could legitimately act as middlemen—simply a handshake or two away from the source of authenticity who had crafted the product. Japanese beadwork, however, which was inauthentic for non-Indian traders, acquired (even when labeled "not-Indian-made") a cachet of authenticity as it passed through the hands of an Indian seller. The purchaser could in fact claim that the object had been purchased from an Indian. The artifact itself mattered less than the Indianness that came with the final handshake that closed the deal.[49]

The hobby economy encapsulated the wide-ranging contradictions that haunted the entire hobbyist enterprise. Relying on a culture-based blurring of social boundaries, hobbyists nonetheless imagined Indians and Indian objects in racial terms that redefined Indians as different. Seeking to escape the inauthenticity of a consumerist, mass production–oriented American economy, they created an equally problematic economy of their own. Hobbyists abstracted a magical quality of Indianness from their material relations with native people and poured it into commodities like Japanese beads. At the same time, they forced Indian crafts marketers to make a material performance of their Indianness—one that visibly defined native people's racial difference. In the craft booths, one could see the inevitable disjunctures between different kinds of imaginary Indians and their real counterparts, between conflicting notions of racial difference and human sameness, and between the interlocked edges of the doubled consciousness of middle-class white Americans during the Cold War.

After World War II, people hobbyists transformed a search for authenticity that had been figured around Indians since the turn of the century. Playing off popular conceptions of culture and tuned into Cold War rhetorics of national consensus and racial assimilation, they nearly eliminated the barriers that differentiated Indians and whites. Indian people themselves broadened the scope of this boundary crossing through their presence in urban wage labor economies. Within this integrationist paradigm, however, one might also find refigurings of racial difference, refigurings that were arguably vital to the notion of a desirable Indian authenticity. If Indianness had been remade as an interior quality, something shared by both Indians and white Americans, it nonetheless relied upon an exterior otherness that marked Indians as Indians and thus different and authentic.

Notwithstanding its omnipresent racialism and contradictory character, the hobby also displayed a degree of mutuality that can only be described as new. At no other time in the long history of Indian play did the arcs of native people and non-Indians swing so close together. But if mutualism characterized the hobby in some ways, differences over such social interaction lay just beneath the surface. I've painted the people hobbyists in broad strokes, but, in truth, they thought very differently about the relations they were willing to establish with Indian people. The elite group that published the journals, handed down the etiquette guidelines, and made the reservation tours reflected the optimistic notions of tolerance and community that undergirded Kroeber's "culture over race" narrative. They seemed to suggest a multicultural ideal—an egalitarian blending of sameness and difference within a range of cultural activities both Indian and white in nature.[50]

Unlike the solitary reproduction of a pair of nineteenth-century moccasins, the sensual sociality of dance and song led many of these individuals to think about themselves and their world in ways that challenged the verities of everyday life. Many such hobbyists developed insights into society and culture that charted their personal and professional lives. Howard and Powers turned to academic anthropology. Norman Feder and Richard Conn became prominent museum curators. Others taught at tribal schools or nearby colleges. Almost all of them came to understand the textures of Indian life, and some went native.

Influential voices in the hobbyist movement, they tried to lead others to their own more reflective, cross-cultural experience, and many of them translated their experience into the nonhobbyist world.

Most hobbyists, however, were more casual actors, enjoying a familiar variety of usable primitivism. Like other Americans, they played Indian in order to address longings for meaning and identity that arose from the anxieties of their time. Powwows granted them freedom from their own culture, but, as with the rebels in Boston, such escape did not result in the solidity of a secure identity. Rather, it left them in an uncertain borderland that was both exhilaratingly creative and frighteningly unstable. Social convention and conformity could be swept joyfully away. The hobbyist Conn has recalled, for example, the spates of "extramarital hanky-panky" and the all-too-frequent drinking binges that accompanied many powwows. On the other hand, such incomplete liberation also suggested "the D. H. Lawrence problem"—a nation unfinished, insecure in its collective and individual identities.[51]

If hobbyists played out such familiar American patterns, they also altered them by engaging native people. Both weekend warriors and superhobbyists made performance—dancing, singing, costume design, and craftsmanship— the basis upon which one might judge the identities they sought to build around Indianness. For the superhobbyists, the critical judges were Indian people as often as they were fellow hobbyists.[52] Weekend warriors, on the other hand, were more reluctant to place Indian people in the position of judging them. Giving up smidgens of social and cultural power to Indians was one thing; giving up the power to define some part of one's identity was quite another. For some, the presence of Indians could even be an annoyance. Powers, for example, fled the movement in disgust after a weekend warrior observed that a powwow would have been great except "there were too many Boy Scouts and too many Indians."[53] Most weekend warriors, however, joined the superhobbyists in making at least some effort to defer to Indian people.

By acknowledging—and yet simultaneously refusing to acknowledge—Indian social and cultural power, people hobbyists nudged the hobby toward what Richard White has termed a middle ground, a complex constellation of intercultural forms that comes into existence when Indian people possess enough power to force non-Indians to accommodate native social and cultural practices.[54] When *American Indian Tradition*'s editors tried to teach etiquette, when Indian dancers invited Puerto Ricans to sing with them, when Indians and non-Indians negotiated their meanings through the exchange of crafts and money—

each time hobbyists and Indians jostled each other they joined in shaping this ambiguous hybrid terrain.

The culmination of this brief tradition may have come in 1953, when the Koshare Scouts prepared the costumes needed to perform the Zuni Shalako dance. Traditionally given only at midwinter, the Shalako ceremony features huge painted costumes that tower over the dancer inside. For the Zunis, however, the dance is not simply a series of steps and a collection of costumes. It is a vital ceremony that, if performed incorrectly or at the wrong time, will bring unpleasant consequences to everyone. The Zunis, who have become leaders in the movement to protect tribal heritage, protested the Koshares' plans, and they threatened to bar non-Indians from all future dances and ceremonies in retaliation. After visiting the Koshare kiva, however, the Zuni people changed their minds. They decided that the scouts' precisely copied Shalakos were authentic and real, and they took the masks back to Zuni and built a special kiva for them.[55]

In making their Shalakos so exact that they met with Zuni approval—and in giving the Zunis the right to pass judgment—the Koshares moved beyond the simple reproduction of Indian material culture to the mimetic production of new intercultural forms. The historian Jay Mechling argues that although the Boy Scouts of La Junta were not Indians, they were also more than simple, straightforward white boys. After having their craft and the identity that accompanied it authenticated by the Zunis, the boys became something peculiarly new—Koshare. And they could have arrived at this odd status only through a process of meaning-making that was collaborative and strikingly cross-cultural.

Yet if some hobbyists recognized Indian power and allowed themselves to be pulled onto the middle ground, and if others sought and accepted Indian affirmation, these experiences were small, personal, and confined largely to the powwow grounds. Outside, Indian people still faced racism, poverty, and coercive government policies aimed at destroying the very qualities hobbyists cherished. In response, native people engaged in a series of political struggles to reclaim their autonomy during the 1950s and 1960s. These battles included the fifteen-year fight to reject the government's termination policy, West Coast "fish-ins" to protest infringement of treaty rights, the highly publicized seizure of Alcatraz Island, the Trail of Broken Treaties march to Washington in 1972, which resulted in the takeover of the Bureau of Indian Affairs building, and, in some tellings, the armed occupation of Wounded Knee.[56]

These social conflicts inevitably changed Indian notions of native identity. As

Indian people once again rejected the idea of assimilation, they began flirting with ethnic separatism and developing their own figurings of racial essentialism. And, as successful political battles gave them increasing confidence, Indian people began installing cultural boundary lines of their own. In the late 1960s and early 1970s, many Indians would exercise real, albeit local, power on reservations and in urban communities by closing many powwows and gatherings to non-Indians. The troublesome question of access to an Indian authentic came eventually to rest squarely in the hands of Indian people.

In 1957, Norman Mailer thought he saw people finding their way out of Cold War America. White hipsters, resisting the traumas of a life devoid of meaning, had "absorbed the existentialist synapses of the Negro." Mailer saw Black Americans as Others of deep psychological import who brought a meaningful "cultural dowry" to a metaphoric marriage with whites. In the same years that Mailer described a glamorous collection of "white negro" cultural rebels, an equally compelling group of middle-class hobbyists were playing with ancient and equally substantive traditions of Indian Americanness. And, as had their cultural forbears, they found Indian Others along contradictory axes—so close as to be part of a slowly forming multicultural society; so distant as to be racially distinct. The contradictory tensions resonated thoroughly in Cold War America. Addressing the problem of inauthenticity meant addressing the problem of race and inclusion; seeing a multicultural, consensual America required a simultaneous vision of racial difference. Americans put paradoxical notions of sameness and difference into material practice on a regular basis, not only at powwows, but at drinking fountains, public restrooms, buses, schools, nightclubs, and on radio and television shows. If Indian play had retreated from the public eye during the economic and military crises of depression and world war, it reemerged as the nation began to struggle once again with its oldest and most contradictory cultural dilemmas—on the one hand, the withholding of liberty in the land of the free and, on the other, the constant tension between the anarchic inclinations of individuals and the social unity of the whole. And, as Indianness pointed back to America's revolutionary origins and to the polar reversal that marked its crises of authenticity and modernity, it also pointed forward to the trials of a world in which meaning became tenuous and meaning-making itself an increasingly problematic enterprise.

six

Counterculture Indians and the New Age

I stood at the entrance to the Beverly Hills Hotel.
The warm wind from the south rippled like clean silk on my skin.
The air smelled like honeysuckle and I took a deep breath.
Every book is rewritten by the reader. If you read a book, it
becomes your personal teacher. You bring to it what you are.

LYNN ANDREWS

Flight of the Seventh Moon: The Teaching of the Shields (1984)

In 1971, a small but dedicated commune lay in the woods outside a college town in the Pacific Northwest. On occasion, my parents would leave for a long weekend, depositing my brother and me there with friends who helped run it. Located on an old farm, the commune had several residents living in the rustic main house and a shifting array of folk wandering in for meals or companionship. In the trees to the south, for instance, a friendly young man had strung together twenty extension cords to power a small circular saw, the only electrical tool he would use to build an octagonal house. Across the nearby stream and up a small hill lay the Indian camp, a set of three Plains tipis that housed a reassembled family of non-Indians who eked out a living making Aleut soapstone carvings.

I liked to visit the Indian camp, where people in headbands, fringed leather jackets, and moccasins padded quietly about, calling each other names I cannot quite recall but that had the kind of faux-Indian ring—Rainbow, maybe, or Green Wood—that I would later associate with suburban tract developments. The tipis were pleasant enough, although they tended to leak when it rained. Perhaps the Indians had been mistaken in choosing the Plains tents, so inappropriate to the wet climate, over the comfortable cedar-plank Indian homes one learned about in the local schools (not to mention the clapboard and shingle homes that housed contemporary people on the nearby reservation). But the tipis were inexpensive and easy to set up, and that was important on a small communal housing budget. More significant, they carried a full cargo of symbolic value. Tipis shouted, "Indian," and all that it entailed, in a way that Northwest coast log homes, even those marked with Indian totem poles, never could.

Heirs of the white middle class of the 1950s, the communalists worked hard to counteract their parents' America, perceived in terms of consumptive excess, alienated individualism, immoral authority, and capitalism red in tooth and claw. As an antidote, they promoted community, and at least some of them thought it might be found in an Indianness imagined as social harmony. The commune, safe to say, was one of hundreds of places in which counterculture rebels turned to Indians to think about a better way of living together. New Mexico's famous New Buffalo Commune, for example, was rife with tipis. Explaining its name, a longtime member, George Robinson, set up a chronology of Indian-white ethnic succession that echoed that of Lewis Henry Morgan and made communalists heirs, not to the 1950s but to nineteenth-century Indians. "The buffalo was the provider for the plains tribes," observed Robinson. "This [commune] is the new buffalo." Ironically, though the members adopted a Plains Indian ancestry, they looked for subsistence not to the bison, but to the corn-beans-squash combination favored by more sedentary native people.

The communalists at New Buffalo and at similar communes across the United States, according to the breathless observer William Hedgepeth, admired "the Indian's feeling of non-acquisitive contentment, his lack of dog-eat-dog Americanized drive, and his tribal sense of sharing and group ritual." Hedgepeth was one of a legion of journalists who hopped from commune to commune, relaying often-prurient tales of drugs, free love, and communal euphoria to a curious public. Many communalists enjoyed such publicity, and they offered writers compelling performances of their tribal lifestyles. When Hedgepeth left New Buffalo for the nearby Lorian community, for example, he found fifteen communalists sitting around a campfire near several tipis: "[The] males clap or slap at their chests and yell 'Yi Yi Yi Yi Yi,' Indian-style, real loud with each voice dropping out when a beer can or joint is passed."[1]

[handwritten marginal note: Like the minstrals again]

In spite of such gestures, most communes disintegrated quickly under the pressures of individual wants and wills. Even as an adolescent, I could see the fissures in the communal facade. Preparing for a "Princess and the Frog" guitar duo concert, for example, someone swept the floors of the main house but did not feel like picking up the enormous dustpile. No one else did either, so we laid a piece of tarpaper over it and did not mention the peculiar mound in the living room. And it was one thing to think in the abstract about the warmth of sharing; a very different thing to think about sharing the same unwashed cereal bowl, spoon, and bottom-of-the-bowl milk with ten other people.

Throughout this history, I have suggested that whenever white Americans have confronted crises of identity, some of them have inevitably turned to Indians. What might it mean to be not-British? The revolutionaries found a compelling array of ideas in Indianness. What did it mean to be American? What did it mean to be modern? To be authentic? Using furs and feathers, headbands and hair, generations of white Americans have, at many levels and with varying degrees of intent, made meanings and, with them, identities. In the world of the communalists, however, meaning itself was often up for grabs. Driven by continuing social transformations—the baby boom, civil rights struggles, consumer culture, the war in Vietnam—older, Cold War quests for personal brands of authentic experience gave way to increasing doubts about the existence of God, authenticity, and reality itself. In the 1960s and early 1970s, many Americans found themselves asking a new question: What is the meaning of meaning? Suppose truth had simply dried up and blown away in the blasting wind of nuclear anxiety, cultural relativism, and psychological self-reflexiveness? What if, as the Beatles had suggested, the world is like Strawberry Fields, a mystical, drug-hazy place where "nothing is real"?[2]

Academic theorists have since devised a vocabulary to describe this skepticism toward meaning. In that vocabulary, one word—*postmodern*—has come to serve as a popular, generic shorthand, describing at once a complicated social world, an equally complex set of intellectual debates, and the interaction between the varied branches of each. That's asking one word to do a great deal of work, and, not surprisingly, *postmodern* has proved to be extraordinarily slippery, its varied definitions emerging from phenomena as diverse as architecture, linguistic theory, philosophy, aesthetics, popular culture, social relations, and global economics.[3]

Why should there be any distinction between the class-bound modernist high culture of the gallery/museum and the vulgar advertisements of mass consumer culture? If language is an arbitrary system of signs, is there any reason to think that the realities it frames are not, in some measure, *created* by the language itself? Why not chop up those signs and rearrange them into a new reality? Was it legitimate to impose the dichotomous worldview of Western philosophy on the rest of the planet? Why was the United States so insistent about global military hegemony? These questions engaged oppositional actors from Andy Warhol to Stokely Carmichael to the communalists at New Buffalo. Likewise, they have challenged a host of intellectual critics seeking to understand and describe a culture in which each was also an actor. In 1972, for example, the theorist Fredric Jameson noted the connections, suggesting "a profound consonance between linguistics as a method and that systematized and disembodied nightmare which is our culture today."[4] At the center of this complicated tangle of ideas and social transformations are three sensibilities that necessarily underpin this final chapter: a crisis of meaning and a concomitant emphasis on the powers of interpretation, a sustained questioning of the idea of foundational truth, and an inclination to fragment symbols and statements and to reassemble them in creative, if sometimes random, pastiche.

What concerns me even more, however, are the ways in which a contradictory notion of Indianness, so central to American quests for identities, changed shape yet again in the context of these postmodern crises of meaning. On the one hand, the refigurings of Indianness produced by the counterculture and the New Age reflect a historical moment unique from those we have already examined. On the other hand, the diverse practices we often subsume under the word *postmodern* may simply echo the familiar toying with meaning and identity we have seen in a long tradition of Indian play. Or maybe both notions are true.

Playing Indian, I've argued, has served as an ultimate tool for grabbing hold of such contradictions, and it has been constantly reimagined and acted out when Americans desire to have their cake and eat it too. Indians could be both civilized and indigenous. They could critique modernity and yet reap its benefits. They could revel in the creative pleasure of liberated meanings while still grasping for something fundamentally American. It should come as no surprise that the young men and women of the 1960s and 1970s—bent on destroying an orthodoxy tightly intertwined with the notion of truth and yet desperate for truth itself—followed their cultural ancestors in playing Indian to find reassuring identities in a world seemingly out of control. Not only in the communes, but in politics, environmentalism, spirituality, and other pursuits, Indianness allowed counterculturalists to have it both ways. In these arenas, we can also witness the continued unraveling of the connections between meanings and social realities. And, as usual, these disjunctures became most obvious when white people in Indian costume turned and found themselves face-to-face with native people.

Even in the reformist utopias of the communes something was not quite right, and it had everything to do with the soggy tipi on the hill and the well-used communal milk at the bottom of the cereal bowl. The gap between communal intention and personal experience widened as contradictions between individual freedom and social order turned into conflict. The doubledness of Indian meanings reflected perfectly the contradictory dimensions of communalism. Indians signified social harmony—one thinks of the stereotype of the peaceful native village, people interacting in seamlessly pleasant and ordered ways. These were the well-worn antimodern Indians of Ernest Thompson Seton and John Collier. But Indianness also carried a full complement of countermeanings. Dating back to the Revolution, these meanings were linked to the very different idea of radical individual freedom.

At the same time the communalists sought social stability, they rejected any notion of authority, a precondition to organizing such stability. Authority was "not only immoral, but functionally incompetent" according to the apologist and social critic Paul Goodman. Young people, he said, "are in an historical situation to which anarchism is the only possible response."[5] Communal life, as it turned out, was usually incompatible with anarchy, yet many communes existed to take individual autonomy to its anarchic edge. In place of a social contract that protected individual freedom through agreed-upon social restraints, communes offered a collective commitment to "doing one's own thing." A powerful counterculture mantra, "Do your own thing" conflated social order—even social consensus—with authority and rejected both.[6] The communalists used Indianness in the hope of establishing a particular kind of organic community, political in its exemplary social nature and self-transforming in practice.

What many of them found instead was an individualism—represented equally powerfully by Indian names, costumes, and tipis—that became supercharged by the very experience of living collectively.

Many communes toyed with symbolic Indianness; they were in reality largely disconnected from Indian people. Communalists searched reservations for authenticity and inspiration, but their visits rarely went as well as those made by many hobbyists. Native communities, often unexpectedly socially restrictive, did not mesh well with the aggressive individualism of many communes. And native people grew weary of constantly reeducating flighty counterculture seekers. Very few of these encounters satisfied either party. Communalists might have learned something about individualism and social order from Indian people, but most preferred a symbolic life of tipis and buckskins to lessons that might be hard-won and ideologically distasteful. The New Buffalos, for example, called their corn-beans-squash experiment a Navajo Diet, ignoring the nearby Pueblos (who had perfected this agriculture) for more symbolically powerful Indians.[7]

Although there were certainly exceptions, communalists tended to value Indian Otherness and its assorted meanings more than they did real native people. And they were not alone. Communal tipis pointed to a broad cultural ethos emphasizing the power of symbolic work over actual labor. When Andy Warhol presented a Campbell's soup label as art, he suggested that the manipulation of symbols had replaced the work of painting and sculpture. When the composer John Cage placed radios on the stage and randomly turned the dials, he did the same, dispensing a chance pastiche of sound in place of a practiced performance. Multinational bankers, advertising designers, politicians, and many others seemed to follow similar paths. In this kind of world, the meanings of Indianness drifted away from actual Indians more quickly and thoroughly than ever (fig. 22).[8]

The dissipation of meaning became particularly clear when Indians appeared in political discourse. Communalism and New Left politics occupied very different wings of the counterculture, but they shared similar tendencies to play with the limits of meaning. In politics, Indianness carried special resonance for antiwar protesters, and it appeared frequently in the collages of symbols they cobbled together with often-creative abandon.[9] The story of nineteenth-century native resistance provided a homegrown model for opposition to the American military imperialism that protesters saw in Vietnam. A popular series of posters,

22. *Gathering of all Tribes for a Human Be-In, 1967. Surrounded by an array of counterculture heroes, the Human Be-In's guitar-playing Indian demonstrated the movement's willingness to paste together symbols—in this case the rebellion encoded in guitar-based rock and roll and the primitive "tribal" community of the Indian. Real Indian people played guitars, but that was hardly the message. Courtesy of Stewart Brand.*

for example, paid tribute to Sitting Bull, Geronimo, and Red Cloud, imagined forerunners of the contemporary protest movement. For Mitchell Goodman, the spirit of impending revolution was akin to that of primitive culture. "Blacks, Vietnamese, Indians," Goodman observed. "From them the young in America have something to learn—and they know it. The young are a *class*, in the neo-Marxian sense—abused, processed, exploited—and they have come to see their common interest. But more important, they are a primitive tribe." And after breaking the LSD guru Timothy Leary out of jail, the would-be warriors of the Weather Underground announced that "LSD and grass, like the herbs and cactus and mushrooms of the American Indians, will help us make a future world where it will be possible to live in peace."[10] When it came to the war, the semantic linkages could hardly have been more appropriate. Racially red Indians matched up well with the ideologically red Vietcong, and both joined youth as pure, antimodern primitives. Guerrilla warfare, practiced to great effect by the Vietnamese and advocated domestically by some radicals, had its parallels in the ambushes and raids of Red Cloud, Geronimo, and others—at least as they were half-imagined and half-remembered from generic western films.

One of the most popular antiwar films of the time was anything but generic, and it used Indianness to model a whimsical postmodern style of resistance and to launch a critique of American military adventurism. In *Little Big Man* (1970), a white-Indian, cross-dressing Dustin Hoffman wanders through the imperial conquest of the West, constantly crossing and breaking down boundaries of race, gender, and nation. As a white pioneer boy, he is adopted by the Cheyenne. As a Cheyenne, he is first adopted and later saved by the vainglorious Col. George Custer. Flexible boundary hoppers with multiple modes and meanings, the Indians are funny, smart, and sexy. Their playfully serious postmodern nature stands in direct contrast to Custer and his army, who die from rigidity and imperial arrogance at the Little Big Horn. Audiences had little trouble figuring out with whom they were to identify.[11]

The notion of an oppositional political culture linked to Indianness attracted young Americans, many of whom had been schooled on the iconic nationalism of the Boston Tea Party.[12] Those original rebels had used Indianness to shift the location of their identities from Britain to America. Since the early twentieth century, people had put on Indian clothes to search for authenticity in a modern America more alienating than welcoming. Now, countercultural rebels became Indian to move their identities away from Americanness altogether, to leap outside national boundaries, gesture at repudiating the nation, and offer what seemed a clear-eyed political critique. The wearing of the symbols of the Indian—the long hair so visible in the poster image of Geronimo and maybe a bandanna headband to go with it—signified that one's sympathies lay with both the past and the present targets of American foreign policy (fig. 23). To play Indian was to become vicariously a victim of United States imperialism. For those confronting National Guardsmen and Army Reserves in the streets, such a position inevitably carried a powerful emotional charge.[13]

Yet, if being Indian offered one an identity as a critic of empire, that position was hardly uncomplicated. Indianness may have lain outside the United States'

There is real power — in his eyes — and so much gentleness too, which is the source of his power!

WHO OWNS THE PARK?

Someday a petty official will appear with a piece of paper, called a land title, which states that the University of California owns the land of the People's Park. Where did that piece of paper come from? What is it worth?

A long time ago the Costanoan Indians lived in the area now called Berkeley. They had no concept of land ownership. They believed that the land was under the care and guardianship of the people who used it and lived on it.

Catholic missionaries took the land away from the Indians. No agreements were made. No papers were signed. They ripped it off in the name of God.

The Mexican Government took the land away from the Church. The Mexican Government had guns and an army. God's word was not as strong.

The Mexican Government wanted to pretend that it was not the army that guaranteed them the land. They drew up some papers which said they legally owned it. No Indians signed those papers.

The Americans were not fooled by the papers. They had a stronger army than the Mexicans. They beat them in a war and took the land. Then they wrote some papers of their own and forced the Mexicans to sign them.

The American Government sold the land to some white settlers. The Government gave the settlers a piece of paper called a land title in exchange for some money. All this time there were still some Indians around who claimed the land. The American army killed most of them.

The piece of paper saying who owned the land was passed around among rich white men. Sometimes the white men were interested in taking care of the land. Usually they were just interested in making money. Finally some very rich men, who run the University of California, bought the land.

Immediately these men destroyed the houses that had been built on the land. The land went the way of so much other land in America — it became a parking lot.

We are building a park on the land. We will take care of it and guard it, in the spirit of the Costanoan Indians. When the University comes with its land title we will tell them: "Your land title is covered with blood. We won't touch it. Your people ripped off the land from the Indians a long time ago. If you want it back now, you will have to fight for it again."

Berkeley, CA!

23. Frank Bardacke, People's Park Manifesto, 1969. Geronimo, long-haired sign of imperial victimization and stalwart resistance, served as backdrop for the linkage of white counterculturalists with the Costanoan Indians. Courtesy of Frank Bardacke.

social boundaries when it came to the exercise of imperial power, but it was also at the very heart of the American identities inherited by the predominantly white, middle-class antiwar protesters. Playing Indian replicated the contradictory tensions established by the Revolution. An interior Indianness that signified national identity clashed with an exterior Indianness linked with the armed struggle to control the continent. The only significant point of difference was the inversion that marked modernity: nineteenth-century savages had become authentic twentieth-century victims and critics.

Real Indian people, many of whom were fighting as American soldiers in Vietnam, complicated the picture still further. The contradictions between real and imagined Indians have always pointed to other contradictions bound up within the contours of Indian Otherness itself. One could read the Red Cloud poster, for example, in terms that were not oppositional, but patriotic. Indianness represented native, American martial skill as well as it reflected the resistance of national enemies. Indeed, such an interpretation was likely among native people, for whom patriotism and military service have been and continue to be highly valued.[14]

Still other Indian people challenged the United States politically themselves, not only on the war, but on native civil rights issues as well. Again, the connections were easily made. "When I walk down the streets of Saigon," observed the Tuscarora activist Wallace Mad Bear Anderson, "those people look like my brothers and sisters." With white radicals appropriating Indian symbols and native people reinterpreting those symbols and launching protests of their own, Indianness became a potent political meeting ground. White antiwar political organizers who sought to harness Indianness often found themselves edging along the periphery of a burgeoning Red Power movement. White radicals helped with logistical details of food and transportation during the Indians of All Tribes' seizure of Alcatraz Island in 1969, for example, and Indian resistance movements appealed to all sorts of non-Indian sympathizers. The actor Marlon Brando reflected that appeal when he sent Sasheen Little Feather to refuse his Academy Award in 1973 (for his portrayal of Don Corleone in *The Godfather*) with a Red Power speech attacking the film industry's portrayals of native people. Brando, she said (hoping to counter charges of trendiness and yet pointing in exactly that direction), had been "a friend of the American Indian long before it was fashionable to pile on the turquoise and the feathers." Eager non-Indians showed up at fishing protests, at the Trail of Broken Treaties caravan to Washington, D.C., and, of course, at Wounded Knee (where Brando himself thought he could be of most use). By the same token, Indian leaders sometimes linked hands with other political movements in gestures of solidarity. In 1968, for example, Indians participated in the Poor People's Campaign, a march on Washington planned by the Southern Christian Leadership Conference that included blacks, Latinos, and poor whites.[15]

But just as often as they engaged real Indian people, white radicals joined the communalists in placing their highest premium upon a detached, symbolic Indianness. Different perspectives on rebellion and rights—Red, Black, and

Brown Power, antiwar, and women's liberation movements, for example—produced sets of symbols that, for all their distinctions, shared similarly mobile meanings. Red Power drew ideological weight from the far more visible Black Power movement. Indeed, the habit of yoking any number of themes with the word—peace power, love power, people power—points to a certain migratory tendency on the part of the signs of revolt. Sixties rebellion rested, in large part, on a politics of symbol, pastiche, and performance. Influenced by media saturation and the co-optative codes of fashion, the emblems of social protest were plucked from different worlds and reassembled in a gumbo of new political meaning. That headband might mean Geronimo, but it also meant Che Guevara and Stokely Carmichael. Indeed, it meant many things, depending on its context and its interpreters. Sacred pipes, Black Power fists, Aztlan eagles, peace signs, Hell's Angels, beers and joints, Peter Max design—everything fed into a whole that signified a hopeful, naive rebellion that often had as much to do with individual expression and fashion as it did with social change.[16]

While in the 1950s Indian lore hobbyists had sought personal freedom by leaping across the boundaries of a behaviorally defined notion of culture, by the mid-1960s, symbolic border-crossings of culture and race had become so painless that the meanings defined by those boundaries began to disintegrate. With them went a certain kind of social awareness. In 1957, for example, Norman Mailer's celebration of the "white negro" transgressions of the beats still carried a sense of the outrageous. The social world worked differently for blacks and whites; everyone knew it, and they recognized that difference. Now, however, one might lay claim to the more heavily laden word *nigger* without blinking an eye. Paul Goodman argued that his homosexuality had "made him a nigger." Writing as a yippie named Free, Abbie Hoffman claimed the word for young white activists harassed by police. A California professor, Jerry Farber, suggested that students themselves were enslaved niggers. Marginalized by antiwar planners, Hoffman and Jerry Rubin complained that they had been treated like niggers. And John Lennon and Yoko Ono would soon pronounce that "woman is the nigger of the world."[17]

Similar dynamics characterized the more positive meanings being attached to and detached from Indianness. White radicals sought political power by appropriating and cobbling together meanings that crossed borders of culture and race. In the process, they devalued words like *Indian* and *nigger* and deemphasized the social realities that came with those words. Such attempts to create political solidarity worked to the benefit of whites, but they could have negative political consequences for Indians and African Americans. After all, those social realities underpinned civil rights protests. And if whites claimed and then diluted the very words that described those social worlds, they could offer in return only a power more linguistic than actual.

This looseness of symbolic meaning, with ideas, statements, and signs chopped up and reassembled in bold, antiestablishment collages, pervaded oppositional rhetoric. Indeed, it characterized not only the counterculture, but much of American culture itself. Children might continue to dress Indian in Camp Fire and Order of the Arrow groups, but when scouts turned to crafts work, they also found themselves cutting up magazines and gluing together picture and word collages, the understandings of which were both personal and evasive. In politics and in scout patrols, such pastiches could be read in multiple ways, depending on angle of view and the identity one half-glimpsed when one passed in front of a mirror. No one owned—or could even lay claim to—long hair and an Indian headband, much less its myriad meanings. So while some counterculture rebels sought to use Indianness to express antiwar sentiments or revolutionary identities, they found that those identities had power only as the symbols crunched together around an ill-defined, culturally centered notion of rebellion. Otherwise, meaning resided with individuals and their interpretations. "Revolution for the hell of it?" asked Free. "Why not? It's all a bunch of phony words anyway. Reality is a subjective experience. It exists in my head."[18]

Free's key notions—an empowered individualism and a flyaway sense of meaning—were closely related. As individuals insisted upon the power of their own interpretations of symbols, those symbols began to lose their collective significance. At the same time, as symbols and signs became increasingly flexible, individuals found themselves asserting the validity of their right to interpret and to find import. Whereas the hobbyists had embraced an open, relativist understanding of culture, oppositional Indian play went farther, assuming that not only behavior but also meaning itself could be relativistic.

The world looks different on the far side of the 1960s, for the diverse ambitions of the counterculture did in fact produce significant changes in American society. Nonetheless, the movement often worked most effectively in the realm of cultural gesture. "Expressly political concerns," suggests the historian Peter Clecak, "existed fitfully, even secondarily." And Charles Chatfield observed that "symbolism was used to challenge social and cultural conformity in general. This left the antiwar movement open to extraneous attack, since the contest over the war was waged more on the level of symbols than on issues."[19] As the signs of rebellion—that bandanna headband, for instance—had filled with an array of common revolutionary meanings, the groups that used those signs followed fragmented social agendas. Indianness had a certain heft for many white, middle-class men and some white women, but its meanings, like those of Black Power and antiwar protest and feminism, once uprooted from social realities, could not bring together people separated by faultlines of gender, race, and ideology. Red Power, for example, which sought to refocus Indianness on larger audiences, came eventually to matter more to Indian people than to non-Indians. In building the political movement, young Indians looked to elders and traditionals, fundamentally altering the ways subsequent native people would construct their identities.

As meanings became liberated from their social moorings, what began to matter most was the relation between the interpreter and the text being interpreted, be it book, rally, disobedient act, or piece of clothing. In that relation, individuals found new ways to define personal identities. Perhaps nowhere were the powerful interpretive links between a text and its readers (as opposed to authors and their intentions) so visible as in the counterculture's environmentalist wing, which made its own a speech purportedly given by the Suquamish/Duwamish leader Seattle in 1855. Widely quoted and reproduced, the speech offered an emotionally powerful manifesto for living on the land and a set of instructions for white Americans:

> Every part of this earth is sacred to my people . . . we are part of the earth and it is part of us . . . Whatever befalls the earth, befalls the sons of earth. If men spit upon the ground, they spit upon themselves. This we know. The Earth does not belong to man. Man belongs to the earth. This we know. All things are connected like the blood which unites one family. When the last red man has vanished from this earth and his memory is only the shadow of a cloud moving across the prairie, these shores and forest will still hold the spirits of my people. For they love this earth as a new born loves its mother's heartbeat. So if we sell you our land, love it as we have loved it. Care for it as we have cared for it. We may be brothers after all.[20]

In an Indian death speech that echoed Metamora, Logan, or Susquesus, the text gave Seattle's purported blessing and a gentle admonishment to white successors. Yet while the speech tendered a classic tale of succession, it also permanently implanted Indians—spiritually at least—in the American landscape. And at the same time that it set up distinct Indian and white American epochs, it linked people in one aboriginal, nature-loving family. Like the vanishing Indian plays of Jacksonian America, Seattle's words erased contemporary social realities and the complicated, often violent history of Indian land loss. Instead, all people were one, bound by a universal web of blood connections and their relations to the earth. The speech, which pasted together the classic tropes of Indian Americanism, proved one of the most powerful artifacts of the time.

As the words journeyed through American popular culture, jumping from magazine articles to posters to Sierra Club calendars to collective folk wisdom, the fact that Chief Seattle never uttered them fell easily by the wayside. In truth, "Seattle's wisdom" came from the pen of a white screenwriter from Texas, and his moving words were the single highlight of an obscure television script on pollution produced by the Southern Baptist Convention in 1972.[21] What really mattered, however, was not the speech's authorship or its history, which was tangled and complex, but the words themselves and the people who encountered them, interpreted them, and derived meaning and import from their emotionally charged cadences. The text seemed to float suspended above the social world of Indians and whites, environmentalists and screenwriters, generating its own culturally resonant meanings. Those meanings could then be acted out in familiar ways—in the tipis at New Buffalo, the Geronimoesque headband, the "Yi Yi Yi Yi Yi" chant, the reassuring purchase of a beautiful calendar.

But Indianness has always been about contradictions, and its uses were hardly confined to this creative, confusing world of free meanings. Indeed, in such a decentered world, many people found themselves searching for something fixed, real, and authentic. Paul Goodman concluded that what really drove the counterculture was a crisis of meaning that was spiritual at base and that "in the end it is religion that constitutes the strength of this generation and not, as I used to think, their morality, political will, and common sense."[22] Playing Indian gave the counterculture the best of both worlds. On the one hand, Indianness—in the form of a communal tipi or a speech by Chief Seattle— seemed as open and unfixed as a sign could be. It could mean whatever one wanted it to mean. On the other hand, and almost alone among a shifting vocabulary of images, Indianness could also be a sign of something unchanging, a first principle. This other kind of Indianness also had a powerful, if often half-conscious, history.

After World War II, these twinned desires gained power relative to the other, for each proved critical to the construction of identities. If everything was fair game, including Indianness, then desire for something fixed—also represented by the Indian—increased proportionately. Seattle's speech, with its mystical evocation of edenic nature and aboriginal Americanness, pointed the way to a particularly spiritual form of Indianness. Likewise, Goodman's revelation came after meeting a young hippie: "He was dressed like an (American) Indian, in fringed buckskin and a headband, with red paint on his face. All his life, he said, he had tried to escape the encompassing evil of our society that was bent on destroying his soul." Although much of the counterculture search for spiritual insight would revolve around hallucinogenic drugs and Eastern mysticism, playing Indian offered a familiar and powerful path to the reassuring fixity of ultimate enlightenment.[23]

In the 1960s and 1970s, many spiritual seekers turned to Sun Bear, Rolling Thunder, and other so-called medicine people for guidance in questing after the Great Spirit. There was nothing innocent about these searches. In an oppositional culture, one targeted Christianity as part of the authoritarian structure from which one sought escape. And, as we saw in political and communal discourse, the symbols and practices of many countertraditions blurred and overlapped. Hallucinogenic drug use could be knit together with Plains Indian vision quest rituals, known for the intense experiences that came with their mental and physical deprivations. The paperback edition of John Neihardt's *Black Elk Speaks* (1972), for example, promised eager seekers an account of a "personal vision that makes an LSD trip pale by comparison," and books like *Lame Deer, Seeker of Visions* by John Fire Lame Deer and *Seven Arrows* by Hyemeyohsts Storm were steady sellers.[24]

Indians represented spiritual experience beyond representation. Ironically, books and instruction proved the standard means of gaining access to that experience. The hobbyists of the 1950s had used texts, but many had also turned to real Indians. Counterculture spiritualists sought out Indians, to be sure, but, like the communalists, the number of people who actually "studied with" Indian teachers was small relative to the many more who read and interpreted the books and periodicals. And the path was not always clear even for those who engaged Indians. As cultural boundaries opened up, the role of mediator, already difficult to pin down, proved almost impossibly slippery. Non-Indians began taking up permanent native identities in order to lay claim to the cultural power of Indianness in the white imagination. Likewise, many native people found empowerment in a white-focused, spiritual mediator's role, and they acted accordingly. It became difficult to sort out who was whom along this continuum, and the question of mediators' Indian identity has been fiercely and frequently contested ever since.[25]

The spiritual entrepreneur Sun Bear is an instructive example. In the late 1960s, his *Many Smokes* magazine had a small circulation of Indian readers. Sun Bear editorialized on all manner of native issues, from Office of Equal Opportunity policy to the role of claims settlement money in economic development.[26] Yet, he was clearly already a mediating figure—his masthead photo showed him playing an Apache on the television show *Death Valley Days*. In the 1970s, however, the nature of Sun Bear's intercultural brokerage changed, and *Many Smokes* metamorphosed into a full-blown New Age periodical aimed at a much larger, non-Indian audience. In 1986, it changed its name to *Wildfire* and proffered a montage of articles dealing with Christian theology, crystal magic, spirit channeling, vision questing, land brokering, Afghan relief, natural childbirth, and smudging one's computer with purifying smoke. Catalogue goods were always on sale, as were stock offerings for the Bear Tribe, which, in a 1980s move, became a visible collective through legal incorporation.[27] The Bear Tribe, primarily a collection of non-Indian followers, offered a path to tribal Indianness that relied not upon spiritual experience, cultural crossing, or accidents of birth, but upon economic exchange. Many Indians rejected Sun Bear and his enterprise.

Like its counterparts in communalism, politics, and environmentalism, this brand of countercultural spiritualism rarely engaged real Indians, for it was not only unnecessary but inconvenient to do so. Ambiguous people like Sun Bear proved acceptable, for they served not to reveal the lines between Indian and non-Indian but to blur them even further. The most prominent landmark in this ambiguous tradition of texts and mediators may have come in 1968, when Carlos Castaneda published *The Teachings of Don Juan: A Yaqui Way of Knowledge*, a faux encounter with a Yaqui sorcerer whose spiritual insights and desert adventures were presented as true ethnography rather than fiction. *The Teachings of Don Juan* became required reading for spiritual seekers, and Castaneda continued to dish out Don Juan's insights in a series of books published throughout the next two decades.[28] Although one heard occasional reports of seekers waiting futilely at grimy downtown bus stations in the Southwest for Don Juan's arrival, most followers were more than content simply to buy the books and discuss them among themselves. Likewise, while many traveled to Harney Peak and Bear Butte, holy places named in other Indian books, they rarely engaged the Lakota or Cheyenne people who also visited these places. Even in a quest for fixed meaning, Indian people were basically irrelevant. Indianness—even when imagined as something essential—could be captured and marketed as a text, largely divorced from Indian oversight and questions of authorship.

The disconnections of the 1960s and 1970s may have reached peak development in the activities of the New Age, a movement for an aging counterculture. Like *counterculture* itself, *New Age* spans an ambiguous time period and serves as a general rubric for a wide range of practices. Although one might trace its roots back to the counterculture or to the self-actualization movements of the 1970s, it was not until the early 1980s, with the popular writings of Shirley MacLaine and the noodlely music of Windom Hill recording artists like George Winston and Will Ackerman, that New Age first became visible under that name. Heavily based in self-help and personal development therapies, its proponents await a large-scale change in human consciousness and a utopian era of peace and harmony. In New Age identity quests, one can see the long shadows of certain strands of postmodernism: increasing reliance on texts and interpretations, runaway individualism within a rhetoric of community, the distancing of native people, and a gaping disjuncture between a cultural realm of serious play and the power dynamics of social conflict. New Age thinking tends to focus on ultimate individual liberation and engagement with a higher power, having little interest in the social world that lies between self and spirit.[29]

Take, for example, the Church of Gaia / Council of Four Directions, a gathering of spiritual seekers in my hometown who found themselves easy targets for a *New York Times* writer:

> In an ancient rite of American Indians, wisps of smoke rise from burning herbs in prayer to Mother Earth and Father Sky, as the woman with the pipe intones solemnly, "Creator, we come to you in a sacred manner." There were Indian chants of "ho," a song about the return of the bison, and some reverent words offered for "the red nation." All that was missing in this gathering on the second floor of an office building over a Boulder pizzeria was an Indian.[30]

When the article was reprinted in Boulder's local paper, Stephen Buhner, one of the church's board members, responded in kind. Emphasizing the pedagogical qualifications of the authors of New Age texts and his own First Amendment rights, Buhner captured the mix of interpretation and self-focus that has characterized many New Age pursuits. "Sun Bear and Ed McGaa," he argued, "[were] given the right to teach traditional native religious ways by their teachers. That right has never been rescinded." According to Buhner, McGaa's Vietnam combat record and medicine "training" legitimated his text, *Mother Earth Spirituality*, while Sun Bear's role as Medicine Chief of the recently incorporated Bear Tribe Medicine Society made his a worthy voice.[31]

These are, one should note, particularly Western views of the ways in which spiritual knowledge can be understood and transmitted. Even as the Church of Gaia sought Indian spiritual essentials, then, its members disengaged themselves both physically and intellectually from native people. Adopting the behavioralist dynamic of the hobbyists, Buhner suggested that spiritual insight resulted from a teacher-learner encounter, and that it was manifested through a certification process in which one's qualifications might be revoked for cause. Yet in many native societies, and especially among the Plains people so beloved by New Age seekers, real spiritual authority comes not so much from tutelage as from spiritual experience itself. Buhner valued Sun Bear and Ed McGaa not only for their spiritual experiences but for their compiling of cultural knowledge— texts that could be purchased, interpreted, mastered, and materialized.[32]

What mattered most was Buhner's claim to be able to acquire and practice sacred traditions. He made the claim not in terms of his own training or experience, but by calling on essential Americanisms—freedom of religion and equal opportunity—that rang with an intensity equal to that of McGaa's military service. "Our church," claimed Buhner, "believes that no person because of their skin color, should be prohibited from worshiping God in the manner they choose."[33] Indianness—coded as a spiritual essential—was the common property of all Americans. Yet for native people Buhner's argument could hardly have been more ironic. Indian First Amendment rights, protected only by a congressional vow of good faith and long the target of white reformers, came under severe attack during the 1980s. In a series of legal decisions, the Supreme Court gutted the already-weak American Indian Religious Freedom Act, curtailing the exercise of Indian religious freedom in favor of federal environmental law, tourism and hydropower production, Forest Service–supported logging operations, and state regulation of controlled substances. Coming from a man who lived in a solar home on thirty-five acres of pricey Boulder real estate and who did as he pleased with regard to native spirituality, the claim of discrimination had to ring hollow.[34]

And yet, was Buhner really wrong? Not in a world in which contingent meanings mixed with the power of individual interpretation, endless information, and good intent. And if New Age followers graze freely on proliferating information about other cultures, they usually do so with a sense of compassion and concern. Like the communalists, they tend to be good people bound up in contradictions. McGaa caught the sincere tenor of New Age participants from a sympathetic Indian perspective: "If we want the white man to change, we must teach him." And, echoing Chief Seattle, "We're all brothers."[35] In this universalist interpretation, cultures inevitably bump up against each other and when they do, they exchange and share cultural material, each becoming a kind of hybrid. Making sense of this hybrid world is less a social activity than a personal one, and individuals should be able to use every available tool in doing so. In a world of free-flowing information and multicultural mixing, no group of people has exclusive rights to culture, even if they bound and define it as their own.

Buhner's final argument drew on such multicultural information, at once universally accessible and personally meaningful: "The religious war in the former country of Yugoslavia, fought over just such differences, should be warning enough of the wisdom of the First Amendment."[36] Moving quickly from individual rights to global crisis, Buhner skipped his own social milieu. It was apparent to most Indians that the Church of Gaia/Council of Four Directions—economically powerful and racially unmarked—was probably the last group needing to wage war in order to practice its religious beliefs. Despite its misleading nod to Muslims, Serbs, and Croats, Buhner's argument was both superficial and common: self-creative cultural free play was the prerogative of individuals, and it had little to do with the relations between social groups or the power inequities among them.

But if Buhner's suggestion was superficial, it was hardly simple. Rather, it drew upon a newly empowered multiculturalism, forcing it into an uncomfortable alliance with a postmodernism that emphasized the openness of meaning. The nation's strength, suggested a long line of multiculturalists from the critics Randolph Bourne and Horace Kallen to the historian Gary Nash, lay not in the genteel tradition of white America, but in its diverse array of different peoples and traditions. Difference, they argued, was not to be rejected, but rather embraced. First framed in the early twentieth century, confronted more directly in the post–World War II years, and quasi-institutionalized during the 1970s and 1980s, multiculturalism had become a key idea around which social meanings could be negotiated.

And yet, multiculturalism itself was hardly clear-cut. Bourne, suggests the historian David Hollinger, spoke for a cosmopolitan tradition that emphasized dynamism and openness. Kallen, on the other hand, planted the seeds for a sterner pluralist focus on the autonomy and singularity of ethnic groups. In the wake of the Civil Rights movements of the 1960s, the pluralist form of multiculturalism came to be persistently linked with the questioning of unequal power and opportunity for the nation's diverse peoples. And, through a variety of institutions and programs, white Americans began to think about ways to remedy those inequities.[37]

With its focus on difference and rigid categorizations, however, a multiculturalism based upon pluralism proved troublesome to those who lived identities along more complicated racial-ethnic, gender, sexual, occupational, and geographic lines. Indeed, the breaking down of inequities and social restrictions enlarged the numbers of people who fit multiple categories at the same time: one might be Swedish, Dakota, and Latino all at once. A cosmopolitan focus on culture-crossings and simultaneities, on the other hand, suggested that one's identity was a matter not so much of descent as of consent and choice. This particular kind of multiculturalism gained increasing power and visibility during the 1980s. And yet, placed in the context of a postmodernism that emphasized relativism and openness, it was easy to read cosmopolitan multiculturalism as a license for *anyone* to choose an ethnic identity—Indian, for example—regardless of family, history, or tribal recognition. When non-Indian New Age followers appropriated and altered a cosmopolitan understanding of Indianness, they laid bare a slow rebalancing away from the collective concerns with social justice that had emerged in the 1960s and toward the renewed focus on individual freedom that has characterized America since the 1980s.[38]

New Age adherents found numerous ways to push the scales toward individual liberty, a notion often materialized through the consumption of other cultures. Committed, sincere people like Stephen Buhner surveyed the traditions the world has to offer, mixing Indian spiritual practices with Zen Buddhism, tantric exercise, neopaganism, druidism, and other exotic brands of knowledge. The New Age men's movement, for example, created a complex brew of interpersonal psychology, group therapy, and sensitivity training in Indian-tinged settings. Gathered out-of-doors, men's movement enthusiasts made and wore masks, chose self-reflecting totem animals (usually big, masculine animals), passed an Indian "talking stick" around as they shared repressed experiences, and meditated alone in the wild in a sort of well-tempered vision quest experience. The focus was on healing a wounded Self. Women's groups had similar bonding rituals, often centered on an essentialist vision of women's intrinsic connection to the earth. And, of course, New Age followers of both sexes bonded over someone else's cultural knowledge in situations ranging from conferences at swank hotels to sweatlodge ceremonies in backyards.[39]

Like their countercultural predecessors, New Age devotees relied on books to package and circulate the cultures they consumed. In the mid-1980s, New Age writing exploded, and followers had a wide array of mediating texts to teach them the ways of Indianness. A familiar format involves an old Indian person who, for whatever reason, turns, not to other Indians, but to a good-hearted white writer to preserve his or her sacred knowledge. John Neihardt's moving and sympathetic *Black Elk Speaks* set the trajectory in 1932, and, if the quality of the writing has deteriorated, the model remains the same. Lynn Andrews's *Medicine Woman* series, for example, began with this format and expanded to include other world cultures. Andrews's pastiche accounts leap wildly around native North America. She finds, for example, a Choctaw woman living near a Canadian Cree community in a Pawnee earth lodge, described in such a way as to sound suspiciously like George Catlin's paintings of Mandan houses from 1832. And it is her Cree teacher, Agnes Whistling Elk, who collapses ancient wisdom with postmodern insight: "Every book is rewritten by the reader. . . . You bring to it what you are."[40] Numerous other books gave readers the opportunity to imagine identities through such rewriting. Clarissa Pinkola Estes suggested ways in which women could "run with the wolves," Robert Bly and Sam Keen offered up equivalent myths for men, and James Redfield's abominable *Celestine Prophecy* showed heroic whites learning deep secrets from disappearing South American Indians amidst an insignificant backdrop of social struggle. Readers of such texts then put the words into concrete forms, performing them through vision quest weekends and pipe ceremonies in National Forest hideaways, many of which carried the heady price tag that signified conspicuous bourgeois consumption.[41]

The tendency of New Age devotees to find in Indianness personal solutions to the question of living the good life meant that Indian Others were imagined in almost exclusively positive terms—communitarian, environmentally wise, spiritually insightful. This happy multiculturalism blunted the edge of earlier calls for social change by focusing on pleasant cultural exchanges that erased the complex histories of Indians and others. Even lingering nineteenth-century images of bloodthirsty savagery have been rendered ambivalent or positive. In spite of almost twenty years of Indian protest against his team's nickname (to cite the most egregious example), the late Washington Redskins owner Jack Kent Cooke insisted that the name honors rather than degrades native people.[42]

For hundreds of years, Indianness had been an open idea, capable of having its meanings refigured by Americans seeking identities. The Orwellian pronouncements of people like Cooke, however, suggested that, for many, postmodern Indianness had become so detached from anything real that it was in danger of lapsing into a bland irrelevance.

What are we to make of this transformation? Since the colonial era, Indian Others had been objects of both desire *and* repulsion, and in that raging contradiction lay their power. Now, they were almost completely flattened out, tragic victims who brought the last powerful remnants of their cultures as ethnic gifts for a pluralistic American whole. I have showed how non-Indians constructed Indian Others along two different scales: First, an axis of distance on which Indians could appear anywhere between a remote inhumanity and a mirror reflection of one's Self, and second, an axis of value on which Indians appeared in gradations of positive and negative. Now, these lines of difference and value threatened to disappear. The social boundaries that marked Indianness as either inside or outside America almost vanished before an all-encompassing universalism. For Stephen Buhner and Lynn Andrews, everything was inside. Likewise, the axis of value occupied by savage and noble Indians also shrank in importance as Indians became genial objects of fashion, style, and cultural play. What was there not to like about Indians?

In the sense that everything in a postmodern world could be seen as a game or a project, playing Indian had reached its contradictory apotheosis. It retained its proven creative power—play is a crucial way in which we shape identity and meaning—but, at the same time, its substance tended to slip away. For while play is a critical experience, it is also a powerful metaphor for that which is frivolous and without significance. Postmodernity—as both concept and cultural moment—embraces play, perhaps, because one of its ultimate modes is almost humorously ironic—a firm belief in the contingency of meaning. Such belief might lead one to argue that the way meanings are made and materialized is vitally important. On the other hand, if no meaning is any better than any other, it might also suggest that the practice of meaning-making matters very little.[43]

New Age meaning-making was reflected in the concrete experience of native costume, always a crucial element in Indian play. It was perhaps indicative of the nature of the movement that its followers tended to play Indian in ways that were low-grade. A bandanna headband, an assumed name, a personal fetish—any one would suffice. Many Indian objects were embedded in the conspicuous consumption campaigns that took shape around Santa Fe Style and American Country West.[44] In contrast, the hobbyists (who had made authenticity into their own kind of fetish) had experienced a particularly social kind of interaction. They had sought out Indians and made and worn painstaking reproductions of native clothing. In the New Age, authenticity had few material or social forms. Rather, it resided—like all good, unknowable essentials—in a person's interpretive heart and soul. Yet, as we have seen, putting on costumes had always been an essential element in Indian play. "We do not stir a step until our equipment is right," insisted Lewis Henry Morgan, referring to his new confederates of the Iroquois. The Camp Fire Girls' self-designed Indian dresses, expressing personal character in a material way, underpinned their entire pursuit. The Improved Order of Red Men cherished the smoky canvas costumes that went into the storage locker after a night's ritual.

The concrete nature of clothing had always insured that, even in the midst of creative play, a thread of social connection bound real Indians to those who mimed them. And indeed, it was the social *reality* of authentic, aboriginal Indians that gave Indian play significance and power. When the New Age turned to disjointed signifiers—a headband rife with associations, a stylized pipe influenced (one would almost swear) by J. R. R. Tolkien, a set of tropes from one's personal library—adherents allowed some of the true creative power of Indianness to slip away. Yet most New Agers, confronting the contradictions between a self-focused world of playful cultural hybridity and a social world of struggle, hatred, winners, and losers (with Indians usually numbered among the losers), understandably tended to the former.[45]

Indianness retained a certain degree of power, however, and that power suggests that markers of Indian difference necessarily remained in place. Ironically, the social realities that New Age devotees tended to avoid helped fuel the sense of Indian–white difference that made Indianness meaningful. Indians lived poverty-stricken lives on faraway reservations. Their poverty and geographical and social distance marked them as different—and thereby authentic. Incorporative multiculturalism, on the other hand, has tended to focus on distinctive *cultural* contributions—food, music, language—and to attenuate cultural differences within a larger human whole. The asymmetrical relations of power that both undergird and undermine the system linger, however, in the uneasy collective unconscious. Mexican food, for example, is a more palatable ethnic gift than Mexican agricultural stoop labor, although in its concrete expression of social inequality and physical distance, it is the latter that defines whatever authenticity one might find in tortillas and frijoles.

Native people who reject this kind of cultural incorporation find themselves in a curious and contradictory position, shunted outside the boundaries of a universalism that purports to be without boundaries. Reluctant to share their cultural heritage as a common property, they are marked as exterior. And yet, as is true of the Mexican agricultural worker, it is the social difference of these Indians that guarantees Indian authenticity. In this relentlessly contradictory interplay, such people have been simultaneously granted a platform and rendered voiceless. In the summer of 1992, for example, the Indian-published newspaper *Indian Country Today* ran a series of articles indicting many New Age "medicine people" as frauds and inviting their response. Most refused to grant any legitimacy to the critiques and failed to respond. Some did, and they were rebutted effectively. But the newspaper's detailed investigative reporting had no appreciable effect on New Age audiences. Indian presence was noted. Complaints, however, were ignored and suggestions rejected.[46]

Yet while these oppositional Indians were ignored, it was nonetheless important that they speak—and speak critically, for in doing so, they offered one of the only indicators of authentic difference functioning in the world of texts, interpretations, and unchained meanings. Whereas Sun Bear and Medicine Woman Lynn Andrews inhabited a cultural world easily shared by Indians and non-Indians, oppositional native people focused on social and political worlds, where the differences between the reservation, the urban ghetto, and the Beverly Hills Hotel, with its silky breezes and honeysuckle air, stood in stark relief. When they tried to force non-Indians to translate from the cosmopolitan language of open cultural meanings to the pluralist languages of power, struggle, and inequality, they rethreaded the material connections that made Indianness so real. And so one multicultural tradition—that of cultural pluralism—provided the "reality" that empowered a distorted, postmodern version of a more cosmopolitan multiculturalism. Indian reality fed back into the textual world, increasing the power of Indianness, even as it contradicted the particular form that Indianness took. The presence of multicultural images and statements, however, let Indian players claim a sincere, but ultimately fruitless, political sympathy with native people. Indeed, the New Age's greatest intellectual temptation lies in the wistful fallacy that one can engage in social struggle by working on oneself.

As the hobbyists demonstrated so clearly, a multicultural order requires markers of difference in order to make its blurrings of that difference meaningful. Even as it is often ignored, then, the critical voice offered by *Indian Country Today's* Tim Giago—an interestingly middle-of-the-road voice, one should note—matters more to both New Age postmodernism and to materialist social criticism than that of Dirk Johnson, the *New York Times* reporter who went after Stephen Buhner's church. Racism, poverty, poor health care, underfunded educational facilities, pollution and toxic dumping, domination by extractive industries— these are the issues through which social and political power has figured difference in Indian Country. When the Indian staffers of *Indian Country Today* report on these topics, they reflect that difference, so easily ignored by postmodern multiculturalism and yet so vital to the authenticity of its Indianness.

The quicksand dynamics of power link these two worlds in intimate and confusing ways, for the power that dominated Indians could, at the same time, be turned to their advantage. *Indian Country Today,* which features Giago's frequent attacks on the lack of Indian voices in the mainstream media, has been partially funded by the Gannett Foundation, a mainstream institution. There was certainly no mistaking the meaning and the money when the paper left behind its original name, the *Lakota Times,* for a connection with that most postmodern of print news outlets, *USA Today.* And yet, *Indian Country Today* is, at the same time, a significant power base for native people. If Indian people found themselves disempowered in one social realm—the mainstream press—they also found power in that same place. It is, paradoxically, the same power, and it makes a difference that it flows through different channels. One channel maintains a social hierarchy; the other maintains a contradictory ethic of multicultural egalitarianism. The power to define and exclude, the power to appropriate and co-opt, the power to speak and resist, and the power to build new, hybrid worlds are sometimes one and the same, and that power flows through interlocked social and cultural systems, simultaneously directed and channeled by humans and yet often beyond strict human control.[47]

Indian people have, for more than one hundred years, lacked military power. Being militarily defeated, they found that social, political, and economic power were often hard to come by as well. Native people have been keenly aware, however, that in their relations to white Americans they do in fact possess some mysterious well of cultural power. When the Red Power activists of the late 1960s and early 1970s took over Alcatraz, marched on Washington and trashed the office of the Bureau of Indian Affairs, and sniped at the besieging army at Wounded Knee, they were not engaging in simply military or revolutionary actions. Above all, they were committing cultural acts in which they sought social and political power through a complicated play of white guilt, nostalgia, and the deeply rooted desire to be Indian and thereby aboriginally true to the spirit of the land. Among American ethnic and racial groups, Indians have occupied a privileged position in national culture, and native people have often put the power that came with this exceptionalism to political and social ends.

That such a politics of culture resonated so thoroughly—even in a world in which symbols had spread their meanings hopelessly thin—suggests the continuing depth and power of Indianness for white Americans. Community and individualism, spiritual essence and precarious meanings, cultural universalism and social difference—paradoxes like these continue to drive contemporary Indian play just as surely as the problem of Briton and aborigine drove the original revolutionaries. Likewise, if the Indian plays of the counterculture and the New Age reflect the cultural moment we have called postmodern, they also reveal the ways in which its practices have a longer history. There is little about the postmodern—linguistic relativism, epistemological crisis, pastiche, and bricolage—that has not appeared in the past. Indeed, many of these interpretive tropes have shown up in the history of Indian play. Indian costume has been the site of a host of language games and remade meanings, and people like Lewis Henry Morgan and Ernest Thompson Seton and Arthur C. Parker have used it to rethink the very ways they understood the world. Writers, fraternalists, Boy Scouts, and bohemian reformers have all chipped off fragments of Indianness, put them into new contexts, and turned them to new uses. Granted, says the theorist Fredric Jameson, but what makes postmodernism a thing unto itself is the changed social realities of the post–World War II world, with its new relations of power, its global character, its inclination to turn culture—and multiculture—into marketable commodities. And indeed, Indian play has reflected such underlying changes, as Americans of all sorts have negotiated, rebuilt, and forgotten the cultural differences that help produce collective and individual identities.[48]

My weekends visiting the tipi camp and slurping used milk from the collective cereal bowl were part of something new in the sense that Indian play has always taken on new shape and focus to engage the most pressing issues of a particular historical moment. I, too, was an actor in a world in which questioning the common sense of everyday life was bidding to *become* the common sense of everyday life. But in other, and perhaps more crucial ways, I was participating in a long, unbroken tradition in American history. My communal Indian friends were attempting to redefine themselves and their local community. In doing so, they hoped, in some small way, to offer an example to the nation as a whole. Like many before them, they had turned to Indianness as the sign of all that was authentic and aboriginal, everything that could be true about America. But they had also turned to Indianness as a way of making an absolutely new start. Yet like those who had come before, they found that Indianness inevitably required real native people, and that those people called everything into question. Playing Indian, as always, had a tendency to lead one into, rather than out of, contradiction and irony.

conclusion

The Grateful Dead Indians

When the colonials dressed as Indians, they sent the signal
of total rebellion. To associate with "savages" (the natives) was
the sign that the colonists would go to the last measure to obtain
their freedom. The Society of Indian Dead invite all peaceful
tribes to send representatives to the New American Revolution.

APACHE RISES FROM THE GRASS
Live and Let Live #9

Entering a Grateful Dead show in the early 1990s, one might have been handed
the latest issue of *Live and Let Live*, published by the Society of Indian Dead. If you
looked up from the hand that proffered the single-sheet newsletter, you might
see paint, buckskin, even feathers. And if you followed the Indian-garbed pamphleteer through the vans and tents in the parking lot surrounding the stadium,
you might have been invited into a tipi pitched atop the asphalt. Chicory coffee,
hummus and pita bread, skulls, bears, roses, and the smell of patchouli oil on
skin. Beat-up guitars, endless rounds of the Dead classic "Fire on the Mountain,"

and the various scents and textures of smoke—Indians fit seamlessly into the mix, but then, so did most everything.

Indeed, one can interpret the Indian Dead as a postmodern phenomenon, a bricolage whirl of color, style, fashionable rebellion, and flyaway meaning. On the other hand, one might just as easily say that, far from reveling in relativism, the members had embarked on an antimodern quest for authentic truth. Given the group's rejection of urbanism, technology, mass culture, environmental degradation, and alienating individualism, that interpretation made sense, too. But if the Indian Dead point in these directions, they also point further back, to the Revolution and the Boston Tea Party, iconic moments that suggest still other interpretations of American history and identity. In fact, the group made the Tea Party connection explicit. In the lines between tattoo art and slogans rejecting the war on drugs, *Live and Let Live* offered a historical analysis of America's first rebellion: "The Indian Dead understand that Indians were the first Americans. As was understood at one time, the turning point in the American Revolution was the Boston Tea Party. It was the symbol: STARVE RATHER THAN SUBMIT."[1]

The familiar phrases of the Society of Indian Dead suggest that, for all the transmutations that have come with two hundred and fifty years of Indian play, certain threads have held continuing power in the weave of American life. Indians *were* first and original Americans, and taking on Indian identity *was* in fact a moment of no return for rebellious colonists. Notions such as these have guided the actions of Tea Party Indians, fraternalists, Camp Fire Girls, hobbyists, and Deadheads alike. And yet, Indian play was hardly clear-cut, for if Indianness was critical to American identities, it necessarily went hand in hand with the dispossession and conquest of actual Indian people.

And this was not the only contradiction undergirding the nation's history and sense of collective identity: what of the constant collisions between personal liberty and social order? the distance between the rhetoric of egalitarianism and the reality of slavery and class struggle? Disjunctures like these are the stuff of which most nations and societies are made. And yet, while its citizens created the United States around such dissonances, many of them found that playing Indian offered a powerful tool for holding their contradictions in abeyance. Indianness gave the nation a bedrock, for it fully engaged the contradiction most central to a range of American identities—that between an unchanging, essential Americanness and the equally American liberty to make oneself into something new.

Indianness has, above all, represented identities that are unquestionably American. Despite the shifting nature of individual, social, and national identities, Indianness has made them seem fixed and final. For the Tea Party Indians and Tammany paraders of the Revolution, aboriginal Indianness made one a citizen, not of an impermanent government, but of the land itself. That half-secret meaning, as D. H. Lawrence half-realized, was as powerful as the timeless earth was real. For those who came here from other countries, the ultimate truths of America's physical nature—rocks, water, sky—were intimately linked to a *metaphysical* American nature that would always be bound up with mythic national identities. The secrets of both natures lay in Indianness. It is in this particular, historical relation between immigrants, natives, land, and political rebellion that Indianness began to acquire its most critical meanings.

The intuitive links that colonists first forged between Indianness and the land held strong as subsequent Americans shaped other associations between Indians and ultimates. In the early years of the new nation, the New York Tammany Society and the Improved Order of Red Men used Indianness to wed themselves to an essential American nationalism. The Society of Red Men dressed Indian to express inexpressible cosmic truths. Lewis Henry Morgan looked to the same place for transcendent American artistry. Leaders of the Woodcraft Indians and Camp Fire Girls garbed children in Indian costume to teach the natural and proper places of men and women and the importance of authenticity in a modern world. Likewise, after World War II, generations of Americans caught up in relativisms that challenged nation, community, and selfhood turned to Indians as markers of something undeniably real. In the end, Grateful Dead Indians, Boston Tea Party Indians, and those who came between drank from the same well of meanings: Indianness offered a deep, authentic, aboriginal Americanness. No matter if the form were proto-American or anti-American, Indianness grounded a number of significant searches for identity on this continent. To play Indian has been to connect with a real Self, both collective and individual, and there was no better way to find such reassurance.

And yet if Americanness has been a collection of found identities, it has just as often been a creative experience of fresh interpretation and vigorous self-reshaping. Those engaged in playing Indian sought essentials, but they were also busily inventing new identities that ranged the gamut from Crèvecoeurian new man to postmodern multiculturalist. Indianness, a powerful indicator of the timeless and the unchanging, has been an equally compelling sign of transformation, rebellion, and creation. Playing Indian did not fail to call fixed meanings—and sometimes meaning itself—into question. As they shed their old clothes in favor of feathers, canvas costumes, intricate "artifakery," and bandanna headbands, white Indians have sported quite literally with the contingency of language, identity, social structure, and understanding itself.

Playing Indian encouraged people to reject the stories and language that helped structure the common sense of everyday life. American freedom meant, above all, a chance to be ultimately free. Aboriginal liberty was not freedom within a system. Rather it rejected every restraint—politics, society, language, meaning itself. And so, when Apache Rises from the Grass laid out the Society of Indian Dead's platform for an ideal America, it was as tightly focused on the abstraction of freedom as the rhetoric of the Tea Party Indians more than two hundred years before: "Celebrate Freedom, Affirm Choice, Take Responsibility, Organize Peaceful People, Spread Love and Understanding, Practice Liberty."[2] The idea that one could make a self-identity through an anarchic approach to meaning has been a cherished American possession from the nation's earliest moments, and it has been frequently played out in Indian costume.

In fact, play proved to be an appropriate vehicle for these contradictory longings for freedom and fixed truth. Play was powerful, for it not only made meanings, it made them *real*. The donning of Indian clothes moved ideas from brains to bodies, from the realm of abstraction to the physical world of concrete experience. There, identity was not so much imagined as it was performed, materialized through one's body and through the witness and recognition of others. Such performances did not resolve contradictions, but they did make their dissonances seem somehow harmonious. In putting on feathers and fur, for example, Indian players were forced to acknowledge at some level the social reality of native peoples. Indeed, those social realities constantly renewed "the Indian" as a marker of essential Americanness. And yet what might have been a serious consideration of the inequities that came with American nation building was harmonized as it was cloaked in the powerful, liberating frivolity of play. Indian play was a temporary fantasy, and the player inevitably returned to the everyday world. But the world to which one returned was not that of Indian people, and, in that sense, play allowed one to evade the very reality that it suggested one was experiencing. It offered the concrete ground on which identity might be experienced, but it did not call its adherents to change their lives. Only a handful of Indian players ever went native, and they tended to do so in the mid to late twentieth century, when the borders were blurry enough to slip across with minimal difficulty.

Much has been made of the related notion of an American synthesis, of the "wilderness marriage" that joined Indian and European and thus resolved the dialectic of civilization and savagery in the form of a new product. As D. H. Lawrence suggested, American writers—Hector St. John de Crèvecoeur, James Fenimore Cooper, Frederick Jackson Turner, and many others—have explored this creative tension fully.[3] But Lawrence's taunts to Crèvecoeur ("Can't be done Hector!") in fact suggest that Crèvecoeur—who wanted both civilization and savagery at once—was also on to something more vitally American. Playing Indian offered Americans a national fantasy—identities built not around synthesis and transformation, but around unresolved dualities themselves. Temporary, costumed play refused to synthesize the contradictions between European and Indian. Rather, it held them in near-perfect suspension, allowing Americans to have their cake and eat it too.

I've laid out a series of dialectical tensions at the heart of American identities: open meaning and essential reality, interior and exterior Otherness, subjectivity and objectivity, desire and repulsion, nobility and savagery, individualism and nationalism. When white Americans played Indian, they brought such oppositions into the world and performed them in equal and balanced measure. Immigrant shoemakers and aboriginal "Indians" existed at the same time, in the same person's body. The same physique could contain both middle-class schoolgirls and Camp Fire Indian maidens. Such simultaneous performances of two identities carried far greater power to create Americanness than did literary racial fusions and occasional episodes of going native. Acting Indian brought dialectical interplay to a standstill. It froze contradictions into equivalence. It made them part of the material world. As it did so, playing Indian gave white Americans—from blackfaced Tea Party Mohawks to buckskinned Grateful Dead fans—a jolt of self-creative power.

And that creativity is exactly what was so compelling about playing Indian. In the end, Indian play was perhaps not so much about a desire to become Indian—or even to become *American*—as it was a longing for the utopian experience of being in between, of living a paradoxical moment in which absolute liberty coexisted with the absolute. It was a quest for a meaningful freedom and a contingent truth. Far removed from a relativist anarchy that dissolved meaning into nothingness, it was equally liberated from the iron grip of social order and entrenched philosophy. Americanness is perhaps not so much the product of a collision of European and Indian as it is a particular working out of a desire to preserve stability and truth while enjoying absolute, anarchic freedom.

Such utopian moments, however, rested fundamentally on asymmetrical relations of power. In every instance, playing Indian represented, evaded, and perpetuated those relations. Indianness was the bedrock for creative American identities, but it was also one of the foundations (slavery and gender relations being two others) for imagining and performing domination and power in America. At the very same moment that it was suggesting Indians' essential place in the national psyche, playing Indian evoked actual Indian people and suggested a history of conquest, resistance, and eventual dependency. Struggles for native land defined and transformed the ways in which Americans viewed their nation, themselves, their Indian opponents, and the webs of power in which all were situated.

In the century following the Revolution, for example, the United States waged wars of territorial consolidation against Indian peoples. Although Indian campaigns were marked by genocidal acts and the genocidal urgings of individuals, the United States never formalized a policy of physical genocide toward native people. It could not, for doing so would have made visible an absolutely destructive power over Indians that Americans wanted desperately to deny. And there was good reason—especially at first—to deny that power and to continue the nation's cultural embrace of Indianness. Behind every Indian war in the Old Northwest lay the specter of the British, who had never left the continent and who reemerged as a presence during the War of 1812. With the shadow of John Bull looming, Americans refused to abandon the logic of Indian Americanness that had helped drive the Revolution and define the nation as something other than a British colony. The reemergence of Indian play among the Society of Red Men during the War of 1812 speaks to the lingering power of this older tradition.

Faced with dual threats—British and Indian—American nationalism developed along particularly weak lines. If Americans had been able to focus exclusively on a British enemy, they might well have developed the powerful nationalist expressions sought by Lewis Henry Morgan. Likewise, a strict genocidal focus on Indians might have produced a similarly strong nationalism, albeit one very different in character. The reality of native resistance, however, came to be defined through the ascendent ideology of the vanishing Indian, which held its contradictions in suspension with ferocious power. Indians had a predestined doom, and that knowledge helped erase or justify the later military campaigns against them. Their disappearance, however, was often bittersweet and lamentable, with the disingenuous air of sadness that Renato Rosaldo has labeled "imperialist nostalgia."[4]

From the very beginning, Indian-white relations and Indian play itself have modeled a characteristically American kind of domination in which the exercise of power was hidden, denied, qualified, or mourned. Not surprisingly, Indian play proved a fitting way to negotiate social struggles within white society that required an equally opaque vision of power. The Revolution, in which Indian play transformed treachery to patriotism, is, of course, the first significant marker of this intramural use of Indianness. The New York Tammany Society used "the Indian" in building a powerful political party with specific class and ethnic inflections. Other working-class fraternal orders played Indian to address anxieties driven by their increasing distance from political power and the threatened loss of economic self-sufficiency. Lewis Henry Morgan's elite Indian fraternalism, on the other hand, allowed him to criticize exactly those people—working-class salt boilers who "profaned" the national landscape. For Ernest Thompson Seton, Indianness was key to an upper-class reformist impulse to nurture children placed in gender danger by the modern city. Boys were to be raised to masculinity through contact with Indianized nature, while Camp Fire Girls were to learn the timeless value of female domesticity. In Cold War America, Indian lore hobbyists sought to come to terms with an uneasy middle-class identity that was at once celebrated and attacked. Each of these enterprises found meaning and power on the contradictory foundations of Indian Americanness and Indian dispossession.

But if a mostly imagined Indianness spoke in compelling ways to issues of class, gender, and nationalism within white America, and if Indianness shaped and was shaped by a series of struggles between the United States and a wide array of very real native people, playing Indian has had even more intricate dimensions. In antebellum America, Ely S. Parker and Lewis Henry Morgan inaugurated a paradoxical mode of Indian–non-Indian interaction based not upon military or political conflict, but upon the idea of playing Indian itself. Even as Indian play has been an invasion of the realities of native people, it has been an intercultural meeting ground upon which Indians and non-Indians have created new identities, not only for white Americans, but for Indians themselves.

[handwritten margin note: to see only what we already know!]

When Parker joined Morgan at the meetings of the New Confederacy of the Iroquois, he revealed the contradictory logics that underpinned the group's Indian play, which relied on the traditions of the Revolution and of vanishing Indianness. Dressing native without ever confronting a native person was an exercise in distance, abstraction, and cultural imagination. Parker changed that world, created by colonial rebels and republican fraternalists alike, by forcing the New Confederacy to participate in a particularly social kind of Indian play.

Parker was the ultimate Indian player. He had no control over the history that had positioned him in the social and cultural borderlands between Indian and American. And yet, while fighting the inequities of white racism, callous land speculation, and government corruption, he had nonetheless made himself into a new person, drawing power from Indianness and Americanness in combination. Morgan and Parker both were hybrid figures, living at the overlapping intersections of Iroquois and white American cultures. When Morgan donned Indian costume and Parker wore his suit and tie, they played with the boundaries of selfhood and meaning, simultaneously breaking down and creating cultural difference. It would be wrong to make the two acts equivalent, however, for they also reflect the asymmetries of Indian–non-Indian power. Lewis Henry Morgan did not *have* to engage Iroquois social conventions. The very future of Parker and his people, on the other hand, depended heavily upon their ability to negotiate American society. Figures like Charles A. Eastman and Arthur C. Parker continued this tradition, pairing cultural quests for social power with the creation of complex identities. So did the native singers and dancers of the 1950s and 1960s who balanced Indian lives with the white world of the hobbyists and with the hybrid social world of postwar native America.[5]

One might argue that this Indian-based tradition of hybridity culminated in La Junta, Colorado, in 1953 when the Zunis and the Koshare Boy Scouts convened to resolve the Shalako problem. That meeting—with its creation of an authentic Koshare identity that was both Indian and white and yet also neither— suggested that white Americans might in fact be able to participate in a hybrid world that was attuned both to creative cultural identity-making and to the asymmetries of social and political power. But the Zunis carried the Scout Shalakos back to Zuni, the Koshares watched them go, and the two groups rarely saw each other again.

If such encounters carried untapped potential to alter white Americans, they were certainly transforming for native people. Ely Parker's successors dressed not only in white shirts, coats, and ties, but in Indian costume. Playing cultural

24. Judge Edward R. Harden, 1858.

politics for social and political ends, Arthur C. Parker, Charles A. Eastman, Sun Bear, and others found themselves acting Indian, mimicking white mimickings of Indianness. As they shifted, altered, crossed, and recrossed cultural boundaries, these native people demolished those boundaries, rendering their own identities slippery and uncertain in the process. This kind of native identity, so complex and rich and yet so often and so easily dismissed, has been especially energized by the transformations I've clustered around the ideas of the modern and the authentic. If being a survivor of the pure, primitive old days meant authenticity, and if that in turn meant cultural power that might be translated to social ends, it made sense for a Seneca man to put on a Plains headdress, white America's marker of that archaic brand of authority.

But while Indian people have refined new traditions that mingle white-Indian difference with a more fluid social and cultural hybridity, white Americans have, for the most part, proved unable to follow their lead. During the past thirty years, playing Indian has been as much about reading books as it has been about meeting native people. As the United States has enshrined a multiculturalism that emphasizes culture more than multi-, simply knowing about Indians, African Americans, Asian-Americans, and Latino/as has become a satisfactory form of social and political engagement. As a result, the ways in which white

They've been forced to make the Best of what they can though!

25. *Judge Edward R. Harden in Omaha Costume,*
1855. As one of Nebraska's first territorial judges,
Harden was indispensable in establishing the
structures of national and state power. Paired with
this paradigmatic narrative of American history,
however, was a parallel story in which Harden
played with his identity by donning the costume of
the Omahas, who were dispossessed by Nebraska
settlement. Courtesy of the Nebraska State
Historical Society.

Americans have used Indianness in creative self-shaping have continued to be pried apart from questions about inequality, the uneven workings of power, and the social settings in which Indians and non-Indians might actually meet.

From the beginning, national identity and the nation itself have relied upon such separations. The plotting out and explaining of the United States have for a long time meant celebrating the nation's growing power and its occasionally wise, often tragic, sometimes well-intentioned deployment of that power on the continent and around the world. The celebration of national character, on the other hand, has frequently involved the erasure of such exercises of power. This story is a very different one: it is more tightly linked to destiny, to Indians who simply vanish, to the relativity of culture and meaning, to a long-standing license to make oneself over. Americans have often been inclined to keep the narratives of American nationhood and American character away from each other. And yet, the two stories are inseparable (figs. 24, 25).

Playing Indian, then, reflects one final paradox. The self-defining pairing of American truth with American freedom rests on the ability to wield power against Indians—social, military, economic, and political—while simultaneously drawing power from them. Indianness may have existed primarily as a cultural artifact in American society, but it has helped *create* these other forms of power, which have then been turned back on native people. The dispossessing of Indians exists in tension with being aboriginally true. The embracing of Indians exists in equal tension with the freedom to become new. And the terms are interchangeable. Intricate relations between destruction and creativity—for both Indian and non-Indian Americans—are themselves suspended in an uneasy alliance. And so while Indian people have lived out a collection of historical nightmares in the material world, they have also haunted a long night of American dreams. As many native people have observed, to be American is to be unfinished. And although that state is powerful and creative, it carries with it nightmares all its own.

Acknowledgments

During the course of this project, I have incurred substantial debts, and many thanks are in order. The committee that supervised this work as a dissertation included Howard Lamar, the most generous adviser to stalk the halls of any university, Ann Fabian, whose quirky insights and compassion for students shine as a model for myself and many others, William Cronon, a good friend and an inspiring mentor, and Jean-Christophe Agnew, a consummate intellectual both on and off the basketball court. Other Yale faculty also proved more than generous, and I thank Jon Butler, Nancy Cott, Michael Denning, James Fisher, Jules Prown, Leslie Rado, Alan Trachtenberg, and especially David Rodowick.

At the University of Colorado, I have been blessed with colleagues who have been both supportive friends and incisive critics. Special thanks to Susan Kent, Fred Anderson, and Patricia Nelson Limerick for reading the manuscript in various forms and offering useful advice. I have also benefited greatly from conversations with Virginia Anderson, Lee Chambers-Schiller, Julie Greene, Susan Johnson, and many others.

I owe much to other scholars who have read and commented on the project or its constituent parts. I am grateful to Daniel Belgrad, Leah Dilworth, Emily

Greenwald, J. Reeve Huston, Margaret Jacobs, William K. Powers, Lewis Segall, Richard Slotkin, Suzanne Smith, David Waldstreicher, Clarence Walker, John Wunder, Alfred F. Young, and especially Alexandra Harmon and Richard White. Many of the ideas in this book came out of conversations with friends and colleagues, including Jeff Auerbach, Ed Balleisen, Gregory Dowd, Amy Green, Kenneth Haltman, Laura Katzman, Tina Klein, Cynthia Ott, Gunther Peck, David Stowe, Glen Wallach, and Louis Warren. Special thanks to Michael Goldberg and Carlo Rotella, who, in their very different ways, have taught me so much.

I've also received advice, assistance, and critique from a wonderful group of students. Students in my cultural history seminar and in Robert Ferry's seminar on historical methods made many cogent suggestions. Michael Cohen offered an acute reading of the final chapter, and Cynthia Sliker read the entire manuscript with insight and care. Thanks also to Lynn Kallos for helping with last-minute loose ends.

I have relied heavily on friends and associates at many different libraries. I am especially grateful to George Miles, the Western Americana curator at Yale's Beinecke Rare Book Library, Karl Kabelac at the University of Rochester's Rush Rhees Library, and Carol Summerfield at the Newberry Library. I would also like to thank the staffs at the Philmont Museum, Columbia University, the Library of Congress, the State Museum of New York, the New York Historical Association, the Boulder Carnegie Library, the National Scouting Museum, the Bostonian Society, the Massachusetts Historical Society, and the University of Colorado, especially archivist Susie Bock and word-cruncher extraordinaire Patricia Murphy. At the Smithsonian Institution, William Sturtevant gave me access to a wonderful collection of play Indian costumes. Rayna Green helped point my way with her pathbreaking work on Indian wannabees.

This project has relied on financial support from both the College of Arts and Sciences and the Implementation of Multicultural Perspectives in Research and Teaching initiative at the University of Colorado. Early stages of the project were partially funded by a Dorothy Danforth Compton Fellowship and a Yale Dissertation Fellowship. I thank my department for granting me a semester of teaching leave to pull the manuscript together. I am especially grateful to Chuck Grench, Otto Bohlmann, Lawrence Kenney, and Laura Burrone at Yale University Press for shepherding me through the intricacies of academic publishing.

Jennifer Price and I found ourselves writing parallel projects, and I have benefited from her intellectual acuity and deep passion for writing in ways I cannot express. The book is far better for her insights, as it is for the help of all who have read, commented, discussed, and assisted. Any missteps in fact or interpretation are mine alone. I thank my family—Vine and Barbara Deloria, Tom Burns and Rosalin Burns—for friendship, babysitting, advice, and support. My children, Jackson and Lacey, have kept me excited about the difficult project of figuring out the workings of the world. My greatest debt, however, is to my wife, Peggy Burns, who has been steadfast in her love and encouragement. She is my model for real-world intelligence and perseverance, and this book is dedicated to her.

Notes

Introduction

1. My account draws on Benjamin Woods Labaree, *The Boston Tea Party* (New York: Oxford, 1964); Dirk Hoerder, *Crowd Action in Revolutionary Massachusetts, 1765–1780* (New York: Academic Press, 1977), 257–64; Francis S. Drake, *Tea Leaves: Being a Collection of Letters and Documents Relating to the Shipment of Tea to the American Colonies in the Year 1773, by the East India Company* (1884; reprint Detroit: Singing Tree Press, 1970); Alfred F. Young, "George Robert Twelves Hewes (1742–1840): A Boston Shoemaker and the Memory of the American Revolution," *William and Mary Quarterly*, 3d ser., 38 (October 1981): 561–623.

2. For the "critical moment" argument, see, for example, Wesley S. Griswold, *The Night the Revolution Began: The Boston Tea Party, 1773* (Brattleboro: Stephen Greene Press, 1972). For Tea Party as icon, see Ruth Miller Elston, *Guardians of Tradition: American Schoolbooks of the Nineteenth Century* (Lincoln: University of Nebraska Press, 1964); Michael Kammen, *A Season of Youth: The American Revolution and the Historical Imagination* (New York: Knopf, 1978), 117–21; Diana Karter Appelbaum, *The Glorious Fourth: An American Holiday, An American History* (New York: Facts on File, 1989), 164–65. The Bicentennial reenactment of the Tea Party in 1973 featured protests from the Sierra Club (polluting the harbor with tea), the Boston Indian Council (perpetuating derogatory stereotypes), the Disabled American Veterans (usurping their traditional celebration), anti-Nixon demonstrators (wiretapping is un-American), and Jeremy Rifkin's People's Bicentennial Committee (general discontent).

3. D. H. Lawrence, *Studies in Classic American Literature* (London: Martin Secker, 1924), 160.

4. D. H. Lawrence, *The Symbolic Meaning: The Uncollected Versions of Studies in Classic American Literature*, ed. Armin Arnold (London: Centaur Press, 1962), 70; Armin Arnold, *D. H. Lawrence and America* (London: Linden Press, 1958), 39–84, 105–62.

5. See Leslie Fiedler, *The Return of the Vanishing American* (New York: Stein and Day, 1968); Albert Keiser, *The Indian in American Literature* (New York: Oxford, 1933); Christopher Castiglia, *Bound and Determined: Captivity, Culture-Crossing, and White Womanhood from Mary Rowlandson to Patty Hearst* (Chicago: University of Chicago Press, 1996).

6. See, for example, Mabel Dodge Luhan, *Edge of Taos Desert: An Escape to Reality* (New York: Harcourt, Brace, 1937); Mary Austin, *The American Rhythm: Studies and Reexpressions of American Songs* (New York: Cooper Square, 1970); John Collier, *From Every Zenith: A Memoir* (Denver: Sage, 1963), 115–35. In New Jersey, William Carlos Williams was moving in similar directions, engaging "the Indian" repeatedly in his refiguring of history. See *In the American Grain* (New York: New Directions, 1953).

7. Lawrence, *Studies*, 40.

8. Jean-Jacques Rousseau, *First and Second Discourses*, trans. Roger and Judith R. Masters (New York: St. Martin's Press, 1964), 103–41. Among the countless treatments of the theme, see Roy Harvey Pearce, *Savagism and Civilization: A Study of the Indian and the American Mind*, 2d ed. (Baltimore: Johns Hopkins University Press, 1965); Robert F. Berkhofer, Jr., *The White Man's Indian: Images of the American Indian from Columbus to the Present* (New York: Vintage Books, 1979); Richard Slotkin, *Regeneration Through Violence: The Mythology of the American Frontier, 1600–1860* (Middletown: Wesleyan University Press, 1973); and *The Fatal Environment: The Myth of the Frontier in the Age of Industrialization, 1800–1890* (New York: Atheneum, 1985); Brian Dippie, *The Vanishing American: White Attitudes and U.S. Indian Policy* (Middletown: Wesleyan University Press, 1982); Tzvetan Todorov, *The Conquest of America: The Question of the Other*, trans. Richard Howard (New York: HarperPerennial, 1992).

9. Lawrence, *Studies*, 40.

10. Ibid., 36.

11. Eric Lott, *Love and Theft: Blackface Minstrelsy and the American Working Class* (New York: Oxford, 1993); David R. Roediger, *The Wages of Whiteness: Race and the Making of the American Working Class* (New York: Verso, 1991); Alexander Saxton, *The Rise and Fall of the White Republic: Class, Politics, and Mass Culture in Nineteenth-Century America* (New York: Verso, 1990); Shelley Fisher Fishkin, *Was Huck Black?: Mark Twain and African-American Voices* (New York: Oxford, 1993); Noel Ignatiev, *How the Irish Became White* (New York: Routledge, 1995). Michael Rogin, *Blackface, White Noise: Jewish Immigrants in the Hollywood Melting Pot* (Berkeley: University of California Press, 1996), 19–44. For a useful review, see Shelley Fisher Fishkin, "Interrogating 'Whiteness,' Complicating 'Blackness': Remapping American Culture," *American Quarterly* 47 (September 1995): 428–66.

12. Oliver Wendell Holmes, "The Ballad of the Boston Tea Party," *Songs of Many Seasons, 1862–1874* (Boston: James R. Osgood and Co., 1875), 31–35.

13. See, for example, Max Millard, "The Snafu over Snapple," *Indian Country Today* 14:1 (June 29, 1995): 1. For the superficiality of the idea of "blaming Indians" among patriots themselves, see Labaree, *Tea Party*, 148.

14. Although John Adams later wrote that he did not know the participants' identities. See Labaree, *Tea Party*, 142. Philip Davidson suggests that behind recognized mob leaders—Ebenezer Mackintosh, Isaac Sears, and Joseph Allicocke—were small groups of organizers

who did in fact keep their identities secret. See "Sons of Liberty and Stamp Men," *North Carolina Historical Review* 9 (January 1932): 39, 51. See also Dirk Hoerder, "Boston Leaders and Boston Crowds, 1765–1776," in *The American Revolution: Explorations in the History of American Radicalism*, ed. Alfred Young (DeKalb: Northern Illinois University Press, 1976); Drake, *Tea Leaves*, lxxiii, xci.

15. Drake, *Tea Leaves*, lxxxi.

16. I am not talking about what Richard White has christened "the middle ground," an interdependent, intercultural world in which Europeans often looked and acted a great deal like "Indians." For a materialist tradition, usefully juxtaposed with works on ideology (see n. 8), see White, *The Middle Ground: Indians, Empires, and Republics in the Great Lakes Region, 1650–1815* (New York: Cambridge, 1991); James Merrell, *The Indian's New World: Catawbas and Their Neighbors from European Contact through the Era of Removal* (Chapel Hill: Institute of Early American History and Culture by University of North Carolina Press, 1989); John Mack Faragher, *Daniel Boone: The Life and Legend of an American Pioneer* (New York: Henry Holt, 1992).

17. See, for example, Judith Butler, *Gender Trouble: Feminism and the Subversion of Identity* (New York: Routledge, 1990), 134–41; Terry Castle, *Masquerade and Civilization: The Carnivalesque in Eighteenth-Century English Culture and Fiction* (Stanford: Stanford University Press, 1986); Michael Bristol, *Carnival and Theater: Plebeian Culture and the Structure of Authority in Renaissance England* (New York: Methuen, 1985). For "playing Indian," see Rayna Green, "The Tribe Called Wannabee: Playing Indian in America and Europe," *Folklore* 99 (1988): 30–55; Robert Baird, "Going Indian: Discovery, Adoption, and Renaming Toward a 'True American,' from *Deerslayer* to *Dances with Wolves*," in *Dressing in Feathers: The Construction of the Indian in America Popular Culture*, ed. S. Elizabeth Bird (Boulder: Westview Press, 1996), 195–209.

18. Carroll Smith-Rosenberg, "Dis-covering the Subject of the 'Great Constitutional Discussion,' 1786–1789," *Journal of American History* 79 (December 1992): 841–73.

19. Like the Tea Partygoers, Mardi Gras Indians use Indianness to signify freedom, inversion, rebellion, and aboriginality, but they do so as part of a multifaceted creole culture that has blended African, Caribbean, and native (possibly Natchez) cultural practices with Indianness—both encountered and imagined—in culturally and historically unique ways. See Samuel Kinser, *Carnival, American Style: Mardi Gras at New Orleans and Mobile* (Chicago: University of Chicago Press, 1990), 151–214; Reid Mitchell, *All on a Mardi Gras Day: Episodes in the History of New Orleans Carnival* (Cambridge: Harvard University Press, 1995), 113–30; Michael P. Smith, "New Orleans Hidden Carnival: Traditional African-American Freedom Celebrations in Urban New Orleans," *Cultural Vistas* (Autumn 1990): 5–7, 19–22; George Lipsitz, *Time Passages: Collective Memory and American Popular Culture* (Minneapolis: University of Minnesota Press, 1990), 223–53; Les Blank, *Always for Pleasure* (Flower Films, 1978).

20. Lawrence, *Studies*, 26.

Chapter 1. Patriotic Indians and Identities of Revolution

1. My account is drawn from David E. Van Deventer, *The Emergence of Provincial New Hampshire, 1623–1741* (Baltimore: Johns Hopkins University Press, 1976); Jere R. Daniell, *Colonial New Hampshire: A History* (Millwood, N.Y.: KTO Press, 1981); Charles H. Bell, *History of Exeter, New Hampshire* (1888; rpt. Heritage Books, 1979), 73–75; Calvin Martin and Steven Crain, "The Indian Behind the Mask at the Boston Tea Party," *Indian Historian* 7 (Winter

1974): 45. See also Jeremy Belknap, *The History of New Hampshire* (The Sources of Science, no. 88, 2 vols., 1831; reprint, New York: Johnson Reprint Corp., 1970), 1–232; Nathaniel Adams, *Annals of Portsmouth* (Exeter, 1825; facsimile reprint, Bowie, Md.: Heritage Books, 1989), 158–66. For broader contexts, see Charles Clark, *The Eastern Frontier: The Settlement of Northern New England, 1610–1763* (New York: Knopf, 1970); Richard Hofstadter and Michael Wallace, eds., *American Violence: A Documentary History* (New York: Knopf, 1970), 110–11; Joseph J. Malone, *Pine Trees and Politics: The Naval Stores and Forest Policy in Colonial New England, 1691–1775* (Seattle: University of Washington Press, 1964), 111–12.

2. *Boston Evening Post*, December 26, 1768, 3.

3. The character of American crowds has interested generations of historians. Key touchstones include Gordon Wood, "A Note on Mobs in the American Revolution," *William and Mary Quarterly* 23 (1966): 639; Pauline Maier, "Popular Uprisings and Civil Authority in Eighteenth-Century America," *William and Mary Quarterly* 27 (1970): 3–35; Edward Countryman, "The Problem of the Early American Crowd," *Journal of American Studies* 7 (1973): 77–90; Thomas Slaughter, "Crowds in Eighteenth-Century America: Reflections and New Directions," *Pennsylvania Magazine of History and Biography* 115 (January 1991): 3–34. See also Edward Countryman, " 'Out of the Bounds of the Law': Northern Land Rioters in the Eighteenth Century," in *The American Revolution: Explorations in the History of American Radicalism*, ed. Alfred F. Young (Dekalb: Northern Illinois University Press, 1976), 37–69; Brian Palmer, "Discordant Music: Charivari and white capping in North America," *Labor / Le Travailleur* 1 (September 1978): 5–62; Susan G. Davis, *Parades and Power: Street Theater in Nineteenth-Century Philadelphia* (Philadelphia: Temple University Press, 1986), 97–98.

4. Samuel Adams to James Warren, January 10, 1774, Warren-Adams Papers, I, 20, Massachusetts Historical Society, as quoted in Labaree, *Tea Party*, 150. See Drake, *Tea Leaves*, lxxxv, for two incidents in New York in April 1774. See Labaree, *Tea Party*, 161–66, for Indians harassing merchants, destroying a tavern, and executing the Second Boston Tea Party in March 1774.

5. For proclamation, see Drake, *Tea Leaves*, cxlvii. For New York Mohawks, see Labaree, *Tea Party*, 95; Drake, xix.

6. Indian-garbed social violence would later appear in western Pennsylvania, upstate New York, Maine, and southern New England and would persist through the 1840s. See, for example, Alan Taylor, *Liberty Men and Great Proprietors: The Revolutionary Settlement on the Maine Frontier, 1760–1820* (Chapel Hill: University of North Carolina Press for the Institute of Early American History and Culture, Williamsburg, 1990); J. Reeve Huston, "Land and Freedom: The Anti-rent Wars, Jacksonian Politics, and the Contest over Free Labor in New York, 1785–1865" (Ph.D. diss., Yale University, 1994); James Fenimore Cooper, *The Redskins: Indian and Injin* (New York: Stringer and Townsend, 1855); Hugh Henry Brackenridge, *Incidents of the Insurrection in the Western Parts of Pennsylvania, in the Year 1794* (Philadelphia: John McCulloch, 1795).

7. *History of the Schuylkill Fishing Company of the State in Schuylkill* (Philadelphia, 1889), in Edwin P. Kilroe, *Saint Tammany and the Origin of the Society of Tammany or Columbian Order in the City of New York* (New York: Edwin P. Kilroe, 1913) n. 74, p. 80. For unpublished Tammany material, see the Edwin Kilroe Papers at Columbia University's Rare Book and Manuscript Library. Especially useful are the extensive collections of colonial newsclippings found in

boxes 26, 28, and 29. Also useful are Francis Von A. Cabeen, "The Society of the Sons of Saint Tammany of Philadelphia," *Pennsylvania Magazine of History and Biography* 25 (1901) 433, and subsequent installments in v. 26 and 27; Jerome Mushkat, *Tammany: The Evolution of a Political Machine, 1789–1865* (Syracuse: Syracuse University Press, 1971); Samuel W. Williams, "The Tammany Society in Ohio," *Ohio Archeological and Historical Publications* 22 (1913): 349. See also Euphemia Vale Blake, *History of the Tammany Society from its Organization to the Present Time* (New York: Souvenir Publishing, 1901); and Rufus Home, "The Story of Tammany," *Harpers New Monthly Magazine* 44:263 (April 1872): 685–96.

8. Kilroe, *Tammany*, 37, 84. Kilroe argues that the fishing club was organized in 1732 but suggests that the earliest date one can assign to the May first festival is 1752 (see 124–25). As a direct descendent of traditional European May Day festivities, the festival may well have been in existence before 1732, the figure of Tammany being grafted on gradually during the first half of the eighteenth century. On the other hand, as Alfred Young has suggested, certain European customs may have become dormant in America and then been reconstituted after periods of disuse. Alfred Young, "English Plebeian Culture and Eighteenth-Century American Radicalism," in *The Origins of Anglo-American Radicalism*, ed. Margaret Jacob and James Jacob (London: Allen and Unwin, 1984), 186–89.

9. For transformation, see Kilroe, *Tammany*, 38. For motto, see ibid., 26. In a verse pamphlet published in 1756, Nicholas Scull explained the motto: "To form some idea of [the word's] signification you may imagine a man with his wife and children about him and with an air of resolution calling out to his Enemy, 'All these God has given me, and I will defend them.' " See Von A. Cabeen, "The Sons of Saint Tammany," 437; Townsend Ward, "Restoration of the Schuylkill gun to the State in Schuylkill, April 23, 1884," *Pennsylvania Magazine of History and Biography* 8 (1884): 199–215.

10. Natalie Zemon Davis, "The Reasons of Misrule: Youth Groups and Charivaris in Sixteenth-Century France," *Past and Present* 50 (1971): 41–75; Peter Burke, *Popular Culture in Early Modern Europe* (New York: New York University Press, 1978), 178–204.

11. Through these temporary definitions, I hope to leave the terms linked tightly while preserving an analytical distinction that allows a separate discussion of the predominantly holiday aspects of the Tammany societies and the equally predominant concern with custom and social transgression that characterized the Mast Tree rioters.

12. For titles, see Davis, "Reasons of Misrule," 42–44. See also Burke, *Popular Culture*, 178–85; Mikhail Bakhtin, *Rabelais and His World* (Cambridge: MIT Press, 1968), 74–78; James G. Frazer, *The Golden Bough: A Study in Magic and Religion*, 3d ed. (New York: Macmillan, 1935) 9:334–38. For rough music, see E. P. Thompson, *Customs in Common: Studies in Traditional Popular Culture* (New York: New Press, 1993), 467–538. For England, see Bernard Capp, "English Youth Groups and 'The Pinder of Wakefield,' " in *Rebellion, Popular Protest and the Social Order in Early Modern England*, ed. Paul Slack (Cambridge: Cambridge University Press, 1984), 212–18.

13. For transformation, see Davis, "Reasons of Misrule," 69; Martin Ingram, "Ridings, Rough Music, and 'Popular Culture,' " *Past and Present* 105 (November 1984): 95, 109. Ingram suggests that by the early eighteenth century in London, ridings were organized by such low-status occupational groups as porters. For *revel*, see Michael Holquist, "Introduction," in Bakhtin, *Rabelais and His World*, xviii. Bakhtin, 119, notes the explicit connections

made by the leaders of the French Revolution between Rabelaisian carnival and revolutionary spirit. For a historical treatment of the links between carnival and social protest, see Emmanuel Le Roy Ladurie, *Carnival in Romans*, trans. Mary Feeney (New York: Braziller, 1979).

14. Bakhtin, *Rabelais*, 10. See also Michael D. Bristol, *Carnival and Theater: Plebeian Culture and the Structure of Authority in Renaissance England* (New York: Methuen, 1985), 41. For a more complex reading of carnival, see Peter Stallybrass and Allon White, *The Politics and Poetics of Transgression* (Ithaca: Cornell University Press, 1986), 1–79.

15. Bakhtin, *Rabelais*, 9, 24, 26, 249, 217. For a compilation of such rituals, see Frazer, *Golden Bough* 3: esp. 246–53.

16. David Ridgely, *Annals of Annapolis* (Baltimore, 1841), as quoted in Kilroe, *Tammany*, 86.

17. See, for example, P. H. Ditchfield, *Old English Customs Extant at the Present Time: An Account of Local Observances, Festival Customs, and Ancient Ceremonies yet Surviving in Great Britain* (1896; reprint Detroit: Singing Tree Press, 1968), 95–110; Roy Christian, *Old English Customs* (New York: Hastings House, 1966), 34–45.

18. New York Journal and Patriotic Register, May 19, 1792. See Kilroe Papers, box 26, "Reproductions" file.

19. Peter Shaw, *American Patriots and the Rituals of Revolution* (Cambridge: Harvard University Press, 1981), 212–13. Shaw connects blackfaced revolutionary riots to the ritual symbols of European fire-sacrificed fertility deities—Robin of the Wood, Jack in the Green, the wodewose (a figure covered with leaves), and the "wild man of the woods." As an American wild man linked to the forest and to American abundance, Tammany's mythic passing recapitulated these older festival traditions of fiery death and new birth. See also Frazer, *Golden Bough* 7:31–33. The Tammany bucktail (the tail portion of a deer), an omnipresent carnival badge worn by Tammany paraders, also had its origins in Europe as a token of good luck.

20. Bakhtin, *Rabelais*, 84–85. With their constant rejoinders to the patron saints of Britain, Tammany members offered their saint up as not only a rival, but, in the best tradition of misrule, as a parody as well. The transfer of power from Indian to colonist appeared frequently in the literary efforts of the late eighteenth and early nineteenth centuries. See Werner Sollors, *Beyond Ethnicity: Consent and Descent in American Culture* (Oxford: Oxford University Press, 1986), 102–30. For representative examples, see Philip Freneau, "The Prophecy of King Tammany" (1782), "The Dying Indian" (1784), "Sketches of American History" (1784), "Death Song of a Cherokee Indian" (1787), "The Indian Burying Ground" (1788), in *The Poems of Philip Freneau, Poet of the American Revolution*, vol. 2, ed. Fred Lewis Patee (Princeton: Princeton Library, 1903); Fitz-Greene Halleck, "Red Jacket," in *The Poetical Writings of Fitz-Greene Halleck* (New York: Appleton, 1869), 46–50.

21. Leacock, *Fall of British Tyranny*, as quoted in Kilroe, *Tammany*, 33–36. See also Carla Mulford, "Introduction," in John Leacock, *The First Book of the American Chronicles of the Times, 1774–1775* (Newark: University of Delaware Press, 1987); Francis Dallett, Jr., "John Leacock and the Fall of British Tyranny," *Pennsylvania Magazine of History and Biography* 78 (1954): 456–75. For Philadelphia context, see Carl Bridenbaugh and Jessica Bridenbaugh, *Rebels and Gentlemen: Philadelphia in the Age of Franklin* (New York: Oxford University Press, 1962), 240–63.

22. Even as the song establishes American difference through food, however, it refuses

to critique English roast beef and the equally tasty figure of John Bull. Caught between Indianness and Britishness, Leacock and many other Americans may have found it difficult to sever their connections so overtly.

23. For liberating feasting, see Bakhtin, *Rabelais*, 276, 281–83. For the "carne in carnival," see Burke, *Popular Culture*, 186. For other Tammany odes, see Kilroe, *Tammany*, 39–46, 79.

24. William Wood, *New England's Prospect*, ed. Alden T. Vaughn (Amherst: University of Massachusetts Press, 1977), 41–57.

25. Most Europeans perceived Indian hunting in a negative manner: If farming was work and hunting leisure, then, as hunters, Indian men were lazy and, as farmers rather than domestics, Indian women were enslaved. Not surprisingly, the St. Tammany societies emphasized the positive, liberating implications of Indian hunting.

26. The politicized Tammany celebrations were confined to the immediate area surrounding Philadelphia and perhaps the Chesapeake. Further south, Tammany revels were less self-conscious about patriotism and national identity.

27. Robert F. Berkhofer, Jr., *The White Man's Indian: Images of the American Indian from Columbus to the Present* (New York: Vintage Books, 1979), 3.

28. For "distance," see Tzvetan Todorov, *The Conquest of America: The Question of the Other*, trans. Richard Howard (New York: Harper and Row, 1992), 3. For Otherness in general, see Edward Said, *Orientalism* (New York: Pantheon, 1978); Johannes Fabian, *Time and the Other: How Anthropology Makes its Object* (New York: Columbia University Press, 1983); William Desmond, *Desire, Dialectic, and Otherness: An Essay on Origins* (New Haven: Yale University Press, 1987); James Axtell, "Imagining the Other: First Encounters in North America," *Beyond 1492: Encounters in Colonial North America* (New York: Oxford University Press, 1992); Stephen Greenblatt, *Marvelous Possessions: The Wonder of the New World* (Chicago: University of Chicago Press, 1991), 119–51; Eve Kornfeld, "Encountering the Other: American Intellectuals and Indians in the 1790s," *William and Mary Quarterly* 3d ser., 52 (April 1995): 287–314.

29. Indians could, for example, signify civilized colonial philosophe (interior/noble), fearsome colonial soldier (interior/savage), noble, natural man (exterior/noble), or barbarous savage (exterior/savage). Americans were hardly monolithic in their engagements with Indians and Indian Otherness. See Carroll Smith-Rosenberg, "Dis-covering the Subject of the 'Great Constitutional Discussion,' 1786–1789," *Journal of American History* 79 (December 1992): 848.

30. On constructing nationalism, see Benedict Anderson, *Imagined Communities: Reflections on the Origin and Spread of Nationalism* (New York: Verso, 1991).

31. Multiple definitional vectors are at work here. The gentrified, urban Tammany societies likely saw themselves in opposition not only to the British, but to the Scotch-Irish "rabble" of the backcountry, whose claims to authority revolved around the elimination of Indian people from the region. Dressing as an Indian could mean liberty in relation to Great Britain, while it simultaneously meant social order in relation to the Paxton Boys and other backcountry Indian-haters. Likewise, Indian-haters like "Black Boy" James Smith might don Indian clothes to kill Indians or attack Indian traders, a statement that carried equally complex resonances for Britons, Philadelphia Quakers, and backcountry residents. The notion of Indianness as a signifier of political control over the landscape is, of course, especially pertinent in this context. See Alan Tully, *Forming American Politics: Ideals, Interests, and*

Institutions in Colonial New York and Pennsylvania (Baltimore: Johns Hopkins University Press, 1994), 182–202. For James Smith, see Francis Parkman, *The Conspiracy of Pontiac and the Indian War after the Conquest of Canada* (Boston: Little, Brown, 1890) 2:98.

32. For Puritan prohibitions, see Shaw, *Rituals*, 198; Ingram, "Ridings," 100–03; Bruce C. Daniels, *Puritans at Play: Leisure and Recreation in Colonial New England* (New York: St. Martin's Press, 1995), 88–91, 100–02; George Lee Haskins, *Law and Authority in Early Massachusetts: A Study in Tradition and Design* (New York: Macmillan, 1960), 76–84; Michael Zuckerman, "Pilgrims in the Wilderness: Community, Modernity, and the Maypole at Merry Mount," *New England Quarterly* 50 (June 1977): 255. See also Roger Abrahams and Richard Bauman, "Ranges of Festival Behavior," in *The Reversible World: Symbolic Inversion in Art and Society*, ed. Barbara Babcock (Ithaca: Cornell University Press, 1978), 194, for a consideration of the role of religious and national origins in different festival behaviors.

33. E. P. Thompson, *Whigs and Hunters: The Origins of the Black Act* (New York: Pantheon, 1975), 58, speculates that the fear of informants may have given rise to "a direct tradition, stretching across centuries, of secret poaching fraternities or associations in forest areas." See also Pat Rogers, "The Waltham Blacks and the Black Act," *History Journal* 17 (1974): 483; P. B. Munsche, *Gentlemen and Poachers: The English Game Laws, 1671–1831* (Cambridge: Cambridge University Press, 1981); and John Brock, "Whigs and Deer-Stealers in Other Guises: A Return to the Origins of the Black Act," *Past and Present* 119 (May 1988): 56.

34. Thompson, *Customs in Common*, 185–258. See also *Whigs and Hunters*, 32, n.1, 39–40, 52–53, 60–62; *Customs in Common*, 1–7; Munsche, *Gentlemen and Poachers*, 53. Esther Cohen, "Law, Folklore, and Animal Lore," *Past and Present* 110 (February 1986): 10, offers an account of blurring of law and custom in the animal trials of the thirteenth through eighteenth centuries.

35. Thompson, *Customs in Common*, 4, 117–20. Ingram, "Ridings," 92, notes that the customary social sanction of the charivari was similar to the official punishments meted out by English courts—both might feature rough music, carting backwards, and ducking. See also Donald R. Kelley, "Second Nature: The Idea of Custom," in *The Transmission of Culture in Early Modern Europe*, ed. Anthony Grafton and Ann Blair (Philadelphia: University of Pennsylvania Press, 1990), 131–72.

36. For elite dominance, see Thompson, *Whigs and Hunters*, 104–14. For competing gentries, see Munsche, *Gentlemen and Poachers*, 1–27. For plebeian resistance, see Thompson, *Whigs and Hunters*, 64. For a counterargument, see Brock, "Whigs and Deer Stealers," 65–70. Brock suggests that Windsor Forest, because of its immediate connection with the Crown, may have seen exceptional enforcement of the Black Act as part of Robert Walpole's attempts to win the political favor of George I by cracking down on Jacobin conspiracies. But see also Thompson, *Whigs and Hunters*, 198–206, for his contextualizing of the Whig-Walpole connection. Thompson argues in *Customs in Common*, 103, that resistance was directed not just at royal incursions but at a general pattern of appropriations of common rights.

37. Davis, "Meanings of Misrule," 55. See also Ingram, "Ridings"; Thompson, "Rough Music"; Violet Alford, "Rough Music or Charivari," *Folklore* 70 (December 1959): 505–18; Davis, "The Reasons of Misrule," 41–75.

38. For Black Act, see Thompson, *Whigs and Hunters*, 21–23. See Eveline Cruickshanks and Howard Erskine-Hill, "The Waltham Black Act and Jacobitism," *Journal of British Studies*

24 (1985): 358–65; and Brock, "Whigs and Deer Stealers," 69–71. For penalties, see Thompson, *Whigs and Hunters*, 75–79.

39. Alfred F. Young, "English Plebeian Culture and Eighteenth-Century American Radicalism," 187–89. For immigration and migration, see Ian Steele, *The English Atlantic, 1675–1740: An Exploration of Communication and Community* (New York: Oxford University Press, 1986); Henry A. Gemery, "European Emigration to North America, 1700–1820: Numbers and Quasi-Numbers," *Perspectives in American History* n.s. 1 (1984): 283–328; Clifford K. Shipton, "Immigration to New England, 1680–1740," *Journal of Political Economy* 44 (1936): 225–39; A. Roger Ekirch, *Bound for America: The Transportation of British Convicts to the Colonies, 1718–1775* (Oxford: Clarendon Press, 1987); Roger Thompson, *Mobility and Migration: East Anglian Founders of New England, 1629–1640* (Amherst: University of Massachusetts Press, 1994); and Bernard Bailyn, *The Peopling of British North America: An Introduction* (New York: Knopf, 1986).

40. In the late 1620s (to turn from Massachusetts Bay to Plymouth Plantation) a similar process unfolded when Thomas Morton planted a maypole at Merry Mount, revived old English holidays, and caroused with local Indian people. The residents of Plymouth responded with vicious attacks—rhetorical, legal, and military—against this Lord of Misrule. Morton represented everything the Pilgrims feared most—acculturation to the paired evils of Indian Otherness and carnival sensuality (not to mention Anglicanism and superior trading relations with New England Indian people). See William Bradford, *Of Plymouth Plantation 1620–1647* (New York: Modern Library, 1981), 226–32; Zuckerman, "Pilgrims in the Wilderness"; Slotkin, *Regeneration Through Violence*, 64; and Thomas Morton, *New English Canaan*, with introductory matter and notes by Charles Francis Adams, Jr. (1883; reprint, New York: Burt Franklin, 1967, Research and Source Works Series No. 131), 276–96.

41. See Shaw, *Rituals*, 198–99; Ingram, "Ridings," 100–03 for English Puritan attacks on charivari. For the relationship between Puritan culture and law, see Haskins, *Law and Authority in Early Massachusetts*, 76–84, and Zuckerman, "Pilgrims in the Wilderness." See Shaw, *Rituals*, 198, for civic holidays, and 204–10 for a detailed recounting of the origins and transformations of Pope Day.

42. Thompson, *Customs in Common*, 6.

43. See, for example, Edward Countryman, *Americans: A Collision of Histories* (Hill and Wang, 1996), 49–65.

44. For a detailed list, see "List of Gentlemen Invited to St. Tammany Celebration, May 1, 1773," Miscellaneous folder, box 26, Edwin Kilroe Papers, Columbia University Rare Book and Manuscript Library. For festival and print culture, see David Waldstreicher, "Rites of Rebellion, Rites of Assent: Celebrations, Print Culture, and the Origins of American Nationalism," *Journal of American History* 82 (June 1995): 37–61.

45. Smith-Rosenberg, "Dis-covering the Subject of the 'Great Constitutional Discussion,'" 841–73. For continuity between European folk traditions and American political protests, see Susan G. Davis, *Parades and Power*, 14, 73–77, 96–109.

46. Daniell, *Colonial New Hampshire*, 162, 202; Bell, *History of Exeter*, 72; Van Deventer, *Provincial New Hampshire*, n. 76, 268.

47. Daniels, *Puritans at Play*, 102–05. Abrahams and Bauman, "Ranges of Behavior," 195, point out the fallacy of seeing inversion festivals as absolute reversals of what is. Inversion creates antitheses of ideal normative systems rather than actual ones. Abrahams and Bau-

man found disorder an ongoing phenomenon in most communities: "The same people who engage in license during festivals are the community agents of disorder during the remainder of the year." The Sons of Liberty and Saint Tammany, then, may be identified as consistent agents of social disorder who took advantage of the license allowed by festival.

48. For comparison, see Lester C. Olson, *Emblems of American Community in the Revolutionary Era: A Study in Rhetorical Iconology* (Washington: Smithsonian Institution Press, 1991), 77. See also E. McClung Fleming, "The American Image as Indian Princess," *Winterthur Portfolio* 2 (1965): 65–81; John Higham, "Indian Princess and Roman Goddess: The First Female Symbols of America," *Proceedings of the American Antiquarian Society* 100 (1990): 45–79; Joan D. Dolmetsch, *Rebellion and Reconciliation: Satirical Prints on the Revolution at Williamsburg* (Williamsburg: Colonial Williamsburg Foundation, 1976).

49. Olson, *Emblems*, 78.

50. Ibid., 115.

51. Castle, *Masquerade and Civilization*, 78. For oppositional identity and the carnivalesque, see Stuart Clark, "Inversion, Misrule, and Witchcraft," *Past and Present* 87 (May 1980): 98–127; Ingram, "Ridings," 98–99.

52. See, for example, James Merrell, *The Indian's New World: Catawbas and Their Neighbors from European Contact through the Era of Removal* (Chapel Hill: University of North Carolina Press for the Institute of Early American History and Culture, 1989), 145–50; Eric Hinderaker, "The 'Four Indian Kings' and the Imaginative Construction of the First British Empire," *William and Mary Quarterly* 3d ser., 53 (July 1996): 487–526. Francis Jennings, William N. Fenton, Mary A. Druke, and David R. Miller, eds., *The History and Culture of Iroquois Diplomacy: An Interdisciplinary Guide to the Treaties of the Six Nations and Their League* (Syracuse: Syracuse University Press, 1985), 115–31, offers a glossary of metaphoric treaty terms and an explanation of some of the key rituals of peacemaking. These included the Indian custom of naming non-Indians, most notably the bestowing upon American representative George Morgan the name/title, "Tammany." New York governor Cadwallader Colden was similarly honored. See Kilroe, *Tammany*, 49, 70; Gregory Schaaf, *Wampum Belts and Peace Trees* (Golden: Fulcrum, 1990), 125. See also George R. Stewart, *Names on the Land: A Historical Account of Place-Naming in the United States* (New York: Random House, 1945), and for metaphor at the Tea Party, Drake, *Tea Leaves*, lxxxi.

53. With a diverse set of origins in linguistics, semiotics, and structural anthropology, this line of thought has become a central issue for scholars. Bakhtin argued that languages possess a specific social nature and that, as words collided, their social content oozed from one context to another. Contact led inescapably to transformation. See *Rabelais*, 456–59. See also Homi K. Bhabha, *The Location of Culture* (New York: Routledge, 1994), 1–18, 40–92; Emily Schultz, *Dialogue at the Margins: Whorf, Bakhtin, and Linguistic Relativity* (Madison: University of Wisconsin Press, 1990); Michael Holquist, *Dialogism: Bakhtin and His World* (New York: Routledge, 1990). Ann Norton, *Reflections on Political Identity* (Baltimore: Johns Hopkins University Press, 1988), 42–49. For a useful survey of theories of language, see Terence Hawkes, *Structuralism and Semiotics* (Berkeley: University of California Press, 1977).

54. For Indian metaphor, see Cadwallader Colden, *History of the Five Indian Nations of Canada* (1747; reprint, Toronto: Coles, 1972), xiii: "The Indians having but few words, and few complex ideas, use many metaphors in their discourse, which interpreted by an unskillful tongue, may appear mean, and strike our imagination faintly; but under the pen of a skilful

representer, might strongly move our passions by the lively images." On metaphor, see Bristol, *Carnival and Theater*, 45. For its limits, see Merrell, *Indian's New World*, 149. For toasts, see *Pennsylvania Packet*, May 11, 1787, as quoted in Von A. Cabeen, "The Sons of Saint Tammany," 463.

55. Metaphor is similar to punning in this respect. Peter Shaw, *Rituals*, 12, notes the prevalence of puns turned during the Stamp Act riots: "In a pun, the meaning of a word is reversed yet retained." On inversion and metaphor, see Barbara Babcock, "Introduction," in *The Reversible World*, 15.

56. *Pennsylvania Evening Herald*, May 6, 1786, as quoted in Von A. Cabeen, "The Sons of Saint Tammany," 453.

57. Although *literal* boundary crossings between colonists and actual Indians were a different matter. Fascination with becoming Other, however, was part of broader cultural practice. A dominant cultural form in England, the Masquerade, devoted itself to the costumed crossing of identity boundaries. Masquerade became popular at about the same time the Blacks asserted their control over Windsor Forest (one of the word's possible roots, *mascherer*, meant in Old French, "to blacken the face"), and it remained in vogue until the late 1780s. See Castle, *Masquerade and Civilization*, for a thorough treatment of masquerade.

58. See Grant McCracken, "Clothing as Language: An Object Lesson in the Study of the Expressive Properties of Material Culture," in *Material Anthropology: Contemporary Approaches to Material Culture*, ed. Barrie Reynolds and Margaret A. Stott (University Press of America, 1987), 108–09; Ruth P. Rubenstein, *Dress Codes: Meanings and Messages in American Culture* (Boulder: Westview Press, 1995), 3–15, 191–220; James Fernandez, "The Performance of Ritual Metaphors," in *The Social Use of Metaphor*, ed. J. David Sapir and J. Christopher Crooker (Philadelphia: University of Pennsylvania Press, 1977) 100–31; Timothy J. Shannon, "Dressing for Success on the Mohawk Frontier: Hendrick, William Johnson, and the Indian Fashion," *William and Mary Quarterly* 3d ser., 53 (1996): 13–42.

59. Shaw, *Rituals*, 11.

60. Structuring identity in terms of Otherness requires dualistic oppositions—on one side a Self, on the other, so to speak, an Other. The relation between the two is usually seen as dialectical. Robert Stam, *Subversive Pleasures: Bakhtin, Cultural Criticism, and Film* (Baltimore: Johns Hopkins University Press, 1989), 5, notes that "even when looking within oneself, one looks in and through the eyes of the other, one needs the other's gaze to constitute oneself as self." Such a dialectic also implies hybridity or even utopian fusion with the Other. Dialectically minded Americans have long toyed with these ideas through the wilderness marriage, a literary and rhetorical device in which American self-identity is constituted through the synthesis of European colonist and indigenous Indian. For a particularly acute reading, see Slotkin, *Regeneration Through Violence*, 191–92.

61. I draw this notion of simultaneity from the writings of Walter Benjamin, especially his formulation of the dialectical image. See, for example, *Illuminations: Essays and Reflections*, ed. Hannah Arendt (New York: Schocken, 1968), esp. 262–64; Susan Buck-Morss, *The Origin of Negative Dialectics: Theodor W. Adorno, Walter Benjamin, and the Frankfurt Institute* (New York: Free Press, 1977). On performance and the doubledness of costume (in this case drag), see Judith Butler, *Gender Trouble: Feminism and the Subversion of Identity* (New York: Routledge, 1990), 136–37. See also Marjorie Garber, *Vested Interests: Cross Dressing and Cultural Anxiety* (New York: Routledge, 1992).

62. See Victor Turner, "Variations on a Theme of Liminality," in *Secular Ritual*, ed. Sally F. Moore and Barbara G. Myerhoff (Amsterdam: Van Gorcum, 1977); and "Notes and Conclusions," in Babcock, *The Reversible World*. See also Norton, *Reflections on Political Identity*, 53–55, 81–84.

63. Bristol, *Carnival and Theater*, 30.

64. See Turner, "Variations on a Theme," 43–46, and "Notes and Conclusions," 281.

65. For the rite of passage element in the Revolution, see Michael Kammen, *A Season of Youth: The American Revolution and the Historical Imagination* (New York: Knopf, 1978), 198–211.

66. Ibid., 3–32, 246–256.

67. For three-way, see Helen Carr, *Inventing the American Primitive: Politics, Gender, and the Representation of American Literary Traditions, 1789–1936* (New York: New York University Press, 1996), 34.

Chapter 2. Fraternal Indians and Republican Identities

1. James Fenimore Cooper, *The Redskins: Indian and Injin: Being the Conclusion of the Littlepage Manuscripts* (New York: Stringer and Townsend, 1855), 272. The book was first published in 1846 by Burgess and Stringer of New York. See Robert E. Spiller and Philip C. Blackburn, *A Descriptive Bibliography of the Writings of James Fenimore Cooper* (New York: R. R. Bowker, 1934), 145. For post-Revolution ambiguity surrounding the idea of revolution, see Michael Kammen, *A Season of Youth: The American Revolution and the Historical Imagination* (New York: Knopf, 1978).

2. For Cooper, see Alan Taylor, *William Cooper's Town: Power and Persuasion on the Frontier of the Early American Republic* (New York: Knopf, 1996), 406–27; Charles Hansford Adams, *"The Guardian of the Law": Authority and Identity in James Fenimore Cooper* (University Park: Pennsylvania State University Press, 1990); William P. Kelly, *Plotting America's Past: Fenimore Cooper and the Leatherstocking Tales* (Carbondale: Southern Illinois University Press, 1983), 1–44; Albert Keiser, *The Indian in American Literature* (New York: Oxford, 1933), 112–17. For Cooper's reimagining of noble Indians, see *Redskins*, 272–74.

3. Franklin Ellis, *History of Columbia County, New York* (Philadelphia: Everts and Ensign, 1878), as quoted in Alfred F. Young, *The Democratic Republicans of New York: The Origins, 1763–1797* (Chapel Hill: Published for the Institute of Early American History and Culture by University of North Carolina Press, 1967), 205. The farmers, who had fled to Connecticut before being apprehended, were later acquitted by a jury. See also Martin Bruegel, "Unrest: Manorial Society and the Market in the Hudson Valley, 1780–1850," *Journal of American History* 82 (March 1996): 1393–1424; J. Reeve Huston, "Land and Freedom: The Anti-rent Wars, Jacksonian Politics, and the Contest over Free Labor in New York, 1785–1865" (Ph.D. diss., Yale University, 1994); Alan Taylor, "Agrarian Independence: Northern Land Rioters after the Revolution," in *Beyond the American Revolution: Explorations in the History of American Radicalism*, ed. Alfred F. Young (Dekalb: Northern Illinois University Press, 1993), 221–45; David Maldwyn Ellis, *Landlords and Farmers in the Hudson-Mohawk Region, 1790–1850* (Ithaca: Cornell University Press, 1946); Henry Christman, *Tin Horns and Calico: A Decisive Episode in the Emergence of Democracy* (New York: Holt, 1945); Jeremy Mumford, "Indian Country: The Construction of a Masquerade Identity in the Hudson River Valley Anti-Rent Movement," M.A. thesis, Columbia University, 1996.

4. Young, *Democratic Republicans*, 103–22, 187–94, 534–38. See also Carroll Smith-Rosenberg, "Dis-covering the Subject of the 'Great Constitutional Discussion,' 1786–1789," *Journal of American History* 79 (December 1992): 841–73.

5. Alan Taylor, *Liberty Men and Great Proprietors: The Revolutionary Settlement on the Maine Frontier, 1760–1820* (Chapel Hill: University of North Carolina Press for The Institute of Early American History and Culture, 1990), 264–79.

6. Ibid., 186–87.

7. Unlike the Maine tenants, the whiskey rebels acknowledged the success of the Revolution, arguing that liberty had been betrayed by a power-hungry federal government. My account of the Whiskey Rebellion is based on Thomas Slaughter, *The Whiskey Rebellion: Frontier Epilogue to the American Revolution* (New York: Oxford, 1986), and on the essays found in *The Whiskey Rebellion: Past and Present Perspectives*, ed. Steven R. Boyd (Westport: Greenwood Press, 1985).

8. Other groups blacked their faces and donned women's clothes—a common practice in Europe. Crossing the boundary of gender rather than Indianness suggested the changing dynamics of race. In the post-Revolution backcountry, racial difference was both more monolithic and far more negative. As an Other, a generic woman was more interior than the now-exteriorized figure of the Indian. The use of gendered dress may also have signified the rebels' more recent European origins. Tom the Tinker—a prominent English figure of agrarian rebellion—played a significant role in the uprising's rhetoric. Slaughter, *Whiskey Rebellion*, 113–15, 184.

9. For treaty, see *Pittsburgh Gazette*, August 23, 1794, as quoted in Hugh Henry Brackenridge, *Incidents of the Insurrection in the Western Parts of Pennsylvania, in the year 1794* (Philadelphia: John McCullock, 1795), 6. That the Whiskey Rebellion was a contest over the location of authority became clear in 1794, when a horseman brandishing a tomahawk rode through the streets of Pittsburgh proclaiming, "This is not all that I want: it is not the excise law only that must go down; your district and associate judges must go down; your high offices and salaries. A great deal more is to be done; I am but beginning yet." See Slaughter, *Whiskey Rebellion*, 186–87.

10. For parallels, see Slaughter, *Whiskey Rebellion*, 115.

11. Eric Hinderaker, *Elusive Empires: Constructing Colonialism in the Ohio Valley, 1673–1800* (New York: Cambridge University Press, 1997), 157–61.

12. For a complex reading of the revolutionary situation as it pertained to Indian people, see Richard White, *The Middle Ground: Indians, Empires, and Republics in the Great Lakes Region, 1650–1815* (Cambridge: Cambridge University Press, 1991), 366–412. For Jane McCrae, see Alfred Young and Terry J. Fife, with Mary E. Janzen, *We the People: Voices and Images of the New Nation* (Philadelphia: Temple University Press, 1993), 95.

13. Hinderaker, *Elusive Empires*, 226–45. See also Reginald Horsman, *The Frontier in the Formative Years, 1783–1815* (New York: Holt, Rinehart, and Winston, 1970).

14. As quoted in Francis Von A. Cabeen, "The Society of the Sons of Saint Tammany of Philadelphia," *Pennsylvania Magazine of History and Biography* 26:4 (1902): 443–47.

15. *Independent*, May 6, 1786. "Common Sense" is one of many italicized words implying intentional double meanings. See also Von A. Cabeen, ibid., 26:3 (1902): 446, 453; 27:1 (1903): 37, 40.

16. Philadelphia had a reconstituted (and long-lived) Tammany Society as early as 1793.

The origins of this group, however, should properly be located in New York. In newspaper accounts of the new group's annual celebrations, one finds references to the New Yorkers as "elder brothers" and the subsidiary name "Columbian Order," which clearly originated in New York. The Philadelphia Tammany group seems to have shared the New Yorkers' later affinity for Democratic-Republican politics. See, for example, The General Advertiser (Philadelphia), May 13, 1793; The Timepiece, May 1797. For other New York references, see Philadelphia Aurora, May 15, 1806, May 15, 1807, and May 14, 1808. Kilroe Papers, box 28, folder of clippings, 1750–1800, and folder of clippings, 1800–1850.

17. For the Tammany society in this time period, see Jerome Mushkat, Tammany: The Evolution of a Political Machine 1789–1865 (Syracuse: Syracuse University Press, 1971). See also Edwin P. Kilroe, Saint Tammany and the Origins of the Society of Tammany or Columbian Order in the City of New York (New York: Edwin P. Kilroe, 1913), and Von A. Cabeen, "The Society of the Sons of Saint Tammany of Philadelphia," Pennsylvania Magazine of History and Biography 25:4 (1901): 433–51, and subsequent installments in vol. 26, nos. 1–4 and vol. 27, no. 1. Also useful are M. R. Werner, Tammany Hall (New York: Doubleday, 1928), and Gustavus Myers, The History of Tammany Hall (New York: Gustavus Myers, 1901). Less useful are Euphemia Vale Blake, History of the Tammany Society from its Organization to the Present Time, 1901 (New York: Souvenir Publishing, 1901), and Rufus Home, "The Story of Tammany," Harper's New Monthly Magazine 44:263 (April 1872): 685–96.

18. For the founding, see Kilroe, Tammany, 118–22. For Tammany dinners, see New York Journal and Patriotic Register, May 14, 1789; New York Daily Gazette, May 14, 1789; and New York Daily Advertiser, May 14, 1789, as quoted in Kilroe, 123–25. For holiday parading, see Werner, Tammany Hall, 12; Mushkat, Tammany, 9; Kilroe, Tammany, 178–92. For the Louisiana Purchase parade in 1804, see The American Citizen, May 12 and May 14, 1804; Kilroe, Tammany, 182. For celebrations of the French Revolution, see Kilroe, ibid., 192. Among these might be placed the first American opera, Tammany, or the Indian Chief, by Ann Julia Hatton, first performed in March 1794. See Kilroe Papers, box 22, Tammany Opera folder.

19. New York Daily Gazette, May 12, 1790, provides the rules for Tammany eligibility. See Kilroe, Tammany, n. 62, 161. Anti-Irish nativism seemed most rooted in the New York chapter. The Philadelphia branch (of the New York group) rapidly became largely Irish-Catholic. See William M. Meigs, "Pennsylvania Politics Early in This Century," Pennsylvania Magazine of History and Biography 17 (1893): 462–80. The Washington chapter, organized in 1807, split apart almost immediately on the question of Irish-Catholic exclusion. See Kilroe, Tammany, 142–45. The Kentucky branch (Lexington), the Rhode Island branch (Providence), and eight different Ohio groups (Chillicothe, Cincinnati, etc.) faded by the 1820s, leaving only the New York order. Kilroe, Tammany, 149; Myers, History, 7. Samuel W. Williams, "The Tammany Society in Ohio," Ohio Archaeological and Historical Publications 22 (1913): 349–69, esp. 364–65. Werner, Tammany Hall, 16, 20–22; Young, Republicans, 202–03, and Mushkat, Tammany, 12–14, characterize the society as "middle class" and "open-ended." In 1791, John Pintard called Tammany "a political institution founded on a strong republican basis whose democratic principles will serve in some measure to correct the aristocracy of our city." By a 2:1 ratio, most new members joining between 1797 and 1801 were artisans. See Mushkat, Tammany, 25; Peter Paulson, "The Tammany Society and the Jeffersonian Movement in New York City, 1795–1800," New York History 34 (1953): 50.

20. For fraternalism, see Dorothy Ann Lipson, Freemasonry in Federalist Connecticut, 1789–

1835 (Princeton: Princeton University Press, 1977); Lynn Dumenil, *Freemasonry and American Culture, 1880–1930* (Princeton: Princeton University Press, 1984); Mary Ann Clawson, *Constructing Brotherhood: Class, Gender, and Fraternalism* (Princeton: Princeton University Press, 1989); Mark C. Carnes, *Secret Ritual and Manhood in Victorian America* (New Haven: Yale University Press, 1989); Paul Goodman, *Towards a Christian Republic: Antimasonry and the Great Transition in New England, 1826–1836* (New York: Oxford University Press, 1988), 12–16. For economic transitions affecting artisans, see Sean Wilentz, *Chants Democratic: New York City and the Rise of the American Working Class 1788–1850* (New York: Oxford University Press, 1984), 3–144. For artisanal performative traditions, see Susan G. Davis, *Parades and Power: Street Theater in Nineteenth-Century Philadelphia* (Philadelphia: Temple University Press, 1986), 34–36; and for the role of labor consciousness, ibid., 113–53.

21. Clawson, *Constructing Brotherhood*, 21–89, has shown the connections between European Abbeys of Misrule, craft and artisan guilds, and the many fraternal variants springing from Freemasonry. She argues against a simple equating of the fraternal system with working-class solidarity, pointing out the existence of more complex symbolic and institutional factors.

22. Ibid., 29–38, 45–52. For semiriotous celebrations, see Werner, *Tammany Hall*, 13; Davis, *Parades and Power*, 103–09. For exclusion from politics, see Mushkat, *Tammany*, 5; Myers, *History*, 4–21. In New York, the state constitution of 1777 restricted voting for governor, lieutenant-governor, and state senators to those owning property worth one hundred pounds. Citizens who paid forty shillings per year in rent or who owned freeholds worth twenty pounds were allowed to vote for assemblymen. The activities of Tammany politicians have been reported in disproportion to those of middle- and lower-class members. Myers claims that Tammany's hostility to "aristocracy" spread throughout the group: middle-class members who had prospered were still denied admittance to the upper class, and the remainder of the society opposed wealth on principle. An essentially middle-class operation, Tammany established its power base by catering to the rich and acting in the name of the poor. Myers, *History*, 15–21.

23. Fitz-Greene Halleck, "Song," *The Poetical Writings of Fitz-Greene Halleck* (New York: Appleton, 1869), 124.

24. John Pintard to Jeremy Belknap, April 6, 1791. Belknap Papers, III:490 as quoted in Kilroe, *Tammany*, 136. See also Kilroe Papers, box 28, American Museum file.

25. As quoted in Von A. Cabeen, "Tammany," 27:1 (1903): 36.

26. The New York *Directory and Register*, published yearly by Hodge, Allen, and Campbell, came out near the end of May. Kilroe suggests that, after the successful St. Tammany's day celebration of 1789, the group met to formalize its name in order to place it in the directory. For name changes, see Kilroe, *Tammany*, 126–28, 148–49, also n. 13, 151.

27. Eric Hobsbawm, "The Invention of Tradition," in *The Invention of Tradition*, ed. Eric Hobsbawm and Terence Ranger (Cambridge: Cambridge University Press, 1982), 1–14; Davis, *Parades and Power*, 9–13; Wilbur Zelinsky, *Nation into State: The Shifting Symbolic Foundations of American Nationalism* (Chapel Hill: University of North Carolina Press, 1988).

28. William L. Vance, *America's Rome* (New Haven: Yale University Press, 1989), 9–20, 302–16; Roger G. Kennedy, *Greek Revival America* (New York: Stewart, Tabori, and Chang, 1989); John Eadie, ed. *Classical Traditions in Early America* (Ann Arbor: Center for Coordination of Ancient and Modern Studies, 1976); Edwin A. Miles, "Young American Nation and the

Classical World," *Journal of the History of Ideas* 35 (April-June 1974): 259–74; George Stewart, *Names on the Land: A Historical Account of Place-naming in the United States* (New York: Random House, 1945), 181–88. For limitations on America as an Augustan age, see Linda K. Kerber, *Federalists in Dissent: Imagery and Ideology in Jeffersonian America* (Ithaca: Cornell University Press, 1970). For West, see John Galt, *The Life and Studies of Benjamin West, Esq.*, as cited in *The Rising Glory of America 1600–1820*, ed. Gordon S. Wood (Boston: Northeastern University Press, 1990), 283. See also Ann Uhry Abrams, *The Valiant Hero: Benjamin West and Grand-Style History Painting* (Washington: Smithsonian Institution Press, 1985), 31–94, esp. 76–80, for an analysis that links West's *Savage Chief, or The Indian Family* (ca. 1761) with Apollo Belvedere.

29. Philip Freneau, *The Poems of Philip Freneau, Poet of the American Revolution*, ed. Fred Lewis Pattee, 3 vols. (Princeton: Princeton University Library, 1903) 2:369. See also Emory Elliot, *Revolutionary Writers: Literature and Authority in the New Republic 1725–1810* (New York: Oxford University Press, 1982), 128–70, esp. 150–52; Barbara Novak, *Nature and Culture: American Landscape and Painting 1825–1875* (New York: Oxford University Press, 1980), 8–77, 189. A clear expression of this use of the classical Indian Other to construct an American past could be found in New York's old City Hall building, where John Pintard had located his Tammany Museum. Founded in 1790 as the second museum in America, the Tammany collection included not only pamphlets and manuscripts of the colonial past, but also artifacts and curiosities of Indian people. See also Roger G. Kennedy, *Hidden Cities: The Discovery and Loss of Ancient North American Civilization* (New York: Free Press, 1994); Werner Sollors, *Beyond Ethnicity: Consent and Descent in American Culture* (Oxford: Oxford University Press, 1986), 117–18.

30. For nineteenth-century fraternal orders, see Albert C. Stevens, *Cyclopedia of Fraternities* (New York: E. B. Treat and Co., 1907); Alvin J. Schmidt, *Fraternal Organizations* (Westport: Greenwood Press, 1980). Many orders appeared after the Civil War, as fraternalism provided a powerful venue for remaking disrupted national family ties. The Odd Fellows (1802), Freemasons (mid-1700s), Foresters (1832), and Druids (1839), however, were all English imports that existed in America in the antebellum Republic.

31. William Pitt Smith, "An Oration, delivered by Dr. William P. Smith, before the Society of St. Tammany, or Columbian Order, at their Anniversary Meeting on Wednesday, the 12th of May, 1790," *New York Magazine or Literary Repository* 1:5 (May 1790): 290–95.

32. See Thomas J. Schlereth, "Columbia, Columbus, and Columbianism," *Journal of American History* 79:3 (December 1992): 937–68; William C. Spengemann, *A New World of Words: Redefining Early American Literature* (New Haven: Yale University Press, 1994), 118–77; David C. Humphrey, *From King's College to Columbia, 1746 to 1800* (New York: Columbia University Press, 1976), 270–72.

33. Madge Dresser, "Britannia," in *Patriotism: The Making and Unmaking of British National Identity III, National Fictions*, ed. Raphael Samuel (London: Routledge, 1989), 26–49; Linda Colley, *Britons: Forging the Nation, 1707–1837* (New Haven: Yale University Press, 1992). For Columbia and Indian images of America, see E. McClung Fleming, "The American Image as Indian Princess, 1765–1783," and "From Indian Princess to Greek Goddess: The American Image, 1783–1815," *Winterthur Portfolio* 2 (1965): 65–81 and 3 (1967): 37–66; John Higham, "Indian Princess and Roman Goddess: The First Female Symbols of America," *Proceedings of the American Antiquarian Society* 100:1 (1990): 45–79.

34. For sexual predation, see William Byrd, *Histories of the Dividing Line Betwixt Virginia and*

North Carolina (Raleigh: North Carolina Historical Commission, 1929), 57, 115, and Richard Slotkin's analysis in *Regeneration Through Violence: The Mythology of the American Frontier, 1600–1860* (Middletown: Wesleyan University Press, 1973), 222–26. For political cartoons, see Lester C. Olson, *Emblems of American Community in the Revolutionary Era: A Study in Rhetorical Iconology* (Washington: Smithsonian Institution Press, 1991).

35. For Tammany's "para-government" argument, see Jabez Hammond, *The History of Political Parties in the State of New York* (Albany, 1842) 1:340; James Bryce, *The American Commonwealth*, 3d ed. (New York, 1901) 2:379; Home, "The Story of Tammany," 636. For calculation of calendar date, see Myers, *History*, 6. That the "year of institution" appears as the twelfth rather than the eleventh in the example signifies that the society was using a date before July to mark its origin.

36. After the Revolution, Georgia officials engineered a fraudulent treaty opening Creek territory to settlement. Speculating companies claimed title to huge tracts of land, some of which included the entire Creek homeland. Creek soldiers attacked settlement parties coming upriver and the Georgians responded. The federal government, which had claimed all the land west of established British boundaries, intervened, in part to rein in the Georgians, who argued that western land belonged to the states rather than the nation, and in part to prevent a war with the still-powerful Creeks. See David H. Corkran, *The Creek Frontier, 1540–1783* (Norman: University of Oklahoma Press, 1967), 288–325; Angie Debo, *The Road to Disappearance* (Norman: University of Oklahoma Press, 1941), 37–55.

37. *New York Daily Advertiser*, July 23, 1790.

38. *New York Journal and Patriotic Register* vol. 44, no. 46, August 10, 1790. See also Kilroe, *Tammany*, 138.

39. For other examples of this kind of diplomatic exchange, see *Weekly Museum*, February 20, 1790, p. 1. In a meeting with the Oneidas, the society suggested exchanging ornaments, blood, and names. See also Eric Hinderaker, "The 'Four Indian Kings' and the Imaginative Construction of Empire in 18th-Century Britain," *William and Mary Quarterly* 3d ser., 53 (1996): 487–526. For McGillivray, see *New York Journal and Patriotic Register*, vol. 44, no. 48, August 17, 1790.

40. For presidential title, see Myers, *History*, 5. For Oneidas, *New York Weekly Museum*, Feb. 20, 1790, in Kilroe, *Tammany*, n. 47, 156. For Cayugas, see *New York Journal and Patriotic Register*, May 14, 1790, in Kilroe, ibid., 168, n. 4, 199. With the removal of the capital to Philadelphia in 1790, the society lost the opportunity to interject itself directly into Indian diplomacy. As tribes occasionally traveled through the city, however, Tammany continued to court them. In 1811, for example, they entertained the Ottawas (Kilroe, ibid., 173).

41. After initial recruiting success between 1789 and 1794, an increasingly politicized Tammany society spent three whole years without inducting a single member. Young, *Democratic Republicans*, 398–99. Tammany was often portrayed as a bulwark against the aristocratic ambitions of the Society of the Cincinnati, a hereditary organization limited to former officers of the Continental Army. See, for example, Judah Hammond's history in Hammond, *History of the Political Parties of the State of New York*, 340. This seems to be mostly political mythmaking. In the late eighteenth century, the two groups shared members, toasted each other, and occasionally paraded together. See Kilroe, *Tammany*, 130–31, 140–41. Mushkat, *Tammany*, 19–20, argues that Citizen Genet's visit in 1793 helped crystallize Tammany's transformation from patriotic fraternity to political group. That year, for exam-

ple, "An Oneida Chief" suggested to his rivals that "Mohawks, Oneidas, and Senekas" might attack the Belvidere Club House, where "enemies to liberty" allegedly toasted the destruction of the rights of man. *New York Journal and Patriotic Register*, May 15, 1793.

42. Washington suggested that "self-created societies" advocated political activity (parades, demonstrations, extrainstitutional vigilantism) that looked more like rebellion than the republican discourse of enlightened citizens. His attack was aimed at groups like the Democratic Society of New York, which had been founded in 1794. While Tammany's involvement in governing was initially confined to the symbolic level, other Democratic-Republican clubs sought to participate in the constitution of authority. Advocating power in the hands of the people, they supported groups like the whiskey rebels. Although the membership of the two groups overlapped to some degree, Tammany leadership sometimes inclined to the Federalists, and the two societies were not close. Yet many Tammany members approved of a more direct approach to politics. The result was increased factionalism, the eventual distinction (tenuous as it was) between the society and the political machine later known as Tammany Hall, and the society's drift into a more defined Democratic-Republican orbit. See James Roger Sharp, "The Whiskey Rebellion and the Question of Representation" in Slaughter, *Whiskey Rebellion*. For shifts in Tammany's political and fraternal activities, see Mushkat, *Tammany*, 12–21; Kilroe, *Tammany*, 195–97; Myers, *History*, 13–23. For "self-created societies," see Young, *Democratic Republicans*, 392–419. Judah Hammond's narrative of the sparsely attended celebration is quoted in Jabez Hammond, *History of the Political Parties of the State of New York*, 340–42. For Philadelphia Tammany's earlier transformation, see Meigs, "Pennsylvania Politics"; James Peeling, "Governor McKean and the Pennsylvania Jacobins (1799–1808)," *Pennsylvania Magazine of History and Biography* 54 (1930): 320.

43. For Columbus, see Kenneth Silverman, *A Cultural History of the American Revolution* (New York: Thomas Crowell, 1976), 579. In *Parades and Power*, Davis argues that public performance establishes and delineates power relations by dramatizing both hierarchical rankings and the presence or absence of representative groups.

44. James Cheetham, *American Citizen and General Advertiser*, July 6, 1809, as quoted in Kilroe, *Tammany*, 182.

45. *New York Evening Post*, July 29, 1809. "Toast to 'Old Massa Tom' [Jefferson] himself: His spirits be no ashamed to be wid us a de council fire which be lighted today—better be here wid a poor honest negur African, wan way out younder wid de deblish democrat." Kilroe Papers, box 28, Newspaper Clippings 1800–1850. For *Rhode Island American*, April 20, 1810, see Kilroe Papers, box 22, African Tammany Society folder.

46. For renunciation of Indian costume, see Kilroe, *Tammany*, 184. For Irish attacks on Tammany nativism, as late as 1817, see Myers, *History*, 55. See also Kilroe, *Tammany*, 145; Werner, *Hall*, 29–30. Mushkat, *Tammany*, 59–66, provides context for Tammany's transition from discrimination to partial acceptance to the use of Irish immigrants as a political base. For end of parade tradition, see Kilroe, *Tammany*, 178.

47. See George Lindsay, Charles Conley, and Charles Litchman, *Official History of the Improved Order of Red Men*, ed. Carl R. Lemke (Waco: Davis Brothers, 1964), 187, for an account of "the Kickapoo Amicable Association, which existed in the city of Washington D.C., in the year 1804, and which not only adopted the usages, forms, ceremonies, and costumes of the Indian race, but also gave to its members Indian names." *A History of the Black Hawk War* by

"An Old Resident of the Military Tract," published at Fort Armstrong, Iowa, in 1832, contains the ciphered or mnemonic ritual of still another "Indian society." The text may be found in the Rare Books room at the Library of Congress.

48. For military Tammany celebrations, see Kilroe Papers, box 22, "Copy of Memo from Anthony Wayne's Orderly Book" folder, which contains a memo from April 30, 1795, stating, "The first day of May being the anniversary of St. Tammany the tutelar saint of America all the troops fit for duty on this ground are due to receive one gill of whiskey per man." For lapse in celebration during war, see Von A. Cabeen, "Tammany," 26:1 (1902): 17–21. For cancellation of holiday, 26:4 (1902): 458.

49. For founding, see Litchman, History of the IORM, 199–201; Robert E. Davis, History of the Improved Order of Red Men and Degree of Pocohontas 1765–1988 (Waco: Davis Brothers, 1990), 73–101. Barker, a tailor by trade, kept an inn at "the Sign of Saint Tammany," from which he led the Saint Tammany Fire Company. Although a solid member of the artisan class, Barker had risen to civic prominence as well. A major general in the Philadelphia militia, he also served as city sheriff, alderman, and mayor. The younger Barker was regular army and seems to have lost touch with the volunteers who made up the key membership of the Society of Red Men. See National Cyclopedia of American Biography 12:276; Von A. Cabeen, "Tammany," 26:2 (1902): 223. For Barker as Tammany sachem, see Philadelphia Aurora, May 14, 1800, Kilroe Papers, box 28, Newspaper Clippings 1800–1850.

50. Litchman, History of the IORM, 201–16.

51. Ibid., 211.

52. Secrecy also changed the way that non–Red Men perceived the group. When Tammany members paraded through New York in costume, they forced the city to confront their potentially revolutionary identities and thus their political position. Making fewer public appearances, the Society of Red Men could be categorized under the less threatening rubric "fraternalism" and filed away with men sporting Masonic aprons or Druid capes. For self-association, see Alexis de Tocqueville, Democracy in America, trans. George Lawrence, ed. J. P. Mayer (New York: Harper Perennial, 1969), 513–17.

53. See Davis, History of the IORM, 140, for an occupational breakdown (ten physicians, six accountants, and four attorneys versus sixty-seven cordwainers, sixty-four hatters, fifty carpenters, and sixty-seven innkeepers; only one city council member shows up on his abbreviated list). Compare this with the Philadelphia Tammany society, which was dominated by William Duane, the radical democratic editor of The Aurora, and Dr. Michael Leib, controversial congressman and senator. See also Davis, ibid., 107, 115–20, for the society's explicit rejection of political action on behalf of a member.

54. Litchman, History of the IORM, 206. There may be an element of burlesque in the Italianate titles and florid hierarchy, most likely directed at the Masons. At the same time, one should also keep in mind that voluntary societies were critical sites for the consolidation and deployment of social power in the Republic.

55. For Loudenslager, see Litchman, History of the IORM, 245; Davis, History of the IORM, 153–64. After the Revolution, the men who (re)assembled structures of power denied women a role in political life and positioned them instead—by virtue of female control over the domestic sphere—as the moral guardians of civic virtue. Broader concerns that could be defined as familial—most notably drinking—fell within the domestic sphere and thus offered some women the opportunity to participate in public discourse. Although

some societies (such as the Improved Order) were able to offer an image of religiosity and temperance, others (such as the Society of Red Men) came under attack. Throughout the nineteenth century, fraternal societies continually reformulated their organizations, adding women's auxiliaries, and repeatedly justifying their exclusion of women and their lodge practices. See Linda Kerber, *Women of the Republic: Intellect and Ideology in Revolutionary America* (Chapel Hill: Published for the Institute of Early American History and Culture by the University of North Carolina Press, 1980); Kerber, "I have Don . . . much to Carrey on the Warr : Women and the Shaping of Republican Ideology after the American Revolution," in *Women and Politics in the Age of the Democratic Revolution*, ed. Harriet Applewhite and Darline G. Levy (Ann Arbor: University of Michigan Press, 1990), 227–58; Mary P. Ryan, *Womanhood in America: From Colonial Times to the Present* (New York: New Viewpoints, 1975); Carnes, *Secret Ritual and Manhood*; Linda K. Kerber, Nancy F. Cott, Robert Gross, Lynn Hunt, Carroll Smith-Rosenberg, Christine M. Stansell, "Beyond Roles, Beyond Spheres: Thinking about Gender in the Early Republic," *William and Mary Quarterly* 3d ser. 46 (July 1989): 565–85.

56. For anti-Masonry, see Lorman Ratner, *Antimasonry: The Crusade and the Party* (Englewood Cliffs: Prentice-Hall, 1969), 7–12. William Preston Vaughn, *The Antimasonic Party in the United States, 1826–1843* (Lexington: University Press of Kentucky, 1983), 14–19, and esp. chap. 8 on Pennsylvania, which experienced anti-Masonic agitation in the early 1830s, slightly later than New York and New England; David Brion Davis, "Some Themes of Counter-Subversion: An Analysis of Anti-Masonic, Anti-Catholic, and Anti-Mormon Literature," *Mississippi Valley Historical Review* 47 (September 1960): 205–24; and Goodman, *Towards a Christian Republic*, 13–14 and passim. For cholera, see Charles E. Rosenberg, *The Cholera Years: The United States in 1832, 1849, and 1866* (Chicago: University of Chicago Press, 1962). See Litchman, *History of the IORM*, 207, for the disintegration of the Charleston tribe in 1820: "Local disease proved fatal and carried off my chief aids, 'Peruvian Bark' and 'Mainspring,' which caused a great chasm in the Council. The plague continued, which caused the Tribe to scatter all over the wilderness, taking with them their squaws and papooses, and since then have never been reunited."

57. Michael Paul Rogin, *Fathers and Children: Andrew Jackson and the Subjugation of the American Indian* (New York: Knopf, 1975); Ronald N. Satz, *American Indian Policy in the Jacksonian Era* (Lincoln: University of Nebraska Press, 1974); Reginald Horsman, *The Origins of Indian Removal, 1815–1824* (East Lansing: Michigan State University Press for the Historical Society of Michigan, 1970).

58. Joseph Story, "Discourse Pronounced at the Request of the Essex Historical Society, Sept. 18, 1828, in Commemoration of the First Settlement of Salem, Mass.," quoted in Brian Dippie, *The Vanishing American: White Attitudes and U.S. Indian Policy* (Middletown: Wesleyan University Press, 1982), 1.

59. George Washington Custis, *The Indian Prophecy, a National Drama in Two Acts* (Georgetown: J. Thomas, 1828). For Indian plays, see Sollors, *Beyond Ethnicity*, 104–21; Keiser, *Indian in American Literature*, 65–100.

60. *Metamora, or The Last of the Wampanoags* by John Augustus Stone, 1829; *The Indian Princess; or La Belle Sauvage* by James Nelson Barker and Raynor Taylor, 1808. Barker would later go on to command the Red Man volunteers at Fort Mifflin. See also *Pocahontas; or, The Settlers of Virginia* by George Washington Custis (1830), Joseph Doddridge, *Logan: The Last of the Race of Shikellemus, Chief of the Cayuga Nation* (Buffalo Creek, Va.: S. Sala, 1823). See also Sollors, *Beyond Ethnicity*,

122; Sally L. Jones, "The First but Not the Last of the 'Vanishing Indians': Edwin Forrest and Mythic Re-creations of the Native Population," in *Dressing in Feathers: The Construction of the Indian in American Popular Culture*, ed. S. Elizabeth Bird (Boulder: Westview Press, 1996), 13–27.

61. Cooper, *The Redskins*, 464.

62. Litchman, *History of the IORM*, 251.

63. Ibid., 797. The practice of denying Indian existence continued, despite a rash of protests by Indian people in the early twentieth century, until 1977, when the order finally recognized Indians as potential members. Philip Deloria, "White Sachems and Indian Masons," *Democratic Vistas* 1 (Autumn 1993): 27–43.

64. For celebrations, see David Waldstreicher, "The Making of American Nationalism: Celebrations and Political Culture, 1776–1820" (Ph.D. diss., Yale University, 1994). For "traditionalizing" the Revolution, see Kammen, *A Season of Youth*, esp. 15–32, 43–58, 154–61.

65. This remaking drained Indianness of much of its overt rebellious content. After the antirent conflicts, white Americans tended to use Indians to reflect an institutionalized nationalism rather than to challenge power and authority. It was not until the late nineteenth century that a more rebellious Indianness took shape in the form of African-American Mardi Gras parading and the cultural struggles of the antimodernists.

Chapter 3. Literary Indians and Ethnographic Objects

1. For Riley letter, see Lewis Henry Morgan Papers, Rush Rhees Library, University of Rochester, box 1, folder 6. Unless otherwise noted, all of the Morgan material used in this chapter will be found in these papers. Hereafter, Morgan Papers. I have drawn on the following works for the details of Morgan's life and his association with the New Confederacy: Carl Resek, *Lewis Henry Morgan: American Scholar* (Chicago: University of Chicago Press, 1960); Bernhard J. Stern, *Lewis Henry Morgan, Social Evolutionist* (Chicago: University of Chicago Press, 1931); Thomas R. Trautmann, *Lewis Henry Morgan and the Invention of Kinship* (Berkeley: University of California Press, 1987); Leslie White, ed., "How Morgan Came to Write *Systems of Consanguinity and Affinity*," *Papers of the Michigan Academy of Science, Arts, and Letters* 42 (1957): 257–68; Robert E. Bieder, "The Grand Order of the Iroquois: Influences on Lewis Henry Morgan's Ethnology," *Ethnohistory* 27:4 (Fall 1980): 349–61; Bieder, *Science Encounters the Indian, 1820–1880: The Early Years of American Ethnology* (Norman: University of Oklahoma Press, 1986), 194–246; Elisabeth Tooker, "The Structure of the Iroquois League: Lewis H. Morgan's Research and Observations," *Ethnohistory* 30:3 (1983): 141–54; Tooker, Foreword to Lewis Henry Morgan, *Ancient Society* (Tucson: University of Arizona Press, 1985), xv–xxvii. Volume 2 of the Rochester Historical Society Publication Fund Series (ed. Edward Foreman, Rochester, 1923) is dedicated to Morgan and includes several essays of varying usefulness. These include Joshua McIllvaine's funeral oration and Algernon Crapsey's "Lewis Henry Morgan: Scientist, Philosopher, Humanist." For the literary mission of the group, see "Report of the Committee of Literary and Social Exercises, October 30, 1846," Morgan Papers, box 23, folder 81. Trautmann, *Kinship*, 40, observes that Morgan was "an inveterate organizer and leader of literary societies." While at Cayuga Lake Academy, he had helped found the Erodephecin Society (see folder 52, box 22, Morgan Papers) and would later found The Club, a group of Rochester intellectuals (see folder 43, box 22,

Morgan Papers). For the frequent use of the fraternal form as an organizing structure, see Mary Ann Clawson, *Constructing Brotherhood: Class, Gender, and Fraternalism* (Princeton: Princeton University Press, 1989), 5.

2. Lewis Henry Morgan, "An Address by Schenandoah, delivered on the Second Anniversary . . . ," August 9, 1843. Morgan Papers, box 21, folder 6. For emotional responses to landscape, see Barbara Novak, *Nature and Culture: American Landscape and Painting, 1825–1875* (New York: Oxford University Press, 1980), 3–77.

3. See Leslie White, "How Morgan Came to Write *Systems*," 260. For Indianness and literature in defining national character, see Constance Rourke, *American Humor: A Study of the National Character* (Tallahassee: Florida State University Press, 1959), 113–15; Lucy Maddox, *Removals: Nineteenth-Century American Literature and the Politics of Indian Affairs* (New York: Oxford, 1991), 36–49; Robert F. Sayre, *Thoreau and the American Indians* (Princeton: Princeton University Press, 1977). The New Confederacy was, in many ways, closer kin to the pre-Revolution Tammany societies of Philadelphia than it was to either New York Tammany or the Red Men. Like the first Tammany organizations, the New Confederacy focused on an interior Indian Other that could be enfolded within the boundaries of American society. Both groups used Indianness to create literature and myth that celebrated a uniquely American identity. But while Tammany often spoke to the uniqueness of American nature, his primary role was to crystalize the oppositions between British and revolutionary identity. Morgan's literary Indian figures functioned in exactly the reverse. American-British oppositions were already clearly and painfully drawn—the preeminence of British literature and the failure of Americans to realize a prophesied artistic destiny were crucial contexts for the New Confederacy's efforts. The primary object of the order's writing, research, and ritual was to create a nonoppositional American identity that, through engagement with land, nature, and the continent's human history, stood on its own.

4. For the name of the group, see Stern, *Morgan*, 10. The group's name changed as members garnered more information about the Iroquois. Initially, it took the "modest name of the 'Order of the Iroquois"; then the 'Grand Order of the Iroquois,' or We-yo-Hao-de-ya-da-nah Ho-de-no-sau-nee; finally, 'The New Confederacy of the Iroquois,' or Ac-qui-nus-chi-o-nee, signifying a united people." The words *ethnography, ethnology,* and *anthropology* have all been used to describe Morgan's practice. His use of native informants, on site research, and linguistic studies and his career trajectory, which began with a specific case study and moved to the general and the comparative, fit familiar contemporary definitions of ethnography. On the other hand, his belief in racial differentiation and his philanthropic, nonscientific roots better fit ethnology. In his study of Victorian anthropology, George Stocking links ethnology loosely with humanitarian concerns and anthropology with scientific ones. He posits a rough transition between the two during the 1860s. I have seen Morgan more in terms of his premodern modernism and his transition from the literary to the scientific, and so I have chosen to use *ethnography* rather than *ethnology* as a key descriptive word. See George W. Stocking, Jr., *Victorian Anthropology* (New York: Free Press, 1987), 239–48.

5. As quoted in Joseph J. Ellis, *After the Revolution: Profiles of Early American Culture* (New York: Norton, 1979), 4. See also Michael Kammen, *A Season of Youth: The American Revolution and the Historical Imagination* (New York: Knopf, 1978), 110–42, 154; Robert E. Spiller, ed., *The American Literary Revolution: 1783–1837* (New York: New York University Press, 1967); Clin-

ton Rossiter, *The American Quest, 1790–1860: An Emerging Nation in Search of Identity, Unity, and Modernity* (New York: Harcourt, Brace, Jovanovich, 1971); James D. Wallace, *Early Cooper and His Audience* (New York: Columbia University Press, 1986), 1–28; Emory Elliot, *Revolutionary Writers; Literature and Authority in the New Republic 1725–1810* (New York: Oxford University Press, 1982), 3–54.

6. Philip Freneau, *The Poems of Philip Freneau, Poet of the American Revolution*, 3 vols., ed. Fred Lewis Pattee (Princeton: Princeton University Library, 1903) 1:48–84. For variant editions, see Pattee's notes on 49–50 and 83–84.

7. Lawrence J. Friedman, *Inventors of the Promised Land* (New York: Alfred A. Knopf, 1975), 4–43. See also William J. Free, *The Columbian Magazine and American Literary Nationalism* (The Hague: Mouton and Co., 1968).

8. Ellis, *After the Revolution*, 7.

9. This freedom, according to Freneau and Brackenridge, was not just political. It was, more importantly, a *commercial* freedom, the ability to do one's business unhindered. See Freneau, *Poems*, 1:51; Ellis, *After the Revolution*, 10.

10. Ann Uhry Abrams, *The Valiant Hero: Benjamin West and Grand-Style History Painting* (Washington: Smithsonian Institution Press, 1985); John Galt, *The Life, Studies, and Works of Benjamin West, Esquire* (1820; reprint, Gainesville: Scholar's Facsimiles and Reprints, 1960); Jules David Prown, *John Singleton Copley*, 2 vols. (Cambridge: Harvard University Press for the National Gallery of Art, 1966).

11. Ralph Waldo Emerson, "The American Scholar," in *Selections from Ralph Waldo Emerson: An Organic Anthology*, ed. Stephen E. Whicher (Boston: Houghton Mifflin, 1957), 64.

12. Morgan was not the only luminary-in-the-making involved in the society. Its membership also included Charles T. Porter, who invented governors and other devices essential to nineteenth-century steam engines, Henry Haight, who served as governor of California, and James S. Bush, grandfather of the future president George Bush.

13. "An Address by Schenandoah," August 9, 1843. On Indianness as ground of national literature, see Helen Carr, *Inventing the American Primitive: Politics, Gender and the Representation of Native American Literary Traditions, 1789–1936* (New York: New York University Press, 1996), 101–13.

14. "An Address by Schenandoah," August 9, 1843.

15. Another resident of western New York, Joseph Smith, had woven together similar elements—ancient tribes of European descent, a renewal of their legacy, a literary product that defined a certain type of Americanness. Smith's Mormonism—and indeed the general ferment in American religious practice—suggests that Americans felt a lack of the larger social meanings Morgan sought to create in the New Confederacy.

16. "Form of Inindianation Adopted, Aurora," August 9, 1844. Morgan Papers, box 21, folder 10.

17. Ibid. After Morgan moved to Rochester and inaugurated the Seneca Turtle Tribe, he wrote a second initiation ceremony, which echoes most of the themes found in the Inindianation. See "Special Form of Initiation, Seneca Nation, Turtle Tribe, 1845," Morgan Papers, folder 19, box 21.

18. For nostalgia, see Novak, *Nature and Culture*, 157–200.

19. "An Address by Schenandoah," August 9, 1843. See also Bieder, "Grand Order of the Iroquois," 358. Ironically, more than a century later, scholars have been debating

exactly this point—the depth of influence the form and procedures of the Iroquois league might have had on founding Americans' ideas about constitutional government. See, for example, Bruce Johansen, *Forgotten Founders: How the American Indian Helped Shape Democracy* (Boston: Harvard Common Press, 1982); Donald A. Grinde, Jr., and Bruce E. Johansen, *Exemplar of Liberty: Native America and the Evolution of Democracy* (Los Angeles: American Indian Studies Center, 1991); Grinde and Johansen, "The Debate Regarding Native American Precedent for Democracy: A Recent Historiography," *American Indian Culture and Research Journal* 14:1 (1990): 61–88; Wilbur Jacobs, "The American Indian Legacy of Freedom and Liberty," *American Indian Culture and Research Journal* 16:4 (1992): 185–93; and, for a different perspective, Elisabeth Tooker, "The United States Constitution and the Iroquois League," *Ethnohistory* 35 (Fall 1988): 305–36; and the resulting exchange, Johansen, "Native American Societies and the Evolution of Democracy in America, 1600–1800," and Tooker, "Rejoinder to Johansen," *Ethnohistory* 37 (Summer 1990): 279–97.

20. "An Address by Schenandoah," August 9, 1843.

21. White, "How Morgan Came to Write *Systems*," 260–62.

22. Lewis Henry Morgan, "The Vision of Karistagia, A Sachem of Cayuga," *The Knickerbocker* 24 (1844): 238–45. For manuscript, see Morgan Papers, box 22, folder 54.

23. "An Address by Schenandoah," August 9, 1943. Morgan Papers.

24. Schenandoah [Lewis Henry Morgan], "Indian trail from Central Council Fire at Onondaga to Buffalo Creek," Morgan Papers, box 21, folder 25; "Address by Skenandoah on the Geography and Trails of the Hodenosaunee, Delivered August 10, 1846 before the Council of Delegates of the New Confederacy of the Iroquois at Aurora, Cayuga County, NY," box 21, folder 26. Isaac N. Hurd, "The Onondaga Nation: Their New Year's feast, the sacrifice of the white dog, their dances, their present condition, the school lately established among them, with a few reflections," and "The Political Organization of the Onondaga Nation," Morgan Papers, box 21, folders 15 and 16. See also Elisabeth Tooker, "Isaac N. Hurd's Ethnographic Studies of the Iroquois: Their Significance and Ethnographic Value," *Ethnohistory* 27:4 (Fall 1980): 363–69. For transformation of the society, see Bieder, "The Grand Order of the Iroquois," 350–51.

25. "Schedule of Warriors, August 14, 1843." Morgan Papers, box 21, folder 12.

26. For "August," see "Constitution of the New Confederacy of the Iroquois, adopted Sr-is-gak-nah 13, 1846." Morgan Papers, box 21, folder 27. For Tadodahoh and clan structure, see Trautmann, *Invention*, 46–49.

27. "Proclamation instituting the Wolf Tribe of the Oneidas," December 4, 1844. Morgan Papers, box 22, folder 55. See Bieder, *Science Encounters the Indian*, 352–59.

28. For Morgan's research agenda, see "Circular at the commencement of the 3rd year," August 1845. Morgan Papers, box 21, folder 65. For plans to send agents West, see "Committee of Research Circular," August 24, 1846. Morgan Papers, box 21, folder 79.

29. Trautmann, *Invention*, 46; Lewis Henry Morgan to Henry Rowe Schoolcraft, April 10, 1845. Morgan Papers, box 1, folder 3. William L. Stone, *Life of Joseph Brant—Thayendanegea*, 2 vols. (New York: Alexander Blake, 1838); Stone, *The Life and Times of Red Jacket, or Sa-go-ye-wat-ha; being the sequel to the History of the Six Nations* (New York: Wiley and Putnam, 1841); B. B. Thatcher, *Indian Biography or An Historical Account of those Individuals who have been distinguished among the North American Nations as Orators, Warriors, Statesmen, and other remarkable characters* (New York: A. L. Fowle, 1832; facsimile reprint Glorieta, N.M.: Rio Grande Press, 1973); Cadwallader

Colden, *History of the Five Indian Nations of Canada* (London: T. Osborne, 1747; facsimile reprint Toronto: Coles, 1972).

30. Whether Morgan—or anyone else—single-handedly deserves to be titled as the founder of the discipline is open to question. He has, however, been awarded the title on more than one occasion. See Bieder, "The Grand Order of the Iroquois," 349; and *Science Encounters the Indian*, 194.

31. "An Address read by Schenandoah," April 17, 1844. Morgan Papers, box 21, folder 9. For Parker and his siblings, see William H. Armstrong, *Warrior in Two Camps: Ely S. Parker, Union General and Seneca Chief* (Syracuse: Syracuse University Press, 1978), 23.

32. See Armstrong, *Two Camps*, 47–48; Lewis Henry Morgan, *League of the Ho-de-no-sau-nee or Iroquois* (New York: Dodd, Mead, 1901), xi–xii.

33. See Nancy Oestreich Lurie, "Relations between Indians and Anthropologists," in *History of Indian-White Relations*, ed. Wilcomb E. Washburn, vol. 4, *Handbook of North American Indians* (Washington: Smithsonian Institution, 1988), 548–56; Trautmann, *Invention*, 10.

34. "An Address by Schenandoah," August 9, 1843. Morgan Papers.

35. For Morgan's account of the Ogden conflict, see *League of the Ho-de-no-sau-nee, or Iroquois*, 30–33. See also Laurence M. Hauptman, "The Historical Background to the Present-Day Seneca Nation—Salamanca Lease Controversy," in *Iroquois Land Claims*, ed. Christopher Vecsey and William A. Starna (Syracuse: Syracuse University Press, 1988), 102–04; Armstrong, *Two Camps*, 10–11.

36. Morgan had informed Senator Cass of his honorary membership only seven days before. Lewis Henry Morgan to Lewis Cass, December 30, 1845. Morgan Papers, box 1, folder 5.

37. For *Rochester Daily Advertiser*, March 11, 1852, see Armstrong, *Two Camps*, 27. For Porter, see Charles T. Porter to Henry Rowe Schoolcraft, January 10, 1846. Morgan Papers, box 1, folder 5. For Parker, see Ely S. Parker to Henry Rowe Schoolcraft, May 2, 1846. Morgan Papers, box 1, folder 6.

38. It is tempting to view Morgan's involvement in the society through the lens of his subsequent anthropological career, dismissing its ritual aspects as by-products of his already serious explorations into ethnography. Armstrong, *Two Camps*, 1, makes this claim. Morgan was serious about both his literary aspirations and his historical and ethnographic salvage operations among the Six Nations. We should not, however, attach scholarly sobriety to him prematurely and thus unbalance what was, at least initially, a curiously strong devotion to secrecy and ritual. See also Lurie, "Relations between Indians and Anthropologists," 549. For a suggestive analysis of Morgan's psyche (and the Improved Order of Red Men) in terms of maternal nurture and masculinity, see Mark Carnes, *Secret Ritual and Manhood in Victorian America* (New Haven: Yale University Press, 1989), 93–127.

39. Lewis Henry Morgan to William Allen, Feb. 11, 1845. Morgan Papers, box 1, folder 4.

40. Tekarihogea [Lewis Henry Morgan], "Proclamation Instituting the Wolf Tribe of the Oneidas," December 4, 1844. Morgan Papers, box 22, folder 55.

41. Lewis Henry Morgan to Henry Rowe Schoolcraft, June 30, 1845. Morgan Papers, box 1, folder 5. The previous year, Morgan had failed to persuade another guest: "I do not think you had better make any preparations of that kind for me," David Powens told Morgan. David Powens to Lewis Henry Morgan, July 18, 1844. Morgan Papers, box 1, folder 3.

42. Morgan himself had moved from Aurora to Rochester, where he started the Turtle Tribe of the Senecas. For the Cayuga position, see C. N. Mattoon, Isaac N. Hurd, George A. Brush to Henry Rowe Schoolcraft, May 5, 1845. Morgan Papers, box 1, folder 5.

43. Henry D. Clark to Lewis Henry Morgan, June 6, 1845. Morgan Papers, box 1, folder 5.

44. Lewis Henry Morgan to Henry Rowe Schoolcraft, April 10, 1845. Morgan Papers, box 1, folder 4.

45. For deferring the question until the following year, see "Message in relation to the secrecy of the annual council," June 16, 1845. Morgan Papers, box 22, folder 59. For membership desiring public display, see B.W. Arnold to Lewis Henry Morgan. May 27, 1846; George Brush to Lewis Henry Morgan. May 9, 1846. Morgan Papers, box 1, folder 7.

46. Tekarihogea [Lewis Henry Morgan], "Message in relation to the Annual council," May 16, 1846. Morgan Papers, box 22, folder 69.

47. Carnes, *Secret Ritual and Manhood in Victorian America*, 96; Stern, *Social Evolutionist*, 10; Resek, *American Scholar*, 4.

48. Lewis Henry Morgan to Henry Rowe Schoolcraft, April 10, 1845. Morgan Papers, box 1, folder 3.

49. For Morgan's contradictions, see Carr, *Inventing the American Primitive*, 147–65; Marvin Harris, *The Rise of Anthropological Theory* (New York: Thomas Crowell, 1968), 137–40, 177–79. For the double standard of authenticity, see James Clifford, *The Predicament of Culture: Twentieth Century Ethnography, Literature, and Art* (Cambridge: Harvard University Press, 1988), 227–346. For the location of the real in an interaction of mutual mimesis—such as that between Indians and non-Indians—see Michael Taussig, *Mimesis and Alterity: A Particular History of the Senses* (London: Routledge, 1993). Many commentators looking retrospectively at Morgan have found him "advanced," "ahead of his time," "strikingly modern." See, for example, Crapsey, "Lewis Henry Morgan, Scientist, Philosopher, Humanist," 22–23; Trautmann, *Invention*, 9; Bieder, *Science Encounters the Indian*, 194.

50. See Maddox, *Removals*, especially the section on Thoreau, 146–58.

51. For nonattendance at the council, see Samuel R. Welles to Lewis Henry Morgan, July 3, 1846; George Brush to Lewis Henry Morgan, May 12, 1846. Morgan Papers, box 1, folder 9. Folder 10 contains a variety of regrets letters. For Hamilton Morgan, see George Brush to Lewis Henry Morgan, May 9, 1846. Morgan Papers, box 1, folder 9. For disappearance, see Charles T. Porter to James S. Bush, October 5, 1846; Charles Hayes to Daniel Beach, October 30, 1846. Morgan Papers, both box 1, folder 10.

52. Morgan, "Letters on the Iroquois Addressed to Albert Gallatin," *American Whig Review* 5 (1847): 177–90, 242–57, and 6 (1848): 477–90, 626–33. For Colton, see Tooker, "The Structure of the Iroquois League," 149. In the decade that followed, Morgan applied himself diligently to his legal career. His future secure, he returned to Indian studies in the late 1850s, and what had been a hobby became a new profession. Morgan's *Systems of Consanguinity and Affinity of the Human Family* (1871) and *Ancient Society* (1877) became landmarks in the developing field of anthropology. He wrote two other books as well, *The American Beaver and His Works* (1868) and *Houses and House-life of the American Aborigines* (1881).

53. Trautmann makes compelling linkages between Morgan's avocation as a lawyer and the types of questions and formats he devised for his ethnography. See *Invention*, 39–40.

54. With the advent of social Darwinism, anthropology developed a scientific interior-exterior contradiction. Indians could be interior, in that they "are what we once were"—temporally and developmentally connected—and exterior in that they exist "out of our time." In the late nineteenth century, the anthropologist Frank Hamilton Cushing breached this barrier, dressing as a Zuni Indian and participating in Zuni rituals. Cushing was an exception, however, and it is only recently, with more self-reflexive anthropologies, that these lines have been effectively problematized. For Cushing, see Jesse Green, "Cushing at Zuni: Beginnings of American Anthropology," in *Cushing at Zuni: The Correspondence and Journals of Frank Hamilton Cushing 1879–1884*, ed. Jesse Green (Albuquerque: University of New Mexico Press, 1990); Sylvia Gronewold, "Did Frank Hamilton Cushing Go Native?" in *Crossing Cultural Boundaries*, ed. Solon T. Kimball and James B. Watson (San Francisco: Chandler, 1972), 46.

55. After the Civil War, Indian people put up a brief but effective fight for the Great Plains, thereby calling the full power of an increasingly powerful image-making press to bear on the Indian as an oppositional savage. This popular reimagining of Indianness dovetailed in intricate and sometimes contradictory ways with parallel reimaginings in ethnography.

56. Actual native people, we should note, refused to be rocklike objects and continually reinserted their own reality and subjectivity—along with that of the ethnographer—into the process of accumulating knowledge.

57. See, for example, Marianna Torgovnick, *Gone Primitive: Savage Intellects, Modern Lives* (Chicago: University of Chicago Press, 1990); George W. Stocking, Jr., *Race, Culture, and Evolution: Essays in the History of Anthropology* (New York: Free Press, 1968); James Clifford and George E. Marcus, eds., *Writing Culture: The Poetics and Politics of Ethnography* (Berkeley: University of California Press, 1986); Adam Kuper, *The Invention of Primitive Society: Transformations of an Illusion* (New York: Routledge, 1988), 42–75.

Chapter 4. Natural Indians and Identities of Modernity

1. For Beard's list, see "Untitled list of comparisons between Beard and Seton." Daniel Carter Beard Papers, Manuscript Division, Library of Congress, box 209, folder 3. For Seton reply, see box 110, "Ernest Thompson Seton" folder. The essay is marked "exhibit A." Hereafter, Beard Papers.

2. "Why Mr. Seton was Dropped," *Scouting* 3 (December 15, 1915): 16, Beard Papers, box 209, folder 3. For Seton, I have relied heavily upon his published works, the Beard-Seton correspondence in the Beard papers, his autobiography, *Trail of an Artist-Naturalist* (New York: Scribners, 1940), and the reminiscences of his second wife, Julia M. Seton, *By a Thousand Campfires* (Garden City: Doubleday, 1967). I have also used the following secondary sources: H. Allen Anderson, *The Chief: Ernest Thompson Seton and the Changing West* (College Station: Texas A&M Press, 1986); Betty Keller, *Black Wolf: The Life of Ernest Thompson Seton* (Vancouver: Douglas and McIntyre, 1984); John Henry Wadland, *Ernest Thompson Seton: Man in Nature and the Progressive Era, 1880–1915* (New York: Arno, 1978); Brian Morris, "Ernest Thompson Seton and the Origins of the Woodcraft Movement," *Journal of Contemporary History* 5 (1970): 183–94. The largest collection of primary source material regarding Seton may be found at the Seton Memorial Library and Museum at the Philmont Scout Ranch near

Cimarron, New Mexico. Other material is located at Seton Village, Santa Fe, New Mexico, and at the National Scouting Museum at Murray State University, Murray, Kentucky.

3. Beard loved to cite the Boston Tea Party as a defining moment in American history, claiming that "when our ancestors threw the tea overboard in Boston harbor, there was a lot of junk, in the way of played-out ideas along with a monarchical form of government, which went overboard with the tea." Untitled fragment, Beard Papers. box 209, folder 3. For a variation, see "Dan Beard's Christmas Duffel Bag," *Boy's Life* (December 1914): 17–18. He also claimed that an ancestor had participated in the Tea Party, giving himself a lineal legitimation. See Beard's autobiography, *Hardly a Man Is Now Alive: The Autobiography of Dan Beard* (New York: Doubleday, Doran, 1939), 9.

4. Ernest Thompson Seton, *The Gospel of the Red Man: An Indian Bible* (Garden City: Doubleday, Doran, 1936), 1–2.

5. Anderson, *The Chief*, 138–41. Ernest Thompson Seton, *Two Little Savages: Being the Adventures of Two Boys Who Lived as Indians and What They Learned* (New York: Grosset and Dunlap, 1903). Much of Seton's prolific writing—especially his anthropomorphized animal stories and his articles on nature study and childhood development—helped advance the goals of the woodcraft movement. Anderson's excellent bibliography of Seton writings (312–33) demonstrates the sheer quantity of Seton's literary output. The Woodcraft Society—to which Seton returned full time after his departure from scouting—had its own series of adolescent novels. See, for example, Lillian Elizabeth Roy and M. F. Hoisington, *Woodcraft Boys at Sunset Island* (New York: George H. Doran, 1919). Roy's other books include *Woodcraft Girls in the City, Woodcraft Girls at Camp,* and *The Little Woodcrafter's Book.*

6. On Beard, see Beard Papers, Library of Congress, and Beard's autobiography, *Hardly a Man Is Now Alive*; I have also profited from Allan Whitmore, "Beard, Boys and Buckskins: Daniel Carter Beard and the Preservation of the American Pioneer Tradition" (Ph.D. diss., Northwestern University, 1970). For Sons of Daniel Boone, see William D. Murray, *History of the Boy Scouts of America* (New York: Boy Scouts of America, 1937), 18.

7. For modernity and antimodernism, see T. J. Jackson Lears, *No Place of Grace: Antimodism and the Transformation of American Culture, 1880–1920* (New York: Pantheon, 1981); James Clifford, *The Predicament of Culture: Twentieth-Century Ethnography, Literature, and Art* (Cambridge: Harvard University Press, 1988); Theodor Adorno and Max Horkheimer, *The Dialectic of Enlightenment,* trans. John Cumming (New York: Continuum, 1993); Marianna Torgovnick, *Gone Primitive: Savage Intellects, Modern Lives* (Chicago: University of Chicago Press, 1990); Leah Dilworth, *Imagining Indians in the Southwest: Persistent Visions of a Primitive Past* (Washington: Smithsonian Institution Press, 1996).

8. Alan Trachtenberg, *The Incorporation of America: Culture and Society in the Gilded Age* (New York: Hill and Wang, 1982), 3–8. For Seton quote, see *Gospel of the Red Man,* 117.

9. See William Cronon, *Nature's Metropolis: Chicago and the Great West* (New York: Norton, 1991).

10. Mary Ann Clawson, *Constructing Brotherhood: Class, Gender, and Fraternalism* (Princeton: Princeton University Press, 1989), 124.

11. Frederick Jackson Turner, "The Significance of the Frontier in American History," in *The Frontier in American History* (New York: Henry Holt, 1920); David M. Wrobel, *The End of American Exceptionalism: Frontier Anxiety from the Old West to the New Deal* (Lawrence: University

Press of Kansas, 1993); Richard Slotkin, *The Fatal Environment: The Myth of the Frontier in the Age of Industrialization, 1800–1890* (New York: Atheneum, 1985).

12. For authenticity, see Lionel Trilling, *Sincerity and Authenticity* (Cambridge: Harvard University Press, 1972), 93–102, 123–27; Lears, *No Place*, 57; Clifford, *Predicament*, 4–17; Dean MacCannell, *The Tourist: A New Theory of the Leisure Class* (New York: Schocken, 1976), 1–16; Miles Orvell, *The Real Thing: Imitation and Authenticity in American Culture, 1880–1940* (Chapel Hill: University of North Carolina Press, 1989), xv–xix. Robin D. G. Kelley, "Notes on Deconstructing the 'Folk,'" *American Historical Review* 97 (December 1992): 1400–08.

13. For child raising, see David Macleod, *Building Character in the American Boy: The Boy Scouts, YMCA, and Their Forerunners, 1870–1920* (Madison: University of Wisconsin Press, 1983). For adolescence, see Joseph Kett, "Adolescence and Youth in Nineteenth-Century America," in *The Family in History*, ed. Theodore K. Rabb and Robert I. Rotberg (New York: Harper and Row, 1971), 95–110; Kett, *Rites of Passage: Adolescence in America 1790 to the Present* (New York: Basic Books, 1977), esp. 215–72; Viviana A. Zelizer, *Pricing the Priceless Child* (New York: Basic Books, 1985); Amy Green, "Savage Childhood: The Scientific Construction of Girlhood and Boyhood in the Progressive Era" (Ph.D. diss., Yale University, 1995). For the related "playground movement," see Dominick Cavallo, *Muscles and Morals: Organized Playgrounds and Urban Reform, 1880–1920* (Philadelphia: University of Pennsylvania Press, 1981); Paul Boyer, *Urban Masses and Moral Order in America, 1820–1920* (Cambridge: Harvard University Press, 1978), 233–51. For back to nature, see Seton, "Boy Scout Origins," Beard Papers, box 209, folder 3; Peter J. Schmitt, *Back to Nature: The Arcadian Myth in Urban America* (New York: Oxford, 1969); David Shi, *The Simple Life: Plain Living and High Thinking in American Culture* (New York: Oxford, 1985), 207–14.

14. For Balch, see "Beginnings of the Movement," in Porter Sargent, *A Handbook of Summer Camps* (Boston: Porter Sargent, 1924), 24. See also Elizabeth Balch, "The Boy's Paradise: A Summer Visitor's Account of Camp Chocorua," *St. Nicholas* 13 (June 1886): 604–07. Sargent's *Handbook of Summer Camps*, published annually beginning in 1924, contains philosophical and historical essays concerning camps and camping. Among the many primary works published between 1880 and 1935, see Carlos E. Ward, *Organized Camping and Progressive Education* (Galax, Va.: C. E. Ward, 1935); Hedley S. Dimock and C. E. Hendry, *Camping and Character* (New York: Association Press, 1929); A. E. Hamilton, *Boyways: Leaves from a Camp Director's Diary* (New York: John Day, 1930); Minott Osborn, ed., *Camp Dudley: The Story of the First Fifty Years* (New York: Huntington Press, 1934); Luther H. Gulick, *A Philosophy of Play* (New York: Association Press, 1920). H. W. Gibson was a leading camp exponent whose works included *Camp Management: A Manual for Camp Directors* (Cambridge: Murray Printing Co., 1923) and *Camping for Boys* (New York: Association Press, 1911). Much of the writing concerning camping appeared in periodicals, including *Camping* (published in Cambridge, Massachusetts, by H. W. Gibson and the Camp Directors Association), *Outing Magazine*, *Association Boys*, *Progressive Education*, *St. Nicholas*, *Ladies Home Journal*, *Good Housekeeping*.

15. "A Boys' Camp by one of the Campers," *Saint Nicholas* 13:8 (June 1886): 607.

16. Ibid.

17. Ibid., 612; Ernest Balch, "The First Camp," in Sargent, *Handbook of Summer Camps*, 32–37.

18. For primitivism and modernity, see Torgovnick, *Gone Primitive*; Helen Carr, *Inventing the American Primitive: Politics, Gender, and the Representation of Native American Literary Traditions, 1789–1936* (New York: New York University Press, 1996), 203–14 and passim; Walter Benjamin, "On Some Motifs in Baudelaire," in *Illuminations: Essays and Reflections*, ed. Hannah Arendt (New York: Schocken, 1968), 155–200; Susan Buck-Morss, *The Origins of Negative Dialectics: Theodor Adorno, Walter Benjamin and the Frankfurt Institute* (New York: Free Press, 1977), esp. chap. 3, "Dialectics without Identity"; and Buck-Morss, *The Dialectics of Seeing: Walter Benjamin and the Arcades Project* (Cambridge: MIT Press, 1989), 177–201. For dialogic relationships, see Mikhail Bakhtin, "Epic and Novel," in *The Dialogic Imagination*, ed. Michael Holquist, trans. Caryl Emerson and Michael Holquist (Austin: University of Texas Press, 1981), 3–40; Michael Holquist, *Dialogism: Bakhtin and His World* (New York: Routledge, 1990), 14–39.

19. For policy, see Bernard Sheehan, *Seeds of Extinction: Jeffersonian Philanthropy and the American Indian* (Chapel Hill: University of North Carolina Press, 1973); Francis Paul Prucha, *American Indian Policy in the Formative Years: The Indian Trade and Intercourse Acts, 1790–1834* (Cambridge: Harvard University Press, 1962); Reginald Horsman, *Expansion and American Indian Policy, 1783–1812* (Lansing: Michigan State University Press, 1967). Duane Champagne, *Social Order and Political Change: Constitutional Governments among the Cherokee, the Choctaw, the Chickasaw, and the Creek* (Stanford: Stanford University Press, 1992); William McLoughlin, *Cherokee Renascence in the New Republic* (Princeton: Princeton University Press, 1986). For attitudes, see Brian Dippie, *The Vanishing American: White Attitudes and U.S. Indian Policy* (Middletown: Wesleyan University Press, 1982); Robert F. Berkhofer, Jr., *The White Man's Indian: Images of the American Indian from Columbus to the Present* (New York: Vintage Books, 1979), 71–165. For removal, see Reginald Horsman, *The Origin of Indian Removal, 1815–1824* (East Lansing: Michigan State University Press, 1970); Michael Paul Rogin, *Fathers and Children: Andrew Jackson and the Subjugation of the American Indian* (New York: Knopf, 1975); and Ronald N. Satz, *American Indian Policy in the Jacksonian Era* (Lincoln: University of Nebraska Press, 1975).

20. Slotkin, *The Fatal Environment*, 301–24; Alex Nemerov, "Doing the 'Old America': The Image of the American West, 1880–1920," in *The West as America: Reinterpreting Images of the Frontier*, ed. William H. Truettner (Washington: Smithsonian Institution Press, 1991), 298.

21. See Frederick Hoxie, *A Final Promise: The Campaign to Assimilate the Indians, 1880–1920* (Lincoln: University of Nebraska Press, 1984); Francis Paul Prucha, *American Indian Policy in Crisis: Christian Reformers and the Indian, 1865–1900* (Norman: University of Oklahoma Press, 1976).

22. See Johannes Fabian, *Time and the Other: How Anthropology Makes its Object* (New York: Columbia University Press, 1983), 25–69; Clifford, *Predicament of Culture*, 277–346.

23. Dilworth, *Imagining Indians*, 77–124.

24. For Indians as children, see Rogin, *Fathers*, 113–25; Dippie, *Vanishing*, 97–98; Hoxie Neale Fairchild, *The Noble Savage: A Study in Romantic Naturalism* (New York: Russell and Russell, 1961). For children as primitives, see George Boas, *The Cult of Childhood* (Dallas: Spring Publications, 1990); Green, "Savage Childhood." Green provides a detailed bibliography of early twentieth-century recapitulationism.

25. For savagery, see G. Stanley Hall, *Adolescence*, 2 vols. (New York: Appleton, 1904) 1:x. For a popular version, see Julian Ralph, "Fun among the Red Boys," *St. Nicholas* 31:91, 720–23. See also Green, "Savage Childhood"; Stephen Jay Gould, *Ontogeny and Phylogeny*

(Cambridge: Harvard University Press, 1977). For rejection of book learning, see Hall, *Adolescence*, xi.

26. For savages and smokers, see Ernest Thompson Seton, "The Boy Scouts in America," *Outlook* (July 1910): 633. Seton's autobiographical novel *Two Little Savages* would serve as the first "manual" for his Woodcraft Indians group. For play, see Seton, *How to Play Indian: Directions for Organizing a Tribe of Boy Indians and Making Their Teepees in True Indian Style* (Philadelphia: Curtis Publishing, 1903), 3. "How to Play Indian" served as the Woodcraft manual during the organization's second year. The next three editions were called the "Red Book," with the better-known name, "Birch Bark Roll of the Woodcraft Indians," being used from 1907 on. See Anderson, *Chief*, 141.

27. Seton, *How to Play Indian*, 5–6. Starting a wildfire, notes Seton, is "a dreadful crime against the State, as well as the Tribe."

28. Ibid., 4–11.

29. For camps, see Porter Sargent, *Sargent's Camps*, 110. For Seton, see Anderson, *Chief*, 149–65; Murray, *History of the Boy Scouts*, 1–47; John L. Alexander, *Boy Scouts* (Buffalo: Niagara Lithograph, 1911); "History and Organization of the Boy Scouts of America," *Handbook for Scoutmasters: A Manual of Leadership* (New York: Boy Scouts of America, 1922), 471–91. See also "Boy Scout Origins," Beard Papers, box 209, folder 3.

30. At best, Beard could make Indians the savages of whom America could be proud: "We freely acknowledge that the Indian is the noblest savage on earth." See Dan Beard, "undated, untitled mss on the difference between English and Americans," Beard Papers, box 209, folder 2.

31. Beard's autobiography, *Hardly a Man Is Now Alive*, emphasizes his skills as a surveyor, an occupation he links to surveyor/scout heroes like George Washington and Daniel Boone. See Beard, *Buckskin Book for Buckskin Men and Boys* (Philadelphia: Lippincott, 1929), 7–31. Beard's *Boy Pioneers: Sons of Daniel Boone* (New York: Scribners, 1909) and *American Boys' Book of Signs, Signals and Symbols* (Philadelphia: Lippincott, 1918) are full of elaborate plans for forts, council houses, and quirky, mysterious signs and games.

32. Seton, "History of the Boy Scouts," as quoted in Anderson, *Chief*, 154. Seton had piqued Baden-Powell's interest during an English speaking tour in 1904. See Anderson, *Chief*, 152–53. For Baden-Powell, see Sir Robert Baden-Powell, *Scouting for Boys* (London: Arthur Pearson, 1909); Baden-Powell, *Boy Scouts beyond the Seas: My World Tour* (London: Arthur Pearson, 1913); Tim Jeal, *The Boy-Man: The Life of Lord Baden-Powell* (New York: Morrow, 1990), esp. 375–414; and Robert H. MacDonald, *Sons of the Empire: The Frontier and the Boy Scout Movement* (Toronto: University of Toronto Press, 1993).

33. Rivals included Leatherstocking Scouts (Cleveland), Peace Scouts (California), National Scouts of America, Jack Crawford Scouts, Boy Scouts of the United States (funded by the National Highway Protective Association in the hope that they would report speeders), and William Randolph Hearst's American Boy Scouts. See Keith Monroe, "Ernest Thompson Seton: Scouting's First Spellbinder," in Seton Material, National Scouting Museum, Murray, Kentucky; Anderson, *Chief*, 157. For weaponry, see Seton, "What it means to be a scout of the Boy Scouts of America," undated draft mss. Beard Papers, box 209, folder 3. For an account of the legal case that eventually enjoined Hearst's organization from using the name Boy Scout, see *Handbook for Scoutmasters*, 475–79. For hostility to Indians, see Anderson, *Chief*, 156.

34. For marginalization, see Anderson, *Chief*, 159–61; Harold P. Levy, *Building a Popular Movement: A Case Study of the Public Relations of the Boy Scouts of America* (New York: Russell Sage Foundation, 1944). See also Seton et al., *The Official Handbook for Boys* (New York: Doubleday, Page, 1912). For literary attempts to reassert Indianness, see Seton, *Rolf in the Woods: The Adventures of a Boy Scout with Indian Quonab and Little Dog Skookum* (Garden City: Doubleday, 1911), which was dedicated to the Boy Scouts of America.

35. Daniel Carter Beard, "Copy for advertisement," Beard Papers, box 208, folder 3.

36. My account of Camp Fire history relies primarily on Helen Buckler, Mary F. Fiedler, and Martha F. Allen, *Wo-He-Lo: The Story of the Campfire Girls 1910–1960* (New York: Holt, Rinehart, and Winston, 1961). For influences of Grace Seton and Lina Beard, see 29–32. Dan Beard remained a Camp Fire ally, contributing to fund-raising campaigns and, later, donating a Blackfoot tipi to the organization. See Beard Papers, box 33, "Camp Fire Girls" folder.

37. On Gulick, see Buckler, *Wo-He-Lo*, 4–60; Ethel Dorgan, *Luther Halsey Gulick, 1865–1918* (New York: Columbia Teachers College, 1934). On camp, see Buckler, *Wo-He-Lo*, 11–12.

38. See also *The Book of the Camp Fire Girls* (New York: Camp Fire Girls, 1913); "Wohelo! Wohelo!" in *St. Nicholas* 40 (April 1913): 556–60.

39. Buckler, *Wo-He-Lo*, 22. The recapitulation theory, as Amy Green has argued, "deepened the myth of the domestic realm as an eternal, unchanging, and ahistorical sphere naturally inhabited by the universal woman." See Green, "Children Building Wigwams: Recapitulation as Childrearing Strategy at the Turn of the Century," paper presented at the American Studies Association conference, November 2, 1991, Baltimore, Md. For the transformation of gender roles under the regime of modernity, see Carroll Smith-Rosenberg, *Disorderly Conduct: Visions of Gender in Victorian America* (New York: Oxford University Press, 1985), 245–96; Sara M. Evans, *Born for Liberty: A History of Women in America* (New York: Free Press, 1989), 145–74. For feather etiquette, see Buckler, *Wo-He-Lo*, 15.

40. Buckler, *Wo-He-Lo*, 39–41. See also, for example, Winthrop D. Lane, "The Camp Fire Girls: A Readjustment of Women," *Survey* 29 (May 1912): 320; "A Happy Thought and its Development," *The Human Factor* 1 (September 1913): 5; *Book of the Campfire Girls*, 8; Kathrene G. Pinkerton, *Woodcraft for Women* (New York: Outing Publishing, 1916), 11.

41. For Collier, see Buckler, *Wo-He-Lo*, 43–44. The language in this claim, ostensibly Gulick's, closely parallels Collier's own rhetoric about Indians as the last social remnant possessing community values. See, for example, John Collier, *From Every Zenith* (Denver: Sage Books, 1963), 97–98, 125–26.

42. Books like *The Wizard of Oz* (1900) and *Peter Pan* (1911) illustrate this fantastic, magical "kid privilege." See also Buck-Morss, *Dialectics of Seeing*, 458.

43. See, for example, Adolph Bandelier, *Hemenway Southwestern Archaeological Expedition: Contributions to the History of the Southwestern Portion of the United States* (Cambridge: J. Wilson and Son, 1890); Bandelier, *The Southwestern Journals of Adolph F. Bandelier*, ed. Charles H. Lange and Carroll L. Riley (Albuquerque: University of New Mexico Press, 1966); *The Excavation of Hawikuh by Frederick Webb Hodge* (New York: Museum of the American Indian, Heye Foundation, 1966); Jesse Walter Fewkes, *Archeological Expedition to Arizona in 1895* (Glorieta, N.M.: Rio Grande Press, 1971); Fewkes, *A Journal of American Ethnology and Archeology* (Boston: Houghton Mifflin, 1891–1908); Carobeth Laird, *Encounter with an Angry God* (1975; reprint, Albuquer-

que: University of New Mexico Press, 1993); Curtis M. Hinsley, *Savages and Scientists: The Smithsonian Institution and the Development of American Anthropology, 1846–1910* (Washington: Smithsonian Institution Press, 1981); Neil Judd, *The Bureau of American Ethnology: A Partial History* (Norman: University of Oklahoma Press, 1967).

44. See, for example, Seton, *Sign Talk* (Garden City: Doubleday, Page, 1918); "Recent Bird Records for Manitoba," *Auk* 25 (October 1908): 450–54; "Notes on the Breeding Habits of Captive Deermice," *Journal of Mammology* 1 (May 1920): 134–38; "Tail Glands of the Canidae," *Journal of Mammology* 3 (August 1923): 180–82; "On the Study of Scatology," *Journal of Mammology* 6 (February 1925): 47–49. For use of ethnography, see Anderson, *Chief*, 146.

45. Walter Benjamin, "On the Mimetic Faculty," *Reflections: Essays, Aphorisms, Autobiographical Writings*, ed. Peter Demetz, trans. Edmund Jephcott (New York: Harcourt, Brace, Jovanovich, 1978), 333–36; Benjamin, "Doctrine of the Similar," trans. Knut Tarnowski, *New German Critique* 17 (Winter 1979): 65–69; Buck-Morss, *The Dialectics of Seeing*, esp. 262–70; Michael Taussig, *Mimesis and Alterity: A Particular History of the Senses* (London: Routledge, 1993).

46. Collier, *From Every Zenith*, 125. Consider, for example, Igor Stravinsky's fascination with primal festival (*The Firebird, The Rite of Spring, Petrouchka*), expressed through the powerful mimetic mediums of music and ballet.

47. Taussig, *Mimesis*, 45, 20.

48. For Muybridge, see Gordon Hendricks, *Eadweard Muybridge: The Father of the Motion Picture* (New York: Grossman, 1975); Kevin MacDonnell, *Eadweard Muybridge: The Man Who Invented the Moving Picture* (Boston: Little, Brown, 1972); Alan Trachtenberg, *Reading American Photographs: Images as History, Mathew Brady to Walker Evans* (New York: Hill and Wang, 1989), 78. For the optical unconscious, see Benjamin, "The Work of Art in the Age of Mechanical Reproduction," *Illuminations*, 217–251, esp. 237.

49. Edward S. Curtis, *Portraits from North American Life* (New York: Promontory Press, 1972); Christopher Lyman, *The Vanishing Race and Other Illusions: Photographs of Indians by Edward S. Curtis* (Washington: Smithsonian Institution Press, 1982); Peter Palmquist, *With Nature's Children: Emma B. Freeman [1880–1928]—Camera and Brush* (Eureka, Calif.: Interface, 1976); Lucy Lippard, ed., *Partial Recall: Photographs of Native North Americans* (New York: New Press, 1992). For Cushing, see Frank Hamilton Cushing, *My Adventures in Zuni* (Santa Fe: Peripatetic Press, 1941); Charles F. Lummis, "The White Indian," *Land of Sunshine: Magazine of California and the West* 13 (June 1900): 8–16.

50. Taussig, *Mimesis*, 46; Jay Mechling, "The Magic of the Boy Scout Campfire," *Journal of American Folklore* 93 (Jan 1980): 35–56; Bill Ellis, "The Camp Mock-Ordeal: Theater as Life," *Journal of American Folklore* 94 (October-December 1981): 486–505; Jay Mechling, "Playing Indian and the Search for Authenticity in Modern White America," *Prospects*, ed. Jack Salzman, 5 (1980): 17–33.

51. *Camp Fire Girl Handbook 1922*, 18. Carrie Eastburn was my great-grandmother. All of her daughters—Louise, Barbara, Catherine, and Peggy—went through the Camp Fire program. For Deloria, see Janette K. Murray, "Ella Deloria: A Biographical Sketch and Literary Analysis" (Ph.D. diss., North Dakota State University, 1974); Julian Rice, *Deer Women and Elk Men: The Lakota Narratives of Ella Deloria* (Albuquerque: University of New Mexico Press, 1992); and the "Biographical Sketch of the Author" by Agnes Picotte and "Afterword" by Ray-

mond J. DeMallie found in Ella Deloria, *Waterlily* (Lincoln: University of Nebraska Press, 1988), 229–44.

52. In turn, the idea that Indian self-definition might somehow not be enmeshed in Indian-Euro-American cultural contact implies the existence of a "pure" Indian. Given the long history of contact, positing such purity is to participate in (re)making Indians as primitive, timeless Others. Her conception of a positive notion of Indianness, then, is impossible to locate in rigidly separatist understandings of either Dakota or American societies.

53. Frederick E. Hoxie, "Native American Journeys of Discovery," *Journal of American History* 79 (December 1992): 969–95.

54. Raymond Wilson, *Ohiyesa: Charles Eastman, Santee Sioux* (Urbana: University of Illinois Press, 1983); Hazel W. Hertzberg, *The Search for an American Indian Identity: Modern Pan-Indian Movements* (Syracuse: Syracuse University Press, 1971): 38–42 and passim; Hoxie, "Native American Journeys of Discovery," 976–82.

55. Charles A. Eastman (Ohiyesa), *Indian Scout Talks: A Guide for Boy Scouts and Camp Fire Girls* (Boston: Little, Brown, 1914), 1–7. For ritual, see 137.

56. For Parker, Hertzberg, *Search for an American Indian Identity*, 48–53 and passim; Hertzberg, "Nationality, Anthropology, and Pan-Indianism in the Life of Arthur C. Parker (Seneca)," *Proceedings of the American Philosophical Society* 123 (February 1979): 47–72; W. Stephen Thomas, "Arthur Caswell Parker: 1881–1955," *Rochester History* 17:3, 1–30.

57. July 3, 1910. Periodical not identified. Arthur C. Parker Private Scrapbook, William Beauchamp Collection, box 12, Manuscripts and Archives, New York State Library.

58. Parker made similar arguments elsewhere. See, for example, his retelling of American history, "How Indians Made the United States," in *The Indian How Book* (1927; reprint, New York: Dover, 1975), 327–35.

59. Hanowah Lodge Newsletter, nd. Arthur C. Parker Papers, box 2, folder 5, "Boy Scouts." Manuscript and Archive Room, Rush Rhees Library, University of Rochester.

60. *Rochester Democrat and Chronicle*, June 8, 1940. Arthur C. Parker Papers, box 1, folder 1, New York State Library, Albany, New York.

61. On hybridity, see Homi K. Bhabha, *The Location of Culture* (New York: Routledge, 1994), 1–18, 102–22.

62. E. Urner Goodman to Dan Beard, May 31, 1916. Beard Papers, box 55, folder 1. I write, as well, out of my own experience as a Brotherhood (second out of three degrees) member of two different Order of the Arrow chapters—and a participant on one of the order's Indian dance teams.

63. Beard Papers, box 216, "Buckskin Men" folder.

Chapter 5. Hobby Indians, Authenticity, and Race in Cold War America

1. Eckford de Kay, "Buffalo Chips," *American Indian Tradition* 7:4 (1961): 143. For Powers, see *Here Is Your Hobby: Indian Dancing and Costumes* (New York: G. P. Putnam's Sons, 1966), 14.

2. The listings for these powwows come from the "Buffalo Chips" section of *American Indian Tradition* 7:3 and 7:4 (1961).

3. For the origins of the American Indian powwow, see Susan A. Krouse, "A Window into the Indian Culture: The Powwow as Performance" (Ph.D. diss., University of Wiscon-

sin, Milwaukee, 1991); William K. Powers, *War Dance: Plains Indian Musical Performance* (Tucson: University of Arizona Press, 1990), 3–60.

4. John Collier, *From Every Zenith: A Memoir and Some Essays on Life and Thought* (Denver: Sage Publications, 1963), 126.

5. David Riesman, Nathan Glazer, and Reuel Denney, *The Lonely Crowd: A Study of the Changing American Character* (New Haven: Yale University Press, 1950), 17–48, esp. 37–38.

6. William Whyte, *The Organization Man* (New York: Simon and Schuster, 1956); Sloan Wilson, *The Man in the Gray Flannel Suit* (New York: Simon and Schuster, 1955) C. Wright Mills, *The Power Elite* (New York: Oxford, 1956). For nuclear anxiety, see Paul Boyer, *By the Bomb's Early Light: American Thought and Culture at the Dawn of the Atomic Age* (Chapel Hill: University of North Carolina Press, 1994), 275–87.

7. Norman Mailer, "The White Negro: Superficial Reflections on the Hipster," *Dissent* 4 (Summer 1957): 277. Warren Susman, *Culture as History: The Transformation of American Society in the Twentieth Century* (New York: Pantheon, 1984), 284.

8. Warren Susman, with the assistance of Edward Griffin, "Did Success Spoil the United States? Dual Representations in Postwar America," in *Recasting America: Culture and Politics in the Age of the Cold War,* ed. Lary May (Chicago: University of Chicago Press, 1989), 25. The 1950s were marked, among other things, by an increasing public engagement with psychological ideas. Among this genre, my personal favorite is Gerald Sykes, *The Hidden Remnant* (New York: Harper Brothers, 1962).

9. Jack Kerouac, *On the Road* (New York: Viking, 1957). See also Daniel Belgrad, *The Culture of Spontaneity: Improvisation and the Arts in American Society, 1940–1960* (Chicago: University of Chicago Press, 1998); George Lipsitz, "Land of a Thousand Dances: Youth, Minorities, and the Rise of Rock and Roll," in May, *Recasting America,* 267–84; W. T. Lhamon, Jr., *Deliberate Speed: The Origins of a Cultural Style in the American 1950s* (Washington: Smithsonian Institution Press, 1990), 67–97, 180–92.

10. Mailer, "White Negro," 279. For Ramona, see David Hurst Thomas, "Harvesting Ramona's Garden: Life in California's Mythical Mission Past," in *Columbian Consequences,* vol. 3, ed. David Hurst Thomas (Washington: Smithsonian Institution Press, 1991), 119–57.

11. See Steven Lawson, *Running for Freedom: Civil Rights and Black Politics in America since 1941* (Philadelphia: Temple University Press, 1991), 1–65; Wilcomb Washburn, *Red Man's Land / White Man's Law: The Past and Present Status of the American Indian,* 2d ed. (Norman: University of Oklahoma Press, 1995), 101–08; Francis Paul Prucha, *The Great Father: The United States Government and the American Indians* (Lincoln: University of Nebraska Press, 1986), 340–44; Rodolfo Acuña, *Occupied America: A History of Chicanos,* 3d ed. (New York: HarperCollins, 1988), 289–90; David G. Gutierrez, *Walls and Mirrors: Mexican Americans, Mexican Immigrants, and the Politics of Ethnicity* (Berkeley: University of California Press, 1995), 152–78.

12. Alfred L. Kroeber, *The Nature of Culture* (Chicago: University of Chicago Press, 1952), 139.

13. George W. Stocking, Jr., *Race, Culture, and Evolution: Essays in the History of Anthropology* (New York: Free Press, 1968), 203. See also Edward Tylor, *Primitive Culture* (Gloucester, Mass.: P. Smith, 1970).

14. Ashley Montagu, *Man's Most Dangerous Myth: The Fallacy of Race,* 5th ed. (New York: Oxford University Press, 1974), 305. In the early twentieth century, many Americans came to believe that their own racially based superiority was threatened by the intermixing

of different bloods, and fhey worried about eugenics and "race suicide." See, for example, Madison Grant, *The Passing of the Great Race; or, the Racial Basis of European History*, 2d ed. (New York: Scribner's, 1922). See also John Higham, *Strangers in the Land: Patterns of American Nativism, 1860–1925* (New York: Atheneum, 1969), 131–57, 270–86.

15. Kroeber, *The Nature of Culture*, 104. Culture, as George Stocking points out, "explained all the same phenomena, but it did so in strictly non-biological terms" (265). Taking the argument to extremes, Boas argued, for example, that the physical shapes of immigrants' heads had been altered through contact with American culture. Stocking, *Essays*, 268.

16. Raymond Williams, *Keywords: A Vocabulary of Culture and Society* (New York: Oxford University Press, 1976), 10.

17. Susman, with Edward Griffin, "Did Success Spoil the United States?" 25. For race, see Montagu, *Man's Most Dangerous Myth*; Ruth Benedict, *Patterns of Culture* (Boston: Houghton-Mifflin, 1934), 1–18; Benedict, *Race and Racism* (London: Labour Book Service, 1943); Margaret Mead, *Coming of Age in Samoa: A Psychological Study of Primitive Youth for Western Civilisation* (New York: New American Library, 1949); and especially Gunnar Myrdal, with assistance from Richard Sterner and Arnold Rose, *An American Dilemma: The Negro Problem and Modern Democracy* (New York: Harper Brothers, 1944). For the 1950s, see Richard Polenberg, *One Nation Divisible: Class, Race, and Ethnicity in the United States since 1938* (New York: Viking Press, 1980); William Chafe, *The Unfinished Journey: America since World War Two*, 3d ed. (New York: Oxford University Press, 1995); Lhamon, *Deliberate Speed*; Taylor Branch, *Parting the Waters: America in the King Years, 1954–63* (New York: Simon and Schuster, 1988); Tom Englehardt, *The End of Victory Culture: Cold War America and the Disillusioning of a Generation* (New York: Harper-Collins, 1995), 69–171; James S. Olson and Raymond Wilson, *Native Americans in the Twentieth Century* (Urbana: University of Illinois Press, 1984), 131–53.

18. I should note that, although my discussion will end in the early 1970s, Indian hobbyism is alive and well today. The "hobby's" leading contemporary voice is that of Jack Heriard of New Orleans, who publishes a magazine called *Whispering Wind: American Indian Past and Present*.

19. For the origins of the hobby, see William K. Powers, "The Indian Hobbyist Movement in North America," in *Handbook of North American Indians*, vol. 4, *History of Indian-White Relations*, ed. Wilcomb Washburn (Washington: Smithsonian Institution Press, 1988), 557–61. Class composition suggested by Richard Conn, interview with author, July 13, 1993. See also "Meet Jay Mahoney," *Powwow Trails* 1 (February 1965): n.p., in which the primary focus of the story is Mahoney's wealth, suggesting that he may be an exceptional case.

20. Jay Mechling, " 'Playing Indian' and the Search for Authenticity in Modern White America," *Prospects*, vol. 5, ed. Jack Salzman (New York: Burt Franklin, 1980), 21. See also Jack Kelly, *Koshare* (Boulder: Pruett, 1975).

21. Powers, "The Indian Hobbyist Movement," 557–59.

22. For the Smokis, see Sharlot Hall, *The Story of the Smoki People* (Prescott: Way Out West, 1922); Charles Franklin Parker, *When the Smoki Dance* (Prescott: The Smoki People, 1941). Both of these may be found in the Special Collections Room, University of Arizona Library. See also Leah Dilworth, *Imagining Indians in the Southwest: Persistent Visions of a Primitive Past* (Washington: Smithsonian Institution Press, 1996), 73–75.

23. I have come to this conclusion after a thorough reading of the artifakery sections of *American Indian Tradition*.

24. The *American Indian Hobbyist* was published by Norman Feder, a former Boy Scout who went on to a career as a curator of American Indian art. William K. Powers has argued that Feder's publication marks a point of self-consciousness around which hobby activity, which had been going on for some forty-five years, crystallized. Powers, "The Indian Hobbyist Movement," 558–59.

25. Ralph Hubbard, *American Indian Crafts* (New York: Plume Trading and Sales, 1935); Hubbard, *Queer Person* (New York: Doubleday, 1930); Nellie Snyder Yost, *A Man as Big as the West* (Boulder: Pruett, 1979).

26. The Koshares and the Smokis had danced, of course, but without the attention to ethnographic detail that characterized later dance and music enthusiasts. If their costumes were often ethnographically detailed, Koshare dances nonetheless emphasized a freer "dramatic reinterpretation." See Mechling, "Playing Indian," 24–25. For published music, see Frances Densmore, *Chippewa Music* (Bureau of American Ethnology, Bulletin 53, 1913); *Teton Sioux Music* (Bureau of American Ethnology, Bulletin 61, 1918); *Mandan and Hidatsa Music* (Bureau of American Ethnology, Bulletin 80, 1923); *Pawnee Music* (Bureau of American Ethnology, Bulletin 93, 1929); *Cheyenne and Arapaho Music* (Los Angeles: Southwest Museum Papers, 1936), 10; and Bruno Nettl, *North American Indian Musical Styles* (Philadelphia: American Folklore Society, 1954).

27. William K. Powers, *War Dance*, xi–xv. Many of the figures profiled in *American Indian Tradition*—Frank Turley, Dennis Lessard, Larry Morgan—began making reservation visits in the late 1940s and early 1950s. For Powers's articles, see *American Indian Tradition* 7 (1960–61): 1, 2, 3, 4, 5. For Howard profile, see *American Indian Tradition* 7 (Spring 1961): 104.

28. Powers, *Here Is Your Hobby*, 11.

29. Kroeber, *Nature of Culture*, 104. For passing, see Chief Buffalo Child Long Lance (Sylvester Long), *Long Lance* (New York: Cosmopolitan Books, 1929); Donald B. Smith, *Long Lance: The True Story of an Imposter* (Lincoln: University of Nebraska Press, 1982); Smith, *From the Land of Shadows: The Making of Grey Owl* (Saskatoon: Western Producer Prairie Books, 1990); James A. Clifton, ed., *Being and Becoming Indian: Biographical Studies of North American Frontiers* (Chicago: Dorsey Press, 1989).

30. For Cushing, see Frank Hamilton Cushing, *My Adventures in Zuni* (Santa Fe: Peripatetic Press, 1941); Jesse D. Green, *Cushing at Zuni: The Correspondence and Journals of Frank Hamilton Cushing, 1879–1884* (Albuquerque: University of New Mexico Press, 1990); Charles F. Lummis, "The White Indian," *The Land of Sunshine: Magazine of California and the West* 13 (June 1900): 8–16. Sylvia Gronewald, "Did Frank Hamilton Cushing Go Native?" in *Crossing Cultural Boundaries*, ed. Solon T. Kimball and James B. Watson (San Francisco: Chandler, 1972). For anthropology, see Susan Sontag, *Against Interpretation* (New York: Farrar, Straus, Giroux, 1966), 69–81. The "wannabe" quality of hobbyist practices that sought to transcend race may have been directed in many cases at anthropologists—seen as quintessential boundary-hoppers—as much as it was at Indian people. Likewise, one should note that James Howard did have to confront the issue from time to time.

31. Carey McWilliams, *North from Mexico: The Spanish-Speaking People of the United States*, 2d ed., updated by Matt S. Meier (New York: Greenwood, 1990), esp. 188–231; Warren Miller, *The Cool World, a Novel* (Boston: Little, Brown, 1959); Norman Mailer, "The White Negro"; William F. Whyte, *Street Corner Society: The Social Structure of an Italian Slum* (Chicago: University of Chicago Press, 1955); John Howard Griffin, *Black Like Me* (New York: New American

Library, 1961); Herbert Gans, *The Levittowners: Ways of Life and Politics in a New Suburban Community* (New York: Pantheon, 1967).

32. Among the many studies of whiteness, see Michael Rogin, *Blackface, White Noise: Jewish Immigrants in the Hollywood Melting Pot* (Berkeley: University of California Press, 1996); Eric Lott, *Love and Theft: Blackface Minstrelsy and the American Working Class* (New York: Oxford, 1993); David Roediger, *The Wages of Whiteness: Race and the Making of the American Working Class* (New York: Verso, 1991) and *Toward the Abolition of Whiteness* (New York, 1994); Ruth Frankenberg, *White Women, Race Matters: The Social Construction of Whiteness* (Minneapolis: University of Minnesota Press, 1993); George Lipsitz, "The Possessive Investment in Whiteness: Racialized Social Democracy and the 'White' Problem in American Studies" and responses by George Sanchez, Henry Louis Taylor, Jr., Walter E. Williams, *American Quarterly* 47 (September 1995): 369–427. See also Shelley Fisher Fishkin's bibliographic essay, "Interrogating 'Whiteness,' Complicating 'Blackness': Remapping American Culture," in the same issue, 428–66.

33. For war, see Alison Bernstein, *American Indians and World War II: Toward a New Era in Indian Affairs* (Norman: University of Oklahoma Press, 1991): 159–66. For policy, see Donald Fixico, *Termination and Relocation: Federal Indian Policy, 1945–1960* (Albuquerque: University of New Mexico Press, 1986). For other treatments of this time period, see Larry W. Burt, *Tribalism in Crisis: Federal Indian Policy, 1953–1961* (Albuquerque: University of New Mexico Press, 1982); James S. Olson and Raymond Wilson, *Native Americans in the Twentieth Century* (Urbana: University of Illinois Press, 1984). Since 1955, mixed Indian communities have been discussed as *pan-Indian*. William K. Powers presents a forceful argument against the term and in favor of *inter-Indian*. I have adopted his usage. See "Pan-Indianism Reconsidered," in *War Dance*, 86–112.

34. Powers, "The Indian Hobbyist Movement," 560.

35. The logic of Indian blood quantum operated in direct opposition to the one-drop rule that applied to African Americans. Most whites denied even the most distant black ancestor. Obscure Indian blood, on the other hand, was eagerly claimed, for it served obvious purposes of aboriginal legitimation. The trick, of course, was not to claim too much Indian blood. Still, one could be white and Indian in ways that one could not be white and black. See Rayna Green, "The Tribe Called Wannabee: Playing Indian in America and Europe," *Folklore* 99:1 (1988): 45–47; Terry P. Wilson, "Blood Quantum: Native American Mixed Bloods," in *Racially Mixed People in America*, ed. Maria P. P. Root (Newbury Park: Sage Publications, 1992), 108–25.

36. "Notes from the Moccasin Telegraph," *Powwow Trails* 1:1 (April 1964): n.p. The list includes singers from Oklahoma, North and South Dakota, and Montana. See also Powers, *Here Is Your Hobby*, 19, 115–16.

37. "Meet Frank Turley," *Powwow Trails* 2:9 (February 1966): n.p.; "Meet Larry Morgan," *Powwow Trails* 3:9 (January 1967): 11. "Meet Dennis Lessard," *Powwow Trails* 2:2 (May 1965): n.p.

38. "Comment," *American Indian Tradition* 7:3 (1961): 76

39. "Comment," *American Indian Tradition* 7:4 (1961): 112; "Comment," 7:5 (1961): 148.

40. Powers, "Indian Hobbyist Movement," 560–61. Powers, Letter to Author, December 16, 1992.

41. Powers, "Songs of the Red Man," *War Dance*, 113–27. One should also note that the recording and copyrighting of oral stories and songs have also been an especially egregious site of the outright theft of native cultural property. Powers vehemently attacked such practices. See "Editorial," *Powwow Trails* 1:2 (May 1964): n.p.

42. Powers letter to author, December 16, 1992.

43. Interview with Tim Giago, publisher of *The Lakota Times* (now *Indian Country Today*), Martin, South Dakota, March 16, 1987.

44. See Jay Mechling, "Florida Seminoles and the Marketing of the Last Frontier," in *Dressing in Feathers: The Construction of the Indian in American Popular Culture*, ed. S. Elizabeth Bird (Boulder: Westview Press, 1996), 149–66. These exchanges were, of course, only one of the many ways that Indian people (re)constituted identities and traditions in the 1950s. Among the many meanings that were shared between whites and Indians, the idea of the reservation as Indian homeland was perhaps the most prevalent. Urban Indians often traveled between city and "rez," and it was the reservations that jump-started the broad-based resistance to termination policy that led to the native cultural and political activism that burst to life in the late 1950s.

45. Powers letter to author, January 29, 1993.

46. "Meet the Medicine Drum Dancers," *Powwow Trails* 1:2 (May 1964): n.p.

47. "When the People Gather," *Powwow Trails* 1:9 (February 1965): n.p.

48. Ibid.

49. Marxian analysis has termed this kind of meaning-implanting through market exchange commodity fetishism, an ironic conjuncture, given that fetishes made up at least some part of the hobby trade.

50. The "salad bowl" metaphor, for example, which has been offered as a multicultural replacement for the familiar melting pot, relies upon both mixture and essential difference for its analogic strength.

51. Interview with Richard Conn, July 13, 1993.

52. Powers, "Indian Hobbyist Movement," 559.

53. Powers letter to author, December 16, 1992.

54. Richard White, *The Middle Ground: Indians, Empires, and Republics in the Great Lakes Region, 1650–1815* (New York: Cambridge University Press, 1991), ix–xvi. I am transforming White's concept slightly here, in that his Indian historical subjects possessed of themselves the military and economic power to force non-Indians to the middle ground. Non-Indian hobbyists ceded their power in order to gain access to Indian culture. In many social settings (reservations, urban meeting places), however, Indians did have the power to tell hobbyists to take their ceded power and go home.

55. See Mechling, "Playing Indian"; Val Gendron, *Behind the Zuni Masks* (New York: Longmans, Green, 1958), an adolescent novel, and William L. Merrill, Edmund J. Ladd, and T. J. Ferguson, "The Return of the Ahayu:da: Lessons for Repatriation from Zuni Pueblo and the Smithsonian Institution," *Current Anthropology* 34 (December 1993): 523–55.

56. See, for example, Robert Burnette and John Koster, *The Road to Wounded Knee* (New York: Bantam, 1974); Alvin Josephy, *Red Power: The American Indian's Fight for Freedom* (New York: McGraw-Hill, 1971); Vine Deloria, Jr., *Custer Died for Your Sins: An Indian Manifesto* (New York: Macmillan, 1969) and *Behind the Trail of Broken Treaties: An Indian Declaration of Independence*, 2d ed. (Austin: University of Texas Press, 1985); Troy R. Johnson, *The Occupation*

of *Alcatraz Island: Indian Self-Determination and the Rise of Indian Activism* (Urbana: University of Illinois Press, 1996); Olson and Wilson, *Native Americans in the Twentieth Century*, 157–219.

Chapter 6. Counterculture Indians and the New Age

1. William Hedgepeth, with photographs by Dennis Stock, *The Alternative: Communal Life in New America* (New York: Macmillan, 1970), 73, 84, 81. For corn, beans, squash, see Robert Houriet, *Getting Back Together* (New York: Coward, McCann, and Geoghegan, 1971), 170–71. Although my understanding of countercultural communalism relies on certain personal experiences, I have also drawn upon Keith Melville, *Communes in the Counterculture: Origins, Theories, Styles of Life* (New York: William Morrow, 1972); Richard Atcheson, *The Bearded Lady: Going on the Commune Trip and Beyond* (New York: John Day, 1971); Lewis Yablonsky, *The Hippie Trip* (New York: Pegasus, 1968); Timothy Miller, *The Hippies and American Values* (Knoxville: University of Tennessee Press, 1991); Benjamin Zablocki, *Alienation and Charisma: A Study of Contemporary American Communes* (New York: Free Press, 1980); Laurence Veysey, *The Communal Experience: Anarchist and Mystical Communities in Twentieth-Century America* (Chicago: University of Chicago Press, 1978), 279–406.

2. The Beatles, "Strawberry Fields Forever," *Magical Mystery Tour* (EMI, 1967).

3. In thinking about this cluster of ideas, I have been informed by, among others, Andreas Huyssen, *After the Great Divide: Modernism, Mass Culture, Postmodernism* (Bloomington: Indiana University Press, 1986), esp. 141–221; David Harvey, *The Condition of Postmodernity: An Enquiry into the Origins of Cultural Change* (Cambridge, Mass.: Blackwell, 1989); Fredric Jameson, *Postmodernism, or The Cultural Logic of Late Capitalism* (Durham: Duke University Press, 1991); Hal Foster, ed., *The Anti-Aesthetic: Essays on Postmodern Culture* (Port Townsend, Wash.: Bay Press, 1983); Jean Baudrillard, *Simulacra and Simulations*, trans. Sheila Faria Glaser (Ann Arbor: University of Michigan Press, 1994); Jean-François Lyotard, *The Postmodern Condition: A Report on Knowledge*, trans. Geoff Bennington and Brian Massumi (Minneapolis: University of Minnesota Press, 1984).

4. Fredric Jameson, *The Prison House of Language: A Critical Account of Structuralism and Russian Formalism* (Princeton: Princeton University Press, 1972), ix.

5. Goodman, as quoted in Melville, *Communes in the Counterculture*, 114. See also Goodman, *The New Reformation: Notes of a Neolithic Conservative* (New York: Vintage, 1969), 143–54; Veysey, *Communal Experience*, 3–73. On Paul Goodman, see Theodore Roszak, *The Making of a Counter Culture: Reflections on the Technocratic Society and Its Youthful Opposition* (Garden City: Anchor Books, 1969), 178–204; Morris Dickstein, *Gates of Eden: American Culture in the Sixties* (New York: Basic, 1977), 74–83.

6. See, for example, Abbie Hoffman[pseud. Free], *Revolution for the Hell of It* (New York: Dial Press, 1968), 10, for "Do your own thing" as a mantra; Goodman, *New Reformation*, 145.

7. Stewart Brand, "Indians and the Counterculture, 1960s-1970s," *Handbook of North American Indians*, vol. 4, *History of Indian-White Relations*, ed. Wilcomb Washburn (Washington: Smithsonian Institution Press, 1988), 570. For "Navajo," see Houriet, *Getting Back Together*, 170.

8. For Warhol, see Robert Rosenblum, "Warhol as Art History," *Andy Warhol: A Retrospective*, ed. Kynaston McShine (New York: Museum of Modern Art, 1989), 25–36, 183–97. See also John Cage, *Imaginary Landscape No. 4* (for twelve radios, twenty-four players, and conduc-

tor), 1951, with performances in 1951 and 1959; Cage, *Radio Music* (for one to eight radios), 1956. On Cage, see *John Cage Catalogue* (New York: Henmar Press, 1962), 36, 38; Eric Salzman, "Imaginary Landscaper," and Richard Kostelanetz, "John Cage as Hörspielmacher" in *Writings about John Cage*, ed. Richard Kostelanetz, (Ann Arbor: University of Michigan Press, 1993), 1–7, 213–21. See also Douglas Crimp, "On the Museum's Ruins," *Anti-Aesthetic*, ed. Hal Foster, 43–56.

9. For antiwar movement, see Todd Gitlin, *The Sixties: Years of Hope, Days of Rage* (New York: Bantam, 1987), esp. 242–60, 285–304; William Chafe, *The Unfinished Journey: America since World War II*, 3d ed. (New York: Oxford, 1995), 320–28; Tom Engelhardt, *The End of Victory Culture: Cold War America and the Disillusioning of a Generation* (New York: HarperCollins, 1995), 244–46; Nancy Zaroulis and Gerald Sullivan, *Who Spoke Up? American Protest against the War in Vietnam, 1963–1975* (Garden City, N.J.: Doubleday, 1984); Charles DeBenedetti with assistance from Charles Chatfield, *An American Ordeal: The Antiwar Movement of the Vietnam Era* (Syracuse: Syracuse University Press, 1990). For the relation between antiwar and counterculture protest, see David Farber, "The Counterculture and the Antiwar Movement," *Give Peace a Chance: Exploring the Vietnam Antiwar Movement*, ed. Melvin Small and William D. Hoover (Syracuse: Syracuse University Press, 1992), 7–21. For a general survey, see Farber, *The Age of Great Dreams: America in the 1960s* (New York: Hill and Wang, 1994).

10. Mitchell Goodman, "What's Happening," *The Movement toward a New America: The Beginnings of a Long Revolution (A Collage) A What?* (Philadelphia: Pilgrim Press/Knopf, 1970), vii. For LSD, see Farber, "Counterculture and Antiwar," 19.

11. *Little Big Man*, directed by Arthur Penn (Fox, 1970).

12. Naomi Feigelson, *The Underground Revolution: Hippies, Yippies, and Others* (New York: Funk and Wagnalls, 1970), 7, 64; Hoffman, *Revolution for the Hell of It*, 37.

13. See Hoffman, *Revolution for the Hell of It*, 71–73, for appropriation of racial victim identity. For crossing to the Vietnamese position, see Gitlin, *The Sixties*, 261–82. See also Karin Ashley et al., "You Don't Need a Weatherman to Know Which Way the Wind Blows" (1969), in *A History of Our Time: Readings on Postwar America*, ed. William H. Chafe and Harvard Sitkoff (New York: Oxford, 1983), 235–38.

14. See Tom Holm, *Strong Hearts, Wounded Souls: Native American Veterans of the Vietnam War* (Austin: University of Texas Press, 1996), 118. One should note as well the tendency of American ground troops to reprise nineteenth-century Plains warfare, designating North Vietnamese territory, "Indian country." See Holm, ibid., 129.

15. For Indian activism, see Indians of All Tribes, ed. Peter Blue Cloud, *Alcatraz Is Not an Island* (Berkeley: Wingbow Press, 1972); Adam Fortunate Eagle, *Alcatraz! Alcatraz! The Indian Occupation of 1969–1971* (Berkeley: Heyday Books, 1992); Vine Deloria, Jr., *Behind the Trail of Broken Treaties: An Indian Declaration of Independence* (Austin: University of Texas Press, 1985); Stanley David Lyman, *Wounded Knee 1973: A Personal Account* (Lincoln: University of Nebraska Press, 1991); Paul Chaat Smith and Robert Allen Warrior, *Like a Hurricane: The Indian Movement from Alcatraz to Wounded Knee* (New York: New Press, 1996). For Anderson, see Troy R. Johnson, *The Occupation of Alcatraz Island: Indian Self-Determination and the Rise of Indian Activism* (Champaign: University of Illinois Press, 1996), 32. For Brando, see "Brando Has Long Backed Rights of Racial Minorities," *New York Times*, March 28, 1973, 40. For Poor People's Campaign, see Paul Cowan, "Indians Meet the Press: It's Pride vs. Prejudice," in Goodman, ed., *Movement toward a New America*, 249–50.

16. Feigelson, *Underground Revolution*, 11; Hoffman, *Revolution for the Hell of It*, 164, for pastiche poster. For revolutionary bandanna, see Jerry Avorn, Robert Freedman, et al., "Up against the Ivy Wall," in *Our Time*, ed. Chafe and Sitkoff, 246. For bandanna in drug and communal culture, see Yablonsky, *Hippie Trip*, 64, 74, 80. See James Clifford, *The Predicament of Culture: Twentieth-Century Ethnography, Literature, and Art* (Cambridge: Harvard University Press, 1988), 346, for Indianness encoded in a bandanna headband. For the compression of high and popular culture, see William L. O'Neill, *Coming Apart: An Informal History of America in the 1960s* (Chicago: Quadrangle Books, 1971), 200–27, 245–49.

17. Paul Goodman, *New Reformation*, 194; Hoffman, *Revolution for the Hell of It*, 71–73; Jerry Farber, "Student as Nigger," in Goodman, ed., *Movement toward a New America*, 303–04; Farber, "Counterculture and Antiwar," 17; John Lennon and Yoko Ono, "Woman is the Nigger of the World," *Shaved Fish* (EMI, 1972).

18. Hoffman, *Revolution for the Hell of It*, 9.

19. Peter Clecak, *America's Quest for the Ideal Self: Dissent and Fulfillment in the 60s and 70s* (New York: Oxford University Press, 1983), 117; Chatfield, "The Antiwar Movement and America," *American Ordeal*, 396.

20. As quoted in Rudolph Kaiser, "Chief Seattle's Speech(es): American Origins and European Reception," in *Recovering the Word: Essays on Native American Literature*, ed. Brian Swann and Arnold Krupat (Berkeley: University of California Press, 1987), 517.

21. For a tracing of the speech's diffusion, see ibid., 497–536, esp. 515.

22. Goodman, *New Reformation*, 59.

23. Ibid., 54; Feigelson, *Underground Revolution*, 50–51, 64–65; Roszak, *Making of a Counter Culture*, 124–77.

24. John Neihardt, *Black Elk Speaks: Being the Life Story of a Holy Man of the Oglala Sioux* (New York: Pocket Books, 1972); John Fire Lame Deer and Richard Erdoes, *Lame Deer: Seeker of Visions* (New York: Simon and Schuster, 1972); Hyemeyohsts Storm, *Seven Arrows* (New York: Ballantine, 1972). On drugs, see William Braden, *The Private Sea: LSD and the Search for God* (Chicago: Quadrangle Books, 1967); Melville, *Communes in the Counterculture*, 223–27; Veysey, *Communal Experience*, 437–39, 442–44.

25. Doug Boyd, *Rolling Thunder: A Personal Exploration into the Secret Healing Powers of an American Indian Medicine Man* (New York: Random House, 1974); Sun Bear, *The Medicine Wheel: Earth Astrology* (Englewood Cliffs: Prentice-Hall, 1980); *Walk in Balance: The Path to Healthy, Happy, Harmonious Living* (New York: Prentice-Hall, 1989). See also James Clifton, *Being and Becoming Indian: Biographical Studies of North American Frontiers* (Chicago: Dorsey Press, 1989).

26. Editorial, *Many Smokes* 2:1 (1st Quarter) 1967: 3; 2:3 (3d Quarter) 1967: 3.

27. I make these observations after reading several issues of both *Many Smokes* and *Wildfire*. For specific examples listed, see *Wildfire*'s inaugural publications, 1:1, 2 (Spring-Summer), and 1:3, 4 (Fall-Winter).

28. Carlos Castaneda, *The Teachings of Don Juan: A Yaqui Way of Knowledge* (Berkeley: University of California Press, 1968); *A Separate Reality: Further Conversations with Don Juan* (New York: Simon and Schuster, 1971); *Journey to Ixtlan: The Lessons of Don Juan* (New York: Simon and Schuster, 1972); *Tales of Power* (New York: Simon and Schuster, 1974); *The Second Ring of Power* (New York: Simon and Schuster, 1977). To date, four other books follow, the most recent being *The Art of Dreaming* (New York: HarperCollins, 1993).

29. MacLaine, *Out on a Limb* (New York: Bantam, 1983); *Dancing in the Light* (New York:

Bantam, 1985). Artists on the tastefully packaged Windom Hill label included the pianists George Winston and Bill Quist, the guitarist Ackerman, and the bassist Michael Manring, among many others. See also Marilyn Ferguson, *The Aquarian Conspiracy* (Los Angeles: J. P. Tarcher, 1980).

30. Dirk Johnson, "Spiritual Seekers Borrow Indians' Ways," *New York Times*, December 27, 1993, A1. Also printed as David Johnston, "New Age Rites Seen as Robbery," *Boulder Daily Camera*, December 27, 1993, 5C.

31. Stephen Buhner, "Protecting the Right to Worship," *Boulder Daily Camera*, January 3, 1994, 2C. See also Ed McGaa, *Mother Earth Spirituality: Native American Paths to Healing Ourselves and Our World* (San Francisco: Harper and Row, 1990); *Rainbow Tribe: Ordinary People Journeying on the Red Road* (San Francisco: Harper-San Francisco, 1992).

32. I do not mean to suggest that there are not teacher-student relationships in native religious traditions. It may be important, especially in discussing northern Plains traditions, to distinguish between healing and spirituality, the former relying more heavily on teaching. Sacred bundles and spiritual power have in fact been subject to transfer, although as often in an economic or kinship exchange as in a master-learner one. See, for example, Peter Nabokov, *Two Leggings: The Making of a Crow Warrior* (New York: Thomas Crowell, 1967), 143–54. For Plains spiritual tradition, see James Walker, *Lakota Belief and Ritual*, ed. Raymond J. DeMallie and Elaine A. Jahner (Lincoln: University of Nebraska Press, 1980); Lee Irwin, *The Dream Seekers: Native American Visionary Traditions of the Great Plains* (Norman: University of Oklahoma Press, 1994); Raymond J. DeMallie, "Lakota Belief and Ritual in the Nineteenth Century," *Sioux Indian Religion*, ed. Raymond J. DeMallie and Douglas R. Parks (Norman: University of Oklahoma Press, 1987), 25–44; Joseph Epes Brown, ed., *The Sacred Pipe: Black Elk's Account of the Seven Rites of the Oglala Sioux* (Norman: University of Oklahoma Press, 1953).

33. Buhner, "Protecting the Right to Worship."

34. See, for example, *Badoni v. Higginson* 638 F.2d 172 (1980); *United States v. Dion* 476 U.S. 734 (1986); *Lyng v. Northwest Indian Cemetery Protective Association* 485 U.S. 439 (1988); *Employment Division, Department of Human Resources of Oregon, et al. v. Alfred L. Smith et al.* 494 U.S. 872 (1990). See John Wunder, *"Retained by the People": A History of American Indians and the Bill of Rights* (New York: Oxford University Press, 1994), 180–99.

35. Johnston, "New Age Rites."

36. Buhner, "Protecting the Right to Worship."

37. Randolph Bourne, "Trans-National America," in *War and the Intellectuals: Essays, 1915–1919*, ed. Carl Resek (New York: Harper Torchbooks, 1964), 107–23; Kallen, "Democracy versus the Melting Pot, *Nation* 100 (February 18–25, 1915): 190–94, 217–20. See also Gary B. Nash, "The Great Multicultural Debate," *Contention* 1 (Spring 1992): 1–28; and Nash, "The Hidden History of Mestizo America," *Journal of American History* 82 (December 1995): 941–64. See also David Hollinger, *Postethnic America: Beyond Multiculturalism* (New York: Basic Books, 1995), 11; Lawrence W. Levine, *The Opening of the American Mind: Canons, Culture, and History* (Boston: Beacon Press, 1996), 105–20 and passim.

38. See, for example, Werner Sollors, *Beyond Ethnicity: Consent and Descent in American Culture* (New York: Oxford University Press, 1986).

39. I make this summary after years of reading Boulder's New Age periodicals and talking with friends who have been involved in New Age activities. Particularly useful have

been *Men's Council Journal, Nexus, The Eagle's Cry: A Journal for Holistic Experiences, Wisdom, and Education,* and the nationally circulated magazines *Shaman's Drum* and *New Age Journal.*

40. Lynn Andrews, *Flight of the Seventh Moon* (New York: Harper and Row, 1984), 26. For others in the series, see, for example, *Medicine Woman* (San Francisco: Harper and Row, 1981); *Jaguar Woman and the Wisdom of the Butterfly Tree* (San Francisco: Harper and Row, 1985); *Star Woman* (New York: Warner, 1986); *Shakki: Woman of the Sacred Garden* (New York: Harper-Collins, 1992).

41. Clarissa Pinkola Estes, *Women Who Run with the Wolves: Myths and Stories of the Wild Woman Archetype* (New York: Ballantine, 1992); Robert Bly, *Iron John: A Book about Men* (Reading, Mass.: Addison-Wesley, 1990); Sam Keen, *Fire in the Belly: On Being a Man* (New York: Bantam, 1991): Diane Stein, *Dreaming the Past, Dreaming the Future: A Herstory of the Earth* (Freedom, Calif.: Crossing Press, 1991); James Redfield, *The Celestine Prophecy: An Adventure* (New York: Warner, 1993); Michael Rossman, *New Age Blues: On the Politics of Consciousness* (New York: Dutton, 1979). For more analytical treatments, see Michael Schwalbe, *Unlocking the Iron Cage: The Men's Movement, Gender Politics, and American Culture* (New York: Oxford, 1996); Michael York, *The Emerging Network: A Sociology of the New Age and Neo-Pagan Movements* (Lanham, Md.: Rowman and Littlefield, 1995). For a critique, see Henry Gordon, *Channeling into the New Age: The "Teachings" of Shirley MacLaine and Other Such Gurus* (Buffalo: Prometheus Books, 1988). Numerous other authors, ranging from "Indian" mystery writers Tony Hillerman and Jean Hagar to high culture writers like M. T. Kelly and W. P. Kinsella, have assumed the literary voice of "the Indian." Others, such as Jamake Highwater and Forrest Carter, have taken Indian identity as their own.

42. For mascots, see Philip Deloria, "Mascots and Other Public Appropriations of Indians and Indian Culture by Whites," *Encyclopedia of North American Indians,* ed. Frederick Hoxie (Boston: Houghton-Mifflin, 1996), 359–61; Dennis Banks, Laurel R. Davis, Synthia Syndnor-Slowikowski, and Lawrence A. Wenner, "Tribal Names and Mascots in Sports," *Journal of Sports and Social Issues* 17 (April 1993): 1–33. For Redskins, see, for example, Ward Churchill, "Crimes against Humanity," *Z Magazine* (March 1993): 43–47.

43. On play, see Johan Huizinga, *Homo Ludens: A Study of the Play Element in Culture* (Boston: Beacon Press, 1955), 8.

44. Christine Mather and Sharon Woods, *Santa Fe Style* (New York: Rizzoli International, 1986); Mary Emmerling and Carol Sama Sheehan, *American Country West: A Style and Source Book* (New York: Clarkson N. Potter, 1985).

45. This is not to say that New Age followers have offered no political help to native people, or to suggest that they have completely failed to engage Indians. Rather, it is the nature of that engagement which is at issue. New Age participation in Plains Sun Dances, for example, has been so overwhelming and so lacking in etiquette that many dances have been closed to non-Indians.

46. *Indian Country Today* 13:3 (July 14, 1992): 1, 2, and subsequent editions throughout the months of July and August.

47. On cultural difference, see Homi K. Bhabha, *The Location of Culture* (New York: Routledge, 1994), 34–35. On power, I have been influenced by Michel Foucault, *The History of Sexuality,* vol. 1, *An Introduction,* trans. Robert Hurley (New York: Random House, 1978); *Discipline and Punish: The Birth of the Prison,* trans. Alan Sheridan (New York: Pantheon, 1977); *The Foucault Reader,* ed. Paul Rabinow (New York: Pantheon, 1984).

48. Jameson, *Postmodernism*, x–xxii, 3–6. See also Huyssen, *After the Great Divide*, viii–x, 178–221.

Conclusion. The Grateful Dead Indians

1. Society of Indian Dead, *Live and Let Live*, #9.

2. Ibid.

3. See Richard Slotkin, *Regeneration through Violence: The Mythology of the American Frontier, 1600–1860* (Middletown: Wesleyan University Press, 1973), 191–92; Christopher Castiglia, *Bound and Determined: Captivity, Culture-Crossing, and White Womanhood from Mary Rowlandson to Patty Hearst* (Chicago: University of Chicago Press, 1996).

4. Renato Rosaldo, *Culture and Truth: The Remaking of Social Analysis* (Boston: Beacon Press, 1993), 68–87.

5. Homi K. Bhabha, *The Location of Culture* (New York: Routledge, 1994), 31–39, 40–65.

Index